AF249083

# CASTE, OCCUPATION AND POLITICS ON THE GANGES

# Anthropology and Cultural History in Asia and the Indo-Pacific

Series Editors:
Pamela J. Stewart and Andrew Strathern
University of Pittsburgh, USA

This series offers a fresh perspective on Asian and Indo-Pacific Anthropology. Acknowledging the increasing impact of transnational flows of ideas and practices across borders, the series widens the established geographical remit of Asian studies to consider the entire Indo-Pacific region. In addition to focussed ethnographic studies, the series incorporates thematic work on issues of cross-regional impact, including globalization, the spread of terrorism, and alternative medical practices.

The series further aims to be innovative in its disciplinary breadth, linking anthropological theory with studies in cultural history and religious studies, thus reflecting the current creative interactions between anthropology and historical scholarship that are enriching the study of Asia and the Indo-Pacific region. While the series covers classic themes within the anthropology of the region such as ritual, political and economic issues will also be tackled. Studies of adaptation, change and conflict in small-scale situations enmeshed in wider currents of change will have a significant place in this range of foci.

We publish scholarly texts, both single-authored and collaborative as well as collections of thematically organized essays. The series aims to reach a core audience of anthropologists and Asian Studies specialists, but also to be accessible to a broader multidisciplinary readership.

*Recent titles in the series*

**The Anthropology of Morality in Melanesia and Beyond**
*Edited by* John Barker
ISBN 978 0 7546 7185 5

**Situating the Uyghurs Between China and Central Asia**
*Edited by* Ildikó Bellér-Hann, M. Cristina Cesàro, Rachel Harris
and Joanne Smith Finley
ISBN 978 0 7546 7041 4

**Gender, Christianity and Change in Vanuatu**
Annelin Eriksen
ISBN 978 0 7546 7209 8

# Caste, Occupation and Politics on the Ganges
## Passages of Resistance

ASSA DORON
*The Australian National University, Australia*

ASHGATE

Published by
Ashgate Publishing Limited
Wey Court East
Union Road
Farnham
Surrey GU9 7PT
England

Ashgate Publishing Company
Suite 420
101 Cherry Street
Burlington,
VT 05401-4405
USA

www.ashgate.com

**British Library Cataloguing in Publication Data**
Doron, Assa
  Caste, occupation and politics on the Ganges : passages of
  resistance. - (Anthropology and cultural history in Asia
  and the Indo-Pacific)
  1. Boatmen - Ganges River Valley (India and Bangladesh) -
  Social conditions 2. Mallah
  I. Title
  305.5'68'09541

**Library of Congress Cataloging-in-Publication Data**
Doron, Assa.
  Caste, occupation, and politics on the Ganges : passages of resistance / by Assa Doron.
    p. cm. -- (Anthropology and cultural history in Asia and the
Indo-Pacific)
  Includes bibliographical references and index.
  ISBN 978-0-7546-7550-1 (hardcover) 1. Mallahs--India--Varanasi (Uttar
Pradesh)--Social conditions. 2. Mallahs--India--Varanasi (Uttar Pradesh)--Economic
conditions. 3. Caste--Political aspects--India--Varanasi (Uttar Pradesh) I. Title.

  DS432.M2495D67 2009
  954'.2--dc22

2008029385

ISBN: 978 0 7546 7550 1

# Contents

# List of Map and Figures

Series Editors' Preface
# Ritual Transformations and the Edges of History

Andrew Strathern and Pamela J. Stewart
*University of Pittsburgh*


We are pleased indeed to record here the advent of the first study in our Indo-Pacific Series that deals with a topic from India; and particularly pleased that the topic is as rich and multi-faceted as the focus in the present volume: the famous Ganges River, celebrated in mythology, ritual practices, and ethnographic studies. Dr. Doron offers his readers a novel perspective on this arena, one entirely appropriate for riverine themes: the perspective of the boatmen who are essential in transporting tourists and pilgrims to and fro along the courses that lead to ritual centres and places of interest in the vicinity of Banaras.

From one point of view these boatmen can be thought of as occupying a liminal space in the cosmological topography of the region. Liminal, that is, in a number of ways: they occupy the flowing trajectory of the river itself which conveys the living and the dead within itself and, as Dr. Doron explains, is seen in ritual terms as a *tirtha*, a site of communication between different parts of the cosmos. The boatmen are also seen as at the edges of margins of order in the society at large, having suffered discrimination, categorization as of low hereditary status, and being accused of criminal behavior (e.g. smuggling, a transgressive act). They are sometimes imaged also as providing arenas for illicit or unconventional forms of social interactions generally. These imputed characteristics add up to what we may call 'the ambivalence of liminality' that surrounds them.

Dr. Doron employs an exemplary historical, as well as analytical, approach in deepening his exposition on the lives of these boat people. He takes us through British colonial times, in which the ideology of development brought by both government officials and missionaries saw the boat people as suitable cases for 'improvement': for example in their boat designs as well as in their supposed moral behaviors, and the desirability of their uplifting themselves vis a vis the dominant Brahmin views of them. The British needed to control river traffic and thus they employed the local boatmen and pilots, attempting to regulate their trade. The boatmen today sometimes ironically embrace the image of their 'criminal' past, re-conceptualizing it under the rubric of 'resistance' to domination. They have also effectively mobilized and re-organized themselves in various associations, through which they are able, for example, to protest and in some cases overturn the actions of local police who may attempt to restrict their activities and forbid their informal role as guides to tourists. The boat people are clearly marginalized ('at the river's edge') and form a classic subaltern category, yet they are not without recourse to their own means of exerting agency; and in this connection Dr. Doron's case study provides an excellent commentary on the well-established issues of 'weapons of the weak' and 'can the subaltern speak?'

How these boat people 'speak' in context is realized in three ways: first, through their own presentation of a validatory mythology; second through their social structuring of access to the river itself via the spatial organization of their patrilineages; and third, most strikingly, by their appropriation of vital ritual practices that give them a privileged place in the cosmos centred on the river as the *tirtha* or transition site and a milieu in which life passages are enacted.

In terms of mythology, Dr. Doron explains, the boat people counter the assertion of their 'lowly' status by claiming a close primordial relationship to Lord Ram and the River Ganga through a narrative of the meeting between Ram, the Divine King, and the boatman Khevat. In this narrative, Khevat conveys Lord Ram across the river and declines to accept payment for it, because they are both 'boatmen' in a sense: conveyers of persons and the spirits of persons across liminal spaces. The narrative thus asserts a tie of the highest spiritual kind, metaphorized from the basic image of the boatmen's own practical trade. In addition, the river itself is seen as a Mother Goddess (Ma Ganga) whom the boatmen serve; and various specific river goddesses are also worshipped.

Access to the river is not random. The boat people are organized into patrilineages, which control particular access points, or *ghats*, on the western bank of the river. Particular groups also cultivate riverine gardens in areas they control. A tourist or the visitor who enters a *ghat* and requires a boat for transport can properly be approached only by a recognized member of the *ghat* for their custom. Given the value of the *ghats* for subsistence, there are rivalries and accusations of malfeasance in the establishment of control over them; but the patrilineal principle as such is very strong.

In the ritual sphere the boat people exercise special claims to status. The boat itself (maligned as a clumsy vessel by the colonial authorities in the past) can be transformed by special decorations into a deity or a temple within which, for example, sacred marriage rituals can be performed. The boat in its sacred guise is called a *taran*, and is seen as a means of crossing the ocean of birth and rebirth. Brahmins give a limited recognition to the boatmen's ritual capacities, likening them to 'needles' by comparison with their own capacities as 'swords', but denying to them the honorific title, which the boatmen claim, of being Gangaputras, 'sons of the Ganges'.

In any event, the story of the boatman Khevat also reveals an image of him as inventive, entrepreneurial, 'cunning'. The boatmen's deployment of myth, rules of descent, and ritual as a means of maintaining their monopolies over the river transport reflects this entrepreneurial theme. Tourists experience the entrepreneurial side, sometimes seen as grasping; pilgrims appreciate the sacred or holy side of the boatmen's activities. This sacred side links the boatmen honorifically to nation-wide symbols in the mythology of Lord Ram and the Ganges River. The creative agency of the boatmen is shown in all of these spheres of action, and their ability to turn their practical craft into a powerful symbol of such agency via the sacred presence of the river is a remarkable testimony to the powers of embodiment and cosmology working together.

In reading Dr. Doron's own enterprising ethnography and analysis we have been struck by a general parallel between the concept of the *tirtha*, or liminal space, and concepts regarding ritual places in the earth among peoples in the Southern Highlands of Papua New Guinea, notably the Huli and the Duna peoples with whom we have conducted extensive research work (see for example Stewart and Strathern 2002, Strathern and Stewart 2004).[1] While the Ganges may occupy a unique place in the Hindu cosmography, in Papua New Guinea such sacred sites that reveal openings into different realms of the cosmos are often conceptualized as being linked in a chain of ritual exchanges. The general idea of a space or opening that gives access to the potentialities of the other world (in reality, another part of the cosmos) is of course very common, and rivers provide an easily accessible symbol of such spaces – the river Styx comes to mind from Greek mythology, along with the idea of the boatman Charon who ferries the souls of the dead across it. Watercourses as the passageways of dead spirits carried westwards in the direction of the setting sun are another accessible symbol. And water, itself a liminal substance of transition, lies at the heart of these images, as expressed in the old Celtic poem invoking an image of geese flying over water and carrying a princess:

> Grey goose and ganner
> Wap yer wings the gidder
> And carry the gude king's dochter
> Ow're the ane-strand river.

In the Highlands of Papua New Guinea, especially in parts of the Southern Highlands, there are numerous places where rivers run underground through limestone rock, emerging at certain points, with caves associated with them. Stephen Frankel, in his study of the Huli people (Frankel 1986), describes the whole ritual complex known as *dindi gamu* ('earth rituals') connected with the idea that these underground flows of water mark the passage of the 'root of the earth', which is seen as a heavy vine intertwined by a python, and 'active points along this pathway are marked by the major sacred sites. Such places are referred to as, literally, 'the knots of the earth' (*dindi pongone*), where the key strands of the earth's fabric interweave, and so gain strength. The root of the earth is said to be accessible to ritual manipulation at these points' (Frankel 1986: 19).

---

1   For further references to related publications of ours in this field area see www.pitt.edu/~strather.

Similar ideas are found among the Duna people, neighbors of the Huli, among whom we conduct research. As with the Huli, important pre-Christian ritual sites are linked notionally as 'pathways', along which certain places were important as means of communication with the powers of the earth. The general idea involved is again that of the opening or passage-way between parts of the cosmos. Those who act as the keepers of these passage-ways are seen as formidable exponents of ritual power, while at the same time they may also be seen as outside of ordinary society. We meet here again the impression of liminality which was remarked on earlier here regarding the boat people in Dr. Doron's study. What is remarkable in Dr. Doron's work is his demonstration of the dual persona of the boat people of the Ganges: on the one hand, and from the perspective of some elements of their society, a low-status group with an ambivalent relationship to the state and its governance; on the other hand, from the perspective of their own appropriation of the cosmos and their ritual practices, an honorable group closely in touch with the ritual ordering of the world , as well as a group supplying a significant practical function, river transport. Living at the edges of the river and its history, they are also key players in their own transformation through the symbolism of the river itself as a site of transformation and escape from the sufferings of samsara: a *tirtha*.

Cromie Burn Research Unit
June 2008
AJS and PJS

## References


Frankel, Stephen (1986) *The Huli Response to Illness*. Cambridge: Cambridge University Press.

Stewart, Pamela J. and Andrew Strathern (2002) *Remaking the World: Myth, Mining and Ritual Change among the Duna of Papua New Guinea*. For, Smithsonian Series in Ethnographic Inquiry, Washington, D.C.: Smithsonian Institution Press.

Strathern, Andrew and Pamela J. Stewart (2004) *Empowering the Past, Confronting the Future, The Duna People of Papua New Guinea*. For, Contemporary Anthropology of Religion Series, New York: Palgrave Macmillan.

# Acknowledgments

This book is about caste, occupations and politics as it is refracted through the lives of the boatmen of Banaras (Varanasi), where I spent more than eleven months between 2001 and 2003, with supplementary fieldtrips conducted between 2004 and 2006. Much of the fieldwork was carried on the ghats (landing steps) across the riverfront. These ghats cannot remain anonymous since the descriptions of the physical and cultural characteristics of the ghats are essential for understanding the conditions and the manner in which boatmen operate on them. I have, however, given pseudonyms to most of the boatmen mentioned in the body of the text. This is because of ongoing disputes and conflicts within and outside the community and I do not wish to harm, distress or offend any of the people involved. For this reason, I have also omitted the names of those people involved in the court disputes referred to in the text. I hold photocopies of all material given to me by members of the boatman community in Banaras and have cited them in this book as Reg. (Author's Register). These include press releases, meeting minutes and lawsuits.

During the course of the research and writing of this book I met many wonderful people whose friendship, support, guidance and inspiration has been unforgettable. First and foremost, my greatest thanks goes to the boatmen. The generosity, care and willingness with which they shared their lives, hopes and fears with me was more than I could ever expect and hope for, and for which I am deeply grateful. In particular I wish to thank Deepak Kumar, Kailashnath Nishad, Bejnath Nishad, Gopal Nishad, Balu, Shiva, Shyam Lal, Shankar Babu, Putur, Chachi, Ramesh, Rajesh, and Pradip. During my time in India many friends and colleagues have been very kind and helpful, Sara and Aslan, Nita Kumar, Rakesh Singh, Virendra Singh, Prof. Rana P.B. Singh, Shanti Devi, Osnat El-Kabir and Tasnim. I would especially like to extend my thanks to Mr. Bharat, Mr. Mehta and Pintu for their assistance in Hindi/Bhojpuri translations. I am deeply indebted to Pinku (Ajay), a friend and my research assistant in Banaras, whose convivial manner and immense knowledge of the city were invaluable.

The book grew out of my dissertation, *Sons of the Ganga: the Boatmen and the Riverscape of Varanasi* (La Trobe University, Melbourne, 2005), which was significantly revised during my postdoctoral fellowship at the National University of Singapore (NUS), until reaching its current avatar at The Australian National University (ANU). I would first like to thank my supervisors, Rowan Ireland and Robin Jeffrey, who supported me throughout the project. To Rowan whose enthusiasm, encouragement, patience and guidance was invaluable and uplifting. To Robin for his generosity and for letting me profit extensively from his in-depth knowledge of India and for scholarly support to this day. To Evie Katz,

Chris Eipper and Joel Kahn for their encouragement and incisive comments on my work and to David Shulman who inspired me to pursue further studies and recommended La Trobe for this purpose. C.J. Fuller and Gyan Pandey and Bob Pokrant provided valuable and constructive comments on this early version. Among the many people who shared their insights with me in conversations, discussion and contributions, I wish especially to thank: Nir Avieli, Yohan Arranson, Greg Bailey, Tanya Boughtflower, Alex Broom, Erez Cohen, Peter Friedlander, Alberto Gomes, Cherry Grimwald, Russel Hawking, Adrian Hearn, Trevor Hogan, Jenny Huberman, Ray Madden, Kama Maclean, Helen Lee, Wendy Mee, John Morton, Kalpana Ram, Max Richter, Sanjay Seth, Karl Smith, Sally Warhaft, Phuong Pham and, in particular, to fellow India aficionados, Madeleine, Maxine, Nalin and Nitika.

At NUS, the South Asian Studies Programme provided a supportive environment for completing the research and I would especially like to thanks Peter Reeves, Gyanesh Kudaisya and Rajesh Rai (*bhya*). The final version of this book has greatly benefited from numerous conversations I had with Patrick Daly who persistently encouraged me to look at the bigger picture and push the arguments further. Richard Barz, Linda Malam, Ira Raja, Kate Sullivan, McComas Taylor and Philip Taylor were extremely generous with their time, offering much valued criticism and advice, as was the ongoing encouragement and invaluable editorial comments of Jessica Williams. I would also like to thank Neil Jordan from Ashgate, Pamela J Stewart, Andrew Strathern and the anonymous reviewer of the book for their suggestions and support. I want to thank *Indica Books* (Varanasi) for allowing me to use the cartoon sketches from the wonderful comic written and illustrated by Gol 1999. *A Pilgrimage to Kashi-Banaras, Varanasi, Kashi: History, Mythology and Culture of the Strangest and most Fascinating City in the World.* The artist/photographer Pierre Toutain-Dorbec was very kind in giving me permission to use his historical photos of sandmining on the riverfront. I am also grateful to the *Journal of South Asian Studies*, and its editor Ian Copland for permission to integrate material from my article, 'The Needle and the Sword: Boatmen, Priests and the Ritual Economy of Varanasi', December 2006, 29:3, 345–365; and to the *Australian Journal of Anthropology*, and Rozanna Lilley for allowing me to incorporate material from my article, 'Encountering the "Other": Pilgrims, Tourists and Boatmen in the City of Varanasi', August 2006, 16:2, 157–178. Of course, all errors and omission are mine.

Finally, I wish to thank my family who encouraged and helped me in so many ways. To Joy Florence, Harry Allen, Jane Barrett, and Viji and Margaret Krishnapillai for helping make the journey an enjoyable one. To Udi and Rachel, and especially to my brother Guy, whose intellectual and emotional support has been invaluable and to my mother who is always there without fail. To my two boys Itai (or Bholinath as the boatmen suggested), and Tomer for imbuing my life with such joy and laughter, and much needed perspective, and lastly to Minnie my wife (*yedidat nefesh*) without whom none of this would have been possible.

# List of Abbreviations

| | |
|---|---|
| *C of I* | Census of India |
| GAP | Ganga Action Plan |
| MBC | Most Backward Classes |
| MSSS | Mallah Samuday Sanghars Samity (the Mass Association for the Struggle of Mallahs) |
| RAV | Regional Archives of Varanasi (U.P) |
| REG | Author's register (A.Doron) |
| U.P. | Uttar Pradesh |

# A Note on Translation and Transliteration

This book was written with the general reader in mind. I have therefore tried to avoid overly technical terms and phrases and omitted any diacritical marks. I have attempted to transliterate the Hindi, Sanskrit and Bhojpuri terms in a way that most closely approximates their local pronunciation. Words and terms that are already accepted in English, and found in the Oxford dictionary, like Ramayana, Shiva and Shastra, remain without academic transliteration. Indian terms are pluralized by adding an 's', as in English. Frequently used names and terms have been listed in the glossary at the end of this book.

*For my late father, Ishai, and my mother, Raya*

# Introduction

From the earliest renditions of the *Ramayana*, boatmen have occupied a special place in the traditional moral universe of India. Murals depicting the legendary story of the boatman, Khevat, ferrying Prince Rama, and his pious wife Sita across the Ganga, can be seen all over Banaras, while historical, literary and travel narratives are replete with accounts of encounters with boatmen. The following excerpt from Pankaj Mishra's (1999, 26) acclaimed novel *The Romantics* is a particularly good example of literary fascination with boatmen:

> Miss West had her own favorite boatman: his name was Ramchand and he came running up the steps as soon as she and I appeared on the ghats that evening. He was a strikingly handsome man with beautifully sculpted muscles on his lean, chocolate-brown body, most of which was bare, his only item of clothing being a dhoti, which he wore like a G-string, tightly wound around his hips and buttocks. He held his palms together before Miss West; he bowed his head; he looked eager to serve.

As the subject of Miss West's orientalist gaze, Ramchand is at once exotic, erotic and subservient. Such indulgence, however, is quickly dispelled in the following paragraph:

> She brought an un-Indian naturalness to her exchange with the boatman, and watching her I felt a trifle awkward. Although I spoke the same language as Ramchand and lived in the same country, the scope for conversation between us was limited. Countless inhibitions of caste and class stood in our way; the only common vocabulary between us was of the service he offered.

For all the predictability of a benign orientalism which mars Miss West's view of Ramchand, she brings a certain informality to her encounter with him, something impossible for the narrator who is steeped in the socio-economic hierarchies which underpin everyday interactions among Indians. For him, the boatman belongs to the low caste occupational group known as the Mallah/Nishad, located near the bottom of the social hierarchy. Miss West's approach to the boatman, however, is unmediated by such conditioning.

While the passage registers a vivid sense of the boatman's physical presence, it offers little insight into the daily struggles which characterize the lives of the boatmen as a group. In this book my concern is to render visible the lives, narratives and practices of the boatmen who have been traditionally marginalized by authoritative descriptions of social life. Through a focus on the social and physical space that boatmen inhabit and constitute as part of the broader river economy of Banaras, I seek to examine the way boatmen consciously attempt to subvert, challenge and oppose structures of domination in everyday life. Everyday life in this case must be conceived as a contested and negotiated arena, where experience, meaning, agency and resistance are expressed and perceived in multiple and often contradictory ways. This is precisely what makes Miss West's encounter with the boatman radically different from that of the middle class Indian. Alternatively, this may be the reason why Ramchand, the boatman, is polite and subservient: a culturally appropriate strategy of engagement with ones' patron (Appadurai 1990). If such a reading raises questions of performance, it must also raise the prospect of different audiences and internal dynamics among boatmen themselves. Accordingly, Ramchand's running up the ghat to greet Miss West, may be read as an assertive act; a clear signal to other competing boatmen around the ghat, that Miss West is his 'known' passenger, and therefore off-limits to them. Of course, it is difficult and perhaps presumptive, to attempt to gain access to Ramchand's mind; nonetheless, my point is that everyday life cannot be simply understood as transparent terrain, where meanings are easily available for scrutiny (Highmore 2002). What this further implies is that any investigation of everyday life must take into account both micro and macro perspectives. In other words, a framework that is sensitive to both the micro-analysis of the boatmen's lives, emphasizing experience, agency and resistance is needed, as well as the broader structures, institutions and discourses of domination (alluded to by the middle class Indian in Mishra's novel) that boatmen are subjected to and constrained by in their everyday life, for example, state policies, caste ideology, occupational opportunities and market economy.

In this study I attempt to provide a multilayered understanding of how such processes of domination and subordination operate and the implications they have for the construction of a boatman identity, the exercise of agency and resistance practices. I do so from a number of perspectives. One perspective investigates the authoritative gaze to which boatmen are subjected by the state – a much more portentous one than that of the romanticizing gaze often reflected in tourist sensibilities. Another perspective analyses the dynamics involved in the formation of the community and its identity through its interactions and encounters with state and non-state actors and institutions. The third perspective looks at the interaction between boatmen and foreign visitors to the city. These perspectives, informed and bound together by theoretical understandings, such as the interplay between (notions of) tradition and modernity and domination and subordination, everyday resistance, moral economy and subalternity, constitute the substance of this book.

**Narratives of Place**

As a city Banaras has been the subject of much foreign rumination, both in and outside the academic world. From colonial descriptions of the city, portraying it as a 'living museum', to the more recent studies which have examined Banaras as a paradigmatic pilgrimage centre (Eck 1983), the city remains one of the most seductive destinations for anthropologists and tourists alike. Among the many anthropological studies on Banaras one finds an impressive array of topics, ranging from craftsmanship (Kumar 1988); the death industry and what constitutes a 'good death' in the holy city (Parry 1994; Justice 1997), issues of environmental, moral and physical degradation (Alley 2002; Cohen 1997), masculinity (for example, expressed through wrestling) and womanhood, examined through the prism of ritual practices (Alter 1992; Pintchman 2005). All of these studies have engaged, to some degree, with issues that are central to area studies pertaining to India, such as the dominant values of purity and pollution, the ideology of caste, and more broadly, the study of religion. Moreover, the fact that the meta-narrative of *hierarchy* (Appadurai 1988) hovers above such studies, does not diminish the rich insights which they generate about the complexities of caste, religious ideology and the way in which cultural practices and meanings are implicated within power relations and in the construction of identity, both for the individual and at the level of community (local, regional and national). Likewise, this book and its examination of the Banaras boatmen – a low caste, territorially bound community – draws much of its currency from these debates, which I hope will further contribute to anthropological knowledge and enhance our understanding of the multifarious factors that militate against the myth of any singular dominant principle of hierarchy ordering South Asia society (cf. Parish 1997). Set against this context, boatmen certainly matter and it is surprising that no study has yet focussed on this community, which as we shall see, has been central to the physical and social construction of Banaras, in terms of its trade, pilgrimage and tourist economy.

While certain identifiable intellectual concerns have preoccupied anthropological research on Banaras, and on India more broadly; many anthropologists like to point out (with some justification) that it is the fieldsite and unanticipated encounters and incidents during the course of fieldwork that ultimately dictate what one should study. However, as Gupta and Ferguson (1997, 11) persuasively argue, what is deemed a 'good fieldsite', and 'proper fieldwork' is also defined by a 'crosshatched intersection of visa and clearance procedures, the interests of funding agencies, and intellectual debates within the discipline and its subfields'. Indeed, as a passport carrying Israeli, barred from travelling to Muslim countries in this region, such incidental geopolitical considerations played a part my 'choice' of area of research. I find this worthwhile mentioning right at the outset of this study, not simply as a narrative device, but rather to alert the reader to how my research on Banaras and its boatmen is shot through with political histories, national experiences and disciplinary considerations. These factors have shaped my subject position as an author, as well as the methods I employed in the field, the knowledge I gathered, and ultimately, the way I chose to interpret and represent Banaras and its boatmen.

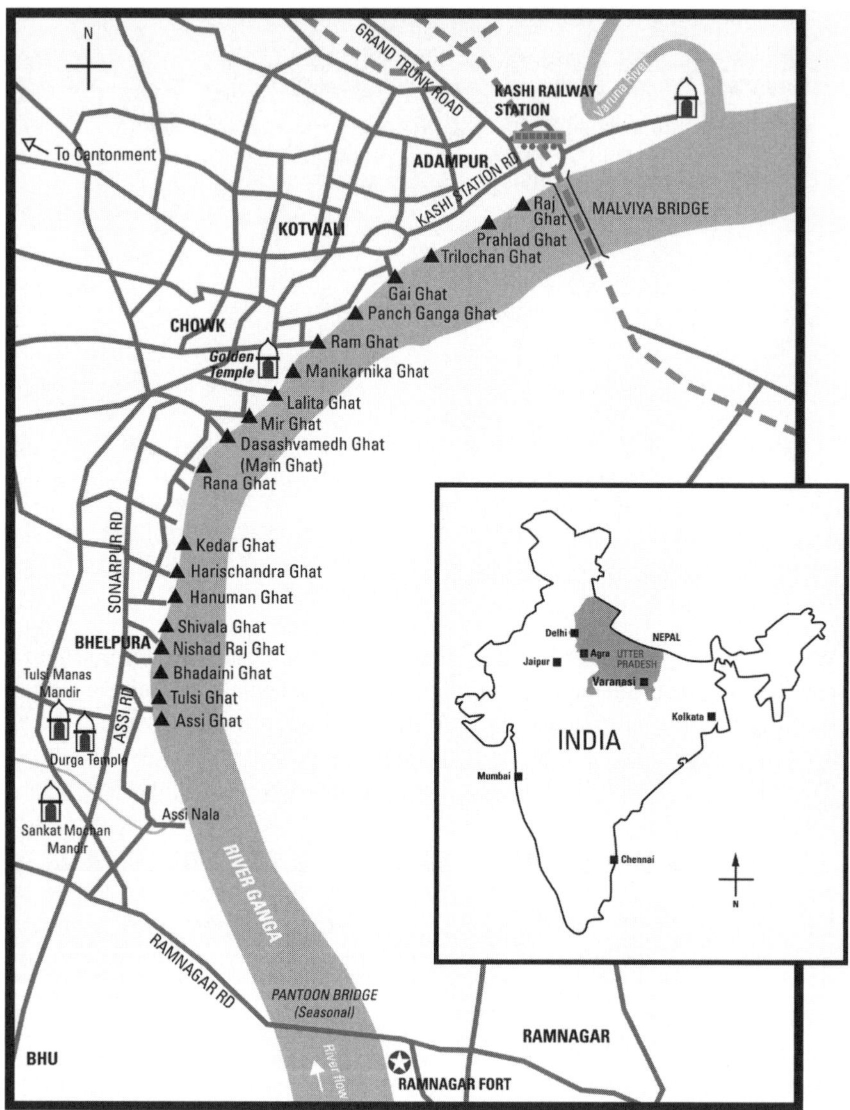


**Map 0.1      Map of Banaras and the River Ganges (with India insert)**

My engagement with the boatmen is therefore not wholly coincidental and, moreover, my examination of issues to do with ideologies of caste, structures of domination and everyday acts of resistance are informed by debates that 'matter to the discipline' and the my area of study (India), at least as much as they matter to the people I have worked with. Indeed, as Malkki (1997) argues, anthropology has developed very sophisticated methodological mechanisms to examine such issues, which animate current debates, particularly as they operate within the durable, day-to-day structures of the social and cultural life of bounded communities. Nevertheless, Malkki is also careful to point out that by 'choosing' such areas of investigation, anthropologists necessarily exclude other, equally valid and important forms of knowledge, phenomena and communities, which may seem difficult to capture through traditional/authoritative fieldwork methodology. The point is that boatmen are no more 'Indian' than those migrant labourers in other parts of India. An ethnographic study of factory workers in India's largest still-plant located in Bhilai is as insightful as the one conducted in 'village India' for understanding the cultural meanings and moral evaluations of the discourse of corruption in India (see Gupta 1995; Parry 2000). Moreover, the fact that boatmen are a territorially bound community, celebrating their belonging to Banaras from time immemorial, must be treated with a degree of historical scepticism, for as recent studies of precolonial India have shown, mobility has long been a strategy of survival, and at times, of resistance, even amongst artisans in their quest for stable and secure livelihoods (Haynes & Roy 1999). In addition, as I argue in Chapter 1, it was under the colonial government that mobile groups, such as boatmen, were progressively incarcerated in, or confined to, specific locations. To this effect then, the very palatability of communities to the anthropological gaze must be subject to close questioning and form part of the narrative of any anthropological study. While the primary concern of this study is to examine the cultural practices of boatmen and their interactions with their immediate social environment within a specific, concrete place; it also seeks to shed light on some of the wider historical and social forces that have produced and reproduced Banaras as a sacred place, in which for many observers, boatmen and their vocation seem almost as eternal as the city itself.

## Encounters with Banaras and the Boatmen

Between 1992 and 2007 I visited Banaras several times in different capacities. Initially as a young 'traveller' fresh out of my Israeli (compulsory) military service, thereafter as a tour-guide and finally as an anthropologist in November 2001. Although it felt strange to visit Varanasi, or Banaras as the city is popularly called, wearing the anthropologist's hat, neither India, nor Banaras were unfamiliar terrain for me.[1] I had been to the city less than one year before (January/February 2001),

---

1 The popular names of the city are Varanasi and Banaras. The first derives from the geographical space marking the boundaries of the city between the Varuna River, which joins the Ganga to the north and the Assi River, nowadays more of a *nala* (drain), to the south. While Varanasi is the official name of the city, the name Banaras (a historical corruption of the Pali version 'Banarasi') continues to be a popularly used name in every day life (Eck 1983, 26). During Muslim and British rule the city was known as Benares. To avoid confusion, I use the names according to the historical period. That is, the name

when, as part of a preliminary research trip, I combined a visit to the Kumbh Mela in Allahabad with a month's stay in Banaras.[2] It was on that trip that I decided to research the boatmen of the city. Banaras was extremely busy in the post-Kumbh period, with multitudes of pilgrims and tourists arriving in the city from Allahabad. Pilgrims came to pay their respects to the visiting Sadhus (holy men) camping on the ghats (landing steps leading to the river). Within this flood of people the boatmen were a conspicuous feature on the riverscape, ferrying passengers back and forth throughout the day. I began to develop an interest in the boatmen and their livelihood, and upon returning to Australia searched for literature on this group of people. To my surprise, I found that, despite Banaras being one of the most researched cities in India (after the major port cities and Delhi), very little had been written on the boatman community. The only information about the boatmen I found was in colonial archives, where the boatmen are documented under the broader category of the Mallah or Nishad caste.[3]

Searching through photos my wife and I had taken on our trips to India, we found several that we had taken on a boat in Banaras. As I began telling people about my project, it seemed that anyone who had been to the city had enjoyed a boat ride and had a story to tell. Such stories further stimulated my interest in the boatmen, particularly their encounters with tourists.

Arriving in Banaras later that year to begin fieldwork, I chose Assi ghat at the southern edge of the city to begin my research. This was done for mainly practical reasons related to my initial research question: What does it mean to be a boatman in Banaras? My question therefore restricted the study to the geographical location in which the boatmen work: the riverscape of Banaras.[4] However, this spatial definition was too broad for my research capacity. Banaras is located on

---

Benares is mainly used in the first chapter, which examines the Mallahs under colonial rule, while Varanasi and Banaras are used interchangeably throughout the book, according to who uses the name and in what context. It is worth noting another well known name for the city, Kashi (the luminous), which is found in the traditional literature (*mahatmya*). For a detailed examination of the city's names, see Eck (1983).

2    The Kumbh Mela is the largest religious gathering in India, occurring every three years, where pilgrims gather near the confluence of sacred rivers to perform ritual ablutions (*snan*).

3    Later in my research I came across one published article specifically focussing on the Mallahs (as a caste) in the Census, see Tiwary (2001). As for material on the boatmen of Varanasi, Katz (1993) looks at the role the boatmen of Assi ghat play in the overall social structure of the Assi neighbourhood and local rituals. Vidyrathi et al. (1979) offer a structural-functionalist account of the boatmen as part of the ritual ecology of Banaras, while Parry's (1994) incisive ethnographic study, *Death in Banaras*, provides some useful details on the role of boatmen in the death industry of Banaras.

4    By riverscape I mean the environment encompassing the ghats on the city side, the river and the other (eastern) side of the river. Along with the physical characteristics of the riverscape, I am also concerned with the social, cultural, economic and symbolic aspects within this space.

the western banks of the River Ganga.[5] There are about 80 ghats along a seven kilometre stretch of river. There are roughly 2000 boatmen and, according to my count, 800 boats in Banaras (the majority being rowboats, with 80 motorboats and 20 houseboats). This meant further limiting my initial investigation to a smaller space and fewer people.

Assi ghat is considered one of the major ghats in the city both on account of its religious importance and physical location. The ghat proved to be a good choice; it was close to where I lived; it was easily accessible by road and had about 40 boatmen plying their trade at any given time, a number that allowed me to get to know most of them personally and learn about their work and lives. I decided to first familiarize myself with this ghat and its boatman community and later venture to other ghats to compare and contrast my findings. I stayed for a period of one year over two visits between 2001 and 2003, and returned for additional shorter periods in 2005 and 2006. During this time I observed and participated in a variety of community events, as well as boating trips with pilgrims and tourists. Most of my initial conversations and interviews were informally conducted around the tea stalls dotting the ghats. In addition, I spoke with various ghat functionaries including priests (*pandas*), washermen (dhobis), buffalo herders (Yadavs) and local shopkeepers. I soon discovered that one of the best places for me to conduct in-depth interviews with individual boatmen was, in fact, on their boats, where they seemed freer of the pressures of the ghat environment. In addition, I collected oral histories and written documentation, such as press releases, lawsuits and archival material from the colonial period. My close association with the boatmen meant I did not have much contact with local police officers or other state officials whose relationships with the boatmen were generally quite tense, hence the story told here is one that emerges mostly from the boatmen's perspective as I understood it.

Two weeks into my research on Assi ghat I established a daily routine. Waking at dawn, I would walk down to the ghat for a cup (or more precisely several cups) of strong, sweet tea (*chai*), to observe and chat with the boatmen I had met. I would then return to my guest house for breakfast, practice Hindi, and write my field notes, which at that point mainly consisted of observations. At around four in the afternoon as the heat began to wane, I would return to the ghat for more observations and cups of tea.

Mornings and evenings are the most active times on the ghats. During the months of October and November, Assi ghat booms with ritual activities associated with the sacred month of Kartik.[6] At the break of dawn local women arrive at the ghat with baskets containing various ritual items. They sit in circles and perform a series of rituals, which involves fashioning idols out of Ganga *mitti* (sacred Ganga

---

5    The anglicized name for Ganga – the River Ganges – is primarily employed in the book when examining the context of British rule. Otherwise, I mostly use the name Ganga, as the river is popularly known.

6    On the festivities involved in the month of Kartik, see Pintchman (2005).

clay), gossiping and singing devotional songs. Alongside these women are the regulars; local residents who come to the ghat daily to practice ritual ablutions. Foreign tourists also visit the ghats in these early morning hours, drinking tea, and taking boat rides to view the majestic vista of the riverscape as it unfolds at sunrise. The evenings are more serene. Locals and tourists generally come to escape the heat and pollution of the city and relax in the spacious and pleasant ghat environment. Not surprisingly therefore, I found that the mornings and evenings were the peak times during which the boatmen busily scouted for potential passengers (*savaris*).

During my first two weeks in the field I occupied myself by observing and writing down the various activities on the ghat in my little notebook. Many of the boatmen took a keen interest in my research and offered to help. They alerted me to the fact that their boats bore the marks of the auspicious season; a time when most boatmen repaint and perform *puja* (worship) for their boats. I began to 'participate' as well as observe, by helping a young boatman named Amit, who later became a key informant, to paint his boat. Thus, my first two weeks in the field were marked by unperturbed observations and a little participation. At the beginning of the third week, however, I made my first dreadful mistake, which ultimately proved to be one of the most meaningful moments of my research.[7]

The incident occurred during the festival of Diwali (15 November, 2001). In the evening the ghat was particularly hectic with people arriving to celebrate the festival. The explosions of fire crackers and small bombs added to the electric atmosphere. As I sat on the steps drinking tea at Lakshmi's small chai stall, Amit arrived, greeting me in the traditional way: 'Diwali mubarak ho' (Diwali greetings), to which I replied in kind. We went down to the water's edge to avoid the noise, and as we were talking a group of foreign tourists approached us. One of them, who must have heard me speaking Hindi and assumed I knew a little more than the average tourist, asked me if I could recommend a big boat for him and his group of friends. I immediately suggested they hire Amit's boat, adding that he was a very knowledgeable guide as well. What I failed to notice, however, was that some members of the group were already negotiating a price with another boatman called Jagdish. I immediately knew that I had overstepped some line. A fierce argument developed between the two boatmen and eventually the tourists left on Amit's boat. Jagdish then turned to me with his green eyes blazing, 'Assi, you should not have done this, these people were mine! And you just gave them to Amit'. Holding my two hands together in a *namaste* gesture, I apologized, trying to explain my ignorance. Jagdish stared at me irately and walked away. That night I could not sleep, rehearsing the unfortunate incident in my mind and thinking of the grave consequences this could have on my future research and relationships with the boatmen. The following day I felt very anxious about appearing on the

---

7    Such mistakes are, of course, a common feature of most ethnographic research. Still, knowing this does not in anyway diminish the emotional angst the follows. On productive, but anxiety ridden mistakes during fieldwork, see for example, Gold (1988).

ghat. When I did eventually go there in the evening, however, nothing seemed to have changed, and even Jagdish greeted me with a *namaste* as if nothing had happened.

*A Productive Mistake*

There are a number of things to be said about this incident, but I shall limit myself here to reflecting on how this incident signalled my 'entry into the field'. At the immediate level, the incident affected my own conduct on the ghat. I was careful thereafter not to involve myself in any tourist-boatman transactions. 'My mistake' offered me a first glimpse into the complex ghat dynamics of the boatmen's livelihood. I became aware that there was a subtle, yet significant socio-economic system operating on the ghat, and a precarious one too, since even a minor and 'ignorant' intrusion like mine could lead to an explosive and contentious outcome. Moreover, I soon discovered that competition, occasionally resulting in violent disputes over passengers, is common among the boatmen of Assi ghat, an issue I explore in Chapter 3.

More generally, this incident also marked a shift in my own status and identity – from tourist to anthropologist-cum-tourist. Upon reflection, it seems all the more obvious to me that the boatmen understood better than I did the ramifications of my long term presence on their livelihoods. They knew that if I intended to stay for an extended period on the ghat I must learn the rules of conduct, and one rule was clear: do not interfere in the work system. My ignorance signalled a turning point, because, as was indicated by the boatmen, I no longer had the 'privileges' of a fleeting tourist. Rather I had to learn their system and act within it – a mark of inclusion.

Such considerations were not only significant in relation to my conduct in the field, but also in relation to my methodology and the trajectory of my overall research interests. It raised important issues concerning social research in general and what Giddens (1984, 284–285) calls the principle of the 'double hermeneutic', that is, the two frameworks of meaning that are involved in any empirical inquiry into what it means to be an 'other'. The first relates to the study of 'phenomena which are already constituted as meaningful' by the actors themselves. In other words, this incident marked my 'entry into the field' in the sense that it was at this point that I began 'to know what actors already know, and have to know, to "go on" with their daily activities in social life' (Giddens 1984, 284). In order to move forward in my endeavour I had to learn about the boatmen's work system, how it operates in their everyday lives, and what meanings they ascribe to their occupation. This generated further questions regarding the broader work system that operates across the riverfront and how it structures the social and economic interactions amongst boatmen within specific ghats and across the riverfront.

The second framework of meaning according to Giddens' principle of the double hermeneutic concerns the 'second order' sociological concepts employed by the researcher to understand and interpret the research results (Giddens 1984, 284). As this incident alerted me to the fierce competition amongst boatmen over resources (passengers), and the difficulties they face in their attempts to maintain and protect their livelihood in the rapidly changing environment of the riverscape, I looked to broad theoretical discussions on power relations, dominance, and the 'relations of actions and structure' (Giddens 1984, 283) as useful interpretive frameworks for conceptualizing my research project.[8] More specifically, the anthropological history of India by Bernard Cohn (1998 [1987]), the scholarship of the Subaltern Studies School, and James Scott's (1985; 1990) ethnographic history detailing everyday forms of resistance have been sources of inspiration for me. The relevant aspects of these theoretical frameworks are elaborated on throughout this book. Here, I shall limit myself to a few general remarks in relation to their views of power and resistance and my own theoretical orientations.

**Theoretical Orientations**

Anthropological studies of Hindu civilization have drawn considerably upon research done in the early 1950s on village India, the primary aim of which was to analyze and explain the process of social change in Indian society. The two most influential theories which emerged from this fertile period were M.N. Srinivas' concept of Sanskritization and Redfield's model of Great and Little Traditions, which posited the existence of an overarching Sanskritic tradition associated with certain pan-Indian beliefs, practices, myths, deities and pilgrimage centres. Both theories have been widely criticized,[9] not least because empirically it is difficult to determine what constitutes a 'great tradition' (Fuller 1992, 25–27). Nonetheless, as I show in this study, pan-Hindu beliefs, symbols and myths continue to figure on a discursive level. They play a prominent part within the indigenous framework where local actors employ such symbols and myths to assert their rights in everyday practice, creatively resisting domination and subordination. In the cases I present, the boatmen refer to such pan-Hindu texts and myths as a source of authority for their claim to respectable social status as well as to challenge ideological domination and, more importantly, to affirm their legitimacy to conduct rituals

---

8    Giddens' (1984) theory of 'structuration' is an important attempt to bridge the structure/agency divide. Similarly, Bourdieu (1982) offered an equally influential model that emphasized conceptions of praxis as central to our understanding of cultural change and the interplay between individual and collective. Others, like Barth (1969), proposed a way around the structure/agency impasse by suggesting a generative approach to account for social change, which is sensitive to how traditions (ideas, events, rituals) work as a process of communicative creativity.

9    The concept of Sanskritization has been subject to much debate. For our purpose it is worth mentioning Hardiman's (1984) criticism of the concept, in which he points out that low castes' selective appropriation of higher caste values, symbols and modes of behaviour must be contextualized within a historical framework acknowledging the dynamic nature of the caste system, which is always informed by power relations.

in the sacred space of the ghats, often considered the exclusive jurisdiction of Brahmin priests (see Chapter 4).[10]

Nevertheless, the strategy of looking at peasant life and the local arena as an entry point into understanding Indian society has remained. In the early 1980s the Subaltern Studies project was launched and peasant society continued to be the focus of inquiry.[11] This time, however, the idea of writing history from below provided both a framework and motivating force for re-examining the 'inadequacy of elitist historiography' (Guha 1982, 2). The examination of the 'privileged discourse' produced in the authoritative accounts of the elites or the experts (e.g., colonial anthropologist or nationalist historian) was counterbalanced by the close attention given to the popular 'archive' (Pandey 2000, 284). Thus, the researcher could reveal not only the power relations embedded in the interaction between colonizer/colonized, dominant/dominated, but also the 'presence of other pasts' (Pandey 2000, 282). These alternative pasts or fragmented histories were often identified by members of the Subaltern Studies School in multiple sites, institutions and activities not readily observed in homogenizing historical narratives.

According to Partha Chatterjee (1993, 171), this critical reading of historical records offered access into the ways in which power and knowledge was exerted over the oppressed, as well as insight into the subaltern consciousness. The aim was to uncover the voice of the subalterns as 'the people on their own, that is, independently of the elite to the making and development of this [Indian] nationalism' (Guha 1982, 2). To do so, the Subaltern Studies project highlighted conflict and subaltern 'resistance to elite domination' (Guha, 5). The project sought a careful de-construction of the elite grand narratives that was attentive to oral histories, myths, rumours and ritual practices; which it conceived as spaces where the subaltern voice could be heard and recognized, independent of elite domination.[12] Thus, the Subaltern Studies project focused on the experience, consciousness and historical agency of marginalized people at the grassroots of society.

However, the obsessive emphasis of the project on conflict, power relations and a separate subaltern sphere has not escaped criticism.[13] Indeed it has been suggested that some members of the Subaltern Studies collective were given to a dichotomous view of subaltern/elite relations, bordering on the essentialist and

---

10 Redfield's model came under scrutiny from various scholars across different disciplines. It seems that the model was especially problematic for anthropologists, as it was said to reduce local practices to the determination of the static, text based, authoritative Great Tradition. See, for example, Lukens-Bull (1999) and van der Veer (1988).

11 The Subaltern Studies project is a complex and varied one. In this book I am mainly concerned with the early volumes of the project, which were almost entirely dedicated to examining peasant struggles and resistance.

12 See, for example, Arnold (1984); Hardiman (1982); Pandey (1983).

13 The debate around these issues has been well drawn out in the recent publication of two edited books: see N. Chaturvedi (2000, ed.) and Ludden (2002, ed.).

ahistorical (Gupta 1985; O'Hanlon 2002). For example, in his engaging analysis of the Santal rebellion of 1855, project founder Ranajit Guha (1983) argues that both colonial and nationalist historiography explain subaltern insurgency in a way that 'amounts to an act of appropriation which excludes the rebel as the conscious subject of his own history and incorporates the latter as only a contingent element in another history with another subject' (Guha 1983, 23). He then goes on to argue that such misleading accounts served to conceal what was the actual essence of subaltern mentality – its religiosity. By uncovering religion as the true and authentic characteristic of the peasant consciousness and resistance, Guha is able to fulfil his stated aim and invest the subaltern with an agency of his own, rather than simply accept elite discourse, which he suggests, represented the rebels as either irrational fanatics or mere passive followers of a secularized leadership (Guha 1983, 24–37). In trying to redress the balance and give voice to underprivileged and hitherto voiceless groups, however, and by declaring religion as the underlying meaning behind subaltern political will, Guha himself reproduces an essentialized or 'ethicized', to use Gupta's (1985: 9–10) term, view of peasant society. Representing elite historiography as biased and contrived implies that the popular domain is the sole repository of what is authentic and original (see also Hansen 1997). In fact, subaltern narratives and identities are equally mediated and constructed; all we can do is attempt to bring to light such constructions and uncover the meanings behind the everyday practices and beliefs of the subordinated groups in society.[14]

In a similar vein, Dipesh Chakrabarty's (1983) discussion of the conditions of Calcutta jute mill workers – while it clearly illuminated the mechanisms and techniques of power and domination exercised by Bengali managerial elites and the colonial state over Calcutta's migrant ex-peasant work force – lacks an equally sophisticated examination of the peasant workers' culture, religious practices and actions. Instead, Chakrabarty briefly tells the reader that the working class was characterized by 'a pre-capitalist culture with a strong emphasis on religion, community, kinship, language and other primordial loyalties' (1983, 208). This uncritical characterization of subaltern culture as based on fixed categories (such as 'community' or 'religion') seems to overlook the possibility of heterogeneity, change and conflict within the subaltern group itself (O'Hanlon 2002, 164–166). Moreover, by simply abstracting the category of subaltern from the complexity of social relations, we are once again restricted by the limitations of structural dichotomies,[15] as peasant cultural identity remains distinct and timeless. In fact, 'primordial' bonds and other cultural systems are never static; rather they

---

14    This was later recognized by members of the Subaltern Studies group itself; see, for example, Pandey (2000).

15    As Copper (2002, 258) argues an analysis that relies on dichotomies, such as elite/subaltern colonizer/colonized, may ultimately limit 'the search for precise ways in which power is deployed and ways in which power is engaged, contested, deflected and appropriated'.

are informed by dynamic social processes, generated both within and outside communities.[16]

Foregrounding agency and resistance of subordinate groups is also a central concern in the influential work of James Scott. Like the cultural historians of the Subaltern Studies project, Scott too is sensitive to the socially constructed nature of archival material, and pays close attention to the culturally specific structures of expectations underpinning relations of domination.[17] While Scott's initial investigation of *The Moral Economy of the Peasant* sought to emphasize the cultural or subjective dimension of peasant rebellions, in his subsequent work, *Weapons of the Weak*, he shifts his attention to what he deems are much more prevalent, but less evident forms of protest employed by subordinated groups. In this fascinating ethnographic study of a Malaysian village, Scott expands our definition of resistance beyond large scale, public and organized acts of resistance, by focusing his analytical lens on the level of everyday life, where he identifies the continuous, covert, undeclared struggle of the poor against various (material and symbolic) forms of domination exercised by the rich. Scott reveals an arsenal of 'unconventional' weapons of the weak, which he argues, 'serves as the means by which subordinates manifest their class interests' (Scott 1989, 5). These mostly individual strategies of resistance include acts such as arson, foot dragging, false compliance, minor sabotage, chicanery, petty pilferage and many more. Scott is thus able to illuminate the subversive discourse and practice of subordinate groups, which despite their apparent compliance, rarely buy into or internalize the norms and definitions imposed by elite ideology:

> By reference to the culture that peasant fashion from their experience – their "offstage" comments and conversations, their proverbs, folksongs, and history, legends, jokes, language ritual and religion – it should be possible to determine to what degree, and in what ways, peasant actually accept the social order propagated by the elites' (Scott 1985, 41).[18]

Scott couches his argument in performative terms (i.e., of on/offstage) which neatly delineate the coherent discourses and practices of rich and poor respectively. Accordingly, the 'offstage' is a guarded, autonomous arena of the poor, where one

---

16   However, some members of the Subaltern Studies collective have shown a greater appreciation of these issues, see, for example, Amin (1984); Arnold (1984); Pandey (1984).

17   For Scott, if one is to understand the nature of popular rebellion, it is imperative to gain an appreciation of the 'emic' perspective of peasants, so that his main concern becomes one of identifying a peasant moral economy, based on 'their notion of economic injustice and their working definition of exploitation' (1976, 2).

18   It is in this context that the notion of 'little traditions' is revived, but this time rather than an adulterated version of the normative tradition; it is conceived as the 'offstage', where dissident culture and subversive activities are found.

can identify a vibrant culture of resistance to the routine oppression of the rich and dominant.

Scott's stress on the everyday life of subordinate people provides excellent insights into the behavior and subjectivity of subordinate groups, and allows him to pinpoint the weaknesses of more formal Marxist analysis. Nonetheless, his own critique of Gramsci's notion of hegemony is not immune from some of the same failings. As Mitchell (1990) points out, Scott's emphasis on the consensual effects of hegemony, where the ideological position of the dominant classes produces harmony and unanimity, is itself reductive, leading Scott to celebrate 'everyday resistance' as an oppositional and autonomous force undermining prevailing ideologies. Gramsci's formulation of hegemony, however, is a more complex and nuanced one, as Williams (1986) carefully observes. Hegemony does not simply mean the subordinate classes imbibing the ideas, values and beliefs propagated by the elites by means of manipulation and indoctrination. Rather, as Williams recovers it, hegemony is 'a whole body of practices and expectations, over the whole of living... It is lived systems of meaning and values – constitutive and constituting... continually resisted, limited, altered, challenged by pressures not at all of its own... it is never either total or exclusive' (1986, 110–113). This is very much in line with Foucault's (1998, 94–96) concept of power, as outside the prerogative of any one group, mechanism or institution, generating a plurality of resistances, which 'includes the dominant *and* the dominated within its circuits' (Hall 2001, 239).

This is related to what several scholars have identified as the class bias in Scott's analysis of resistance, failing to consider other equally important elements of social identity and inequality, such as gender, age, kinship relations and ethnicity (Ortner 1995; Hart 1991; Tsing 1993). Let me provide a brief example to illustrate the point. The following chapters show that the majority of boatmen are acutely aware of what they perceive as their systematic exploitation by the state, as well as the emerging opportunities and potential threats posed by market economy and outside competition to their livelihood. One of the ways in which boatmen have attempted to cope with such challenges is by formalizing their 'traditional' work system across the riverfront. But while such a strategy seems prudent to some, other members of the boatman community have resisted this standardizing project, that to succeed needs broad community consensus. This, I argue, is due to the implications such a formalization has for kinship ties, territorial boundaries, customary practices, status considerations and power relations within the community itself. My argument, then, is that for the concept of resistance to retain its analytical utility, it is pertinent to recognize that subalterns hold overlapping, and sometimes contradictory identities, anchored in concrete settings, where social actors are simultaneously powerful and powerless; unitary and fragmented (Mittelman & Chin 2005, 23). A close examination of the 'shared tradition' of subordinated groups such as boatmen, based on common values, customs, kinship relations and work practices must not be simply conceived as 'given' structures or institutions that either inhibit or enable resistance. Rather, as

Mitchell (1990) is right to suggest, these are themselves 'mechanisms of power' that shape and transform meaning, practices and identities, and should be analyzed as such to reveal 'the means in which relations of dependence and exploitation disguise themselves' (1990, 557). Such a perspective must therefore attend to these culturally specific mechanisms of power, which may at once challenge existing authority structures and notions of hierarchy, while reproducing them at the same time. These ambiguities and contradictions cannot be adequately captured within the binary oppositions of onstage/offstage, resistance and domination, but rather necessitate an examination of the dynamic process involved in the production, circulation, negotiation and contestation of meaning in everyday life (Kondo 1990; Reed Danhey 1993).

The Subaltern Studies School method of reading standardized elite historiography 'against the grain' provides valuable insights into the subjectivity and agency of the subaltern classes as active participants in South Asian history and society (Raheja & Gold 1994). Likewise, Scott's work remains highly suggestive because of its potential for unravelling the practices and meanings underpinning the day-to-day struggles of ordinary people, who seek to secure their livelihoods and enhance their social status. Such considerations have informed my own ethnographic study of the boatmen, where their unique position in Banaras' political and ritual economy exposes them to the forefront of social change and transformation in unpredictable and complicated ways. I argue that in order to fully appreciate the complexities of India's social structure, we must critically examine subaltern identity, not as a single category of experience, but rather as one that accommodates multiple and sometimes competing facets of identity and difference. Boatmen are exposed to and operate within a wide range of forces and social relationships, in which traditional authority structures and state policies play a significant role. Resistance and non-conformity are best understood as oppositional strategies designed to challenge particular forms of oppression, rather than emerging out of an authentic experience, fixed position or autonomous social site (Gal 1995; Moore 1998).

Boatmen have historically been a marginalized community. They are subalterns in the sense that they have limited access to modern institutions, including education, public services and political representation. They experience domination not only under postcolonial state power, but also under traditional authority and the ideological system of caste. In other words, boatmen are disadvantaged in both 'modern' and 'traditional' terms.

**The Day-to-Day Reality of the Boatmen's Lives**

The Boatmen's marginality also stems from their material conditions. The majority of boatmen experience poverty in their day-to-day lives. A brief sketch of the domestic arrangements of boatmen will illustrate the point. As mentioned, the number of boatmen working regularly on the riverfront is approximately 2000, with most residing near the ghats on which they work. Nowadays, because of rising rental prices on the riverfront itself, some boatmen are being forced to move further inland. The majority of boatmen live with their extended families and their houses are generally no more than one or two cramped rooms (3 by 3 metres). Due to family size, which is generally too large to be accommodated in such small quarters, many young boatmen choose to sleep on their boats or in neighbourhood temples. It is important to emphasize that the overwhelming majority of boatmen lead a hand-to-mouth existence. This is partly because of the seasonal nature of their work. Apart from those boatmen who work on the central ghats, most boatmen earn very little during the monsoon months, when few tourists or pilgrims visit Banaras. During these difficult months some rely on their savings, while others resort to casual (manual) work to make ends meet.

Most households have only very basic necessities, with no running water and erratic electricity (usually 'stolen', that is, illegally sourced from wealthier neighbours). Their diet is basic, mostly vegetarian with fish served on special occasions. Boatmen generally marry within their own caste (Mallah/Nishad), and while all boatmen belong to the Mallah caste (*jati*), not all Mallahs are boatmen. In fact, the majority of Mallahs in Banaras are engaged in occupations not connected to the river economy. According to boatmen, however, marriage is no longer clan-bound and they marry across these sub groups. As such, their marriage networks are becoming increasingly wider in geographical terms. Whether a prospective wife comes from a boatman family or not, or a different locale or occupational group is unimportant. What matters, as the boatmen and their mothers told me, is that the prospective wife belongs to a 'good' and 'respected' family and is able to provide the dowry required.[19] This is not to say that marriage into a prosperous boatman family from another ghat is not beneficial or desired, but it is infrequent due mainly to practical reasons, such as the boatmen being comparatively few, while the Mallahs overall are numerous and span the entire Uttar Pradesh and Bihar regions.

Education among the older generation is uncommon and most are illiterate. Among the younger boatmen, however, the majority have primary schooling (up to 5th standard) and basic reading and writing skills. Not surprisingly, therefore, the prospect for skilled/qualified employment is slight. Moreover, while many boatmen claim they want their children to be educated and to attain such qualified work (preferably government jobs, which provide pensions and benefits), the socio-economic reality of everyday life, as well as caste discrimination, prevents them from achieving such goals and, perhaps, the general lack of conditioning to gain an education. Boatmen are an underprivileged and subordinate group and as such their structural and material position constrains their lives and shapes their

---

19    A 'good family' is a somewhat vague definition, but as far as I could gauge it broadly means that the prospective wife's family has a respectable standing in the community, similar socio-economic status and that the woman is well mannered, does not work outside the household, is preferably educated (primary schooling) and fair skinned.

stories/narratives (Pandey 2000, 288). In other words, boatmen do not possess the assets that higher status, educated and credentialed people do, which makes their predicament rather different from that of local middle class elites, for example. For boatmen, their major assets are their expertise and skills as boatmen, in a particular place where these are needed.

This book examines the boatmen's labour patterns and resistance practices as they transpire on the River Ganga. It examines their social conditions and the systematic marginalization and discrimination they experience in their everyday lives. The book does not, however, explore the domestic sphere of the boatmen's lives or the role of women in the community.[20] This is because, firstly, as a male I have very little access to female members of the community, and secondly because there are no women who ply boats: boating is a gendered occupation.[21] Likewise, in this book I am not concerned with issues surrounding masculinity, the body and consumption and how these are related to identity construction (see Alter 1992; Mehta 1997). I am not suggesting that such issues are irrelevant to the study of the boatmen's lives and livelihood. Rather, my own ethnographic study focuses on a specific aspect of the boatmen's lives – their work – and the relationship between occupation and identity. I am interested in the boatman community as it is formed over time in work relations. Because 'work' here is in the public sphere, it directly involves relations with institutions and individuals outside the immediate community. One of the most influential of 'outside' institutions affecting the boatman community has been and is the state.

## Contours of the Book

The first two chapters examine the encounter between boatmen and the modern colonial and postcolonial state. Chapter 1 historically contextualizes the boatmen, discussing the construction of the Mallah caste under colonial rule, offering critical insights into the workings of the colonial state and its discursive principles. It discusses the implications of such policies and practices for the historical and social construction of a unified Mallah caste and the possibility of dissent and resistance under such restrictive conditions. Chapter 2 focuses on the encounter between boatmen and the modern Indian state at the local level. It examines the response and reactions of the boatman community to state policies and an

---

20    On women contesting hegemonic representations and exercising agency within what is largely considered a male dominated environment in North India, see Pintcham (2005); Moore, E (1998); Raheja & Gold (1994). Nita Kumar's (1988) analysis of the world of the artisans of Banaras remains one of the most nuanced interrogations of social categories such as gender, work and popular cultural practice. For a more psychologically oriented analysis of male dominance in Banaras, see Derne (1995).

21    By boating I am referring to an activity that involves the regular use of boats, such fishing, carrying cargo and sightseeing.

environmental development scheme, known as the Ganga Action Plan, which effectively deprived the boatmen of their traditional rights to fish and cultivate on the riverbeds. The chapter examines the boatman community's interpretation and experience of modernity and the development of a 'marginalized' boatman identity, stressing poverty, oppression, and exclusion.

Chapter 3 describes the fascinating work system used by boatmen along the riverfront of Banaras. It reveals a unique and sophisticated socio-economic system, which enables the boatmen to regulate space, mitigate conflict and retain their monopoly over the boating industry in the city. Operating within a bustling and commercially competitive pilgrimage and tourism environment, this innovative system works as a 'moral economy', providing an economic safety net for boatmen and preventing the modern state, local actors and commercial entrepreneurs from infringing on their livelihood. The critical exploration into the workings of space through social practice in this chapter also reveals tension and competition from within the boatman community itself, highlighting both institutionalized and more diffuse forms of resistance.

Chapter 4 examines the role of boatmen as ritual specialists within the ritual economy of Banaras and their devotional relationship with the River Ganga. It discusses how the boatmen invoke caste identity, myth and other cultural symbols to contest Brahminical authority and assert their rights to conduct rituals and maintain control over sacred space. Chapter 5 looks at the relationship between the boatmen and those with whom they interact in their daily lives: pilgrims, domestic tourists and foreign tourists. I examine how the subaltern boatmen exercise agency within what is essentially an asymmetrical power relation, by deploying a range of innovative and calculated strategies to control and influence tourists and pilgrims arriving at the riverfront. It is on an interpersonal level that the dominant tourist discourse emerging from First World countries is often creatively appropriated, subverted and manipulated by marginal groups, such as the boatmen, to further their own economic and social interests. The existence of uneven power relations does not necessarily entail the subordination and passivity of the subaltern 'other'.

The concluding chapter offers further discussion on resistance, particularly in relation to the question of when and under what circumstances subaltern groups, such as the boatmen, switch between everyday modes of resistance to more overt and systematic confrontation. Throughout the book I argue for the need to leave aside binary assumptions implicit in studies of resistance, in favour of a more nuanced approach which is attentive to the inherent ambiguities and complexities involved in the practice of resistance. Such an approach enables us to emphasize the plural articulation of resistance in 'everyday' life, which may, according to the context, serve to reproduce, sustain, subvert and naturalize religious and cultural ideologies. By drawing on ethnographic material about the boatmen of Banaras, an analysis of the multifaceted nature of subaltern identity serves to highlight the place of appropriation, innovation and accommodation as alternative forms of resistance operating within existing structures of power. Furthermore, it is only when we consider extraneous forces (e.g., caste uplift movements, globalization) as well as ongoing politics within the subaltern community itself that we can better understand social change and the changing nature of domination in contemporary India. A scrutiny of these changes is essential for our appreciation of the complex dynamics involved in the construction of subaltern communities all over India and their attempt to make meaning and sense of their lives within the constraints of a rapidly changing socio-economic order.

# Chapter 1
# The Criminal Type:
# Domesticating the Ganges Boatmen

I invited Vivek, a part-time journalist, for a cup of tea at a restaurant by the river. I had heard that he was interested in working for me as a research assistant and translator. When I told him of my plan to study the boatmen of Banaras, he replied, somewhat condescendingly, that one must be wary of boatmen, as they are well-known cheats, drunks and thieves. He pressed me to reconsider my research topic, saying that this group of people are of the 'criminal type'. Well, I thought to myself, perhaps this is the reason why no anthropologist has travelled this murky path before. I was, however, intrigued by the prospect of working with 'criminals' that inspired such strong sentiments. This would indeed be a fascinating project to pursue.

Admittedly, I wasn't overly surprised to hear this from Vivek; I was aware of the fact that under colonial rule people belonging to fishing and boating communities were legally classified under the ominous category of 'criminal castes'. Still, I was somewhat taken aback by the conviction and immediacy conveyed by such derogatory statements. To what extent contemporary views of boatmen are coloured by the colonial legacy is hard to determine. Nevertheless, the targeting and categorizing of a group as a 'criminal' caste is significant if we are to understand the way in which under colonial social order boatmen and numerous other low castes were systematically marginalized, oppressed and stigmatized. The colonial view of boatmen as 'criminals' continues to echo in popular perceptions, not only among the middle classes (as Vivek's comments show), but also among local officials and even within government institutions. To trace this process of marginalization and stigmatization of boatmen, I turn to the colonial archives for they reveal the historically and socially constructed nature of crime and criminality in colonial India. As recent studies have shown (Yang 1985; Radhkrishna 2001), ideas regarding criminality and what constituted illegal behaviour in the imperial system were shaped by the British experience of criminality in their own society, as well as by the colonial perceptions of Indian society itself – one dictated by the despotic rule of 'tradition' and the caste system.

In this chapter I describe the British encounter with the boatmen of the River Ganges, offering insights into the role of the colonial anthropology of India and its categories of knowledge in substantiating the imperial social order, and its regime of discipline and control over the subject population. I chart the way in which such forms of knowledge were instrumental in identifying boatmen as belonging to a wider group of 'criminal tribes', enabling the imperial state to exercise its authority and power to relegate these boatmen to the margins of society.[1]

While British concerns with trade and subsequently statecraft required an unprecedented degree of documentation, codification and disciplinary measures to control and administer space and people; it would be misleading to attribute the British with sole authorship over changes to social and economic structures in India.[2] In our case, the historical perspective reveals that boatmen have long been implicated in the process of social and economic change, one that far pre-dates British colonialism. During the pre-modern period there is evidence to suggest that boat people were formed into guild-like groups, which engaged in river trade and commerce throughout the Gangatic Valley (see Darian 1970). It is during the early modern period that we find evidence of an intensifying network of coastal and inland trade, with the spatial distribution of goods, animals and people along the length of the River Ganges. This was a time when much of the subcontinent came under the centralized administrative structure of the Mughal rulers, with its impressive military, fiscal and monetary systems and vibrant urban culture (Alam & Subramayam 1998 [eds]; Richards 1993). In fact, during the decline of the Mughal state in the early 18th century, internal trade continued to flourish, largely because of the successor states and their monastic armies, which were able to control and extract revenue from a well developed network of pilgrimage routes, rural markets and town bazaars in the Gangatic region (Bayly 1983; Pinch 1996).[3]

While the complex cultural and political landscape of India has gone through many historical transformations, with every ruling power attempting to contain, survey and control it, the colonial era is worth looking at in greater depth for it sought to conceive India, and Indian society, on a grand scale, with a systemic probing of all 'Things Indian' (Crooke 1906).

---

1    Under the British the terms tribe and caste were commonly interchanged.

2    Some scholars have argued that the recent spate of literature advocating the 'colonial constructionist' arguments pertaining to caste, community and identity is overdrawn and historically inaccurate, see Bayly (1985) and Gilmartin & Lawrence (eds 2002). To my mind the issue is more about emphasis, rather than a fundamental difference. For a comprehensive summary of the historiographical debates in South Asia, see Datta (1999) and Pinch (1999).

3    According to Bayly, the British were thus able to take advantage of the opportunities afforded to them at the time. Indeed, company officials were socially, economically and emotionally involved with their local counterparts, generating a favourable environment for Indian merchant families to forge commercial partnerships with European enterprises (Bayly 1983, 239; see also Dalrymple 2003).

## Encountering the British

The boatmen were one of the first groups to encounter the British as they entered the Indian subcontinent. Before the advent of roads and railways, rivers were the main arteries of communication across India. The River Ganges was the chief commercial and communication route on which travellers and military personnel could advance north from the Bay of Bengal. Boats were the primary vehicles for transporting goods, natural resources and people.

While Europeans travelling along the river marvelled at the scenic beauty of the Ganges, their impressions of natives – boatmen included – were often much less favourable, as Lieutenant Thomas Bacon (1837, 233) from the Bengal Horse Artillery noted with exasperation:

> It is utterly impossible to induce the natives to build their boats after any improved system. Year after year, though they have beautiful European models before their eyes, the obstinate fools persist to turn out hundreds of these execrably-devised boats… and why? Because their fathers and their grandfathers before them, and their grandfathers before them, from time immemorial, have continued to build their boats so.

Bacon's impressions strongly echo the colonial Orientalist view of India as unchanging and primitive, in which the natives and their technologies are depicted as archaic – the polar opposite of their European counterparts. India was depicted as frozen in time and the boatmen portrayed as irrational and stubborn people, unable to free themselves from the shackles of tradition. In this case, it is indeed 'tradition' that seems to be the cause of their backwardness, but the notion that such behaviour is one transmitted through an immutable hereditary system already begins to surface.

The 'backwardness' of the natives, however, was not something the colonial officials could simply ignore or tolerate; after all the East India Company had practical considerations in mind. As the Company took over the responsibility of collecting tax revenue, ensuring the safety of boats carrying goods and tax profits became a chief concern.

Colonial fears of the threat of robbery committed by thuggees, dacoits and 'predatory' castes on the rivers are evident in many writings from the period. Boats were the primary targets for such crimes and boatmen seen as principal suspects or at least collaborators. Nevertheless, while boatmen were commonly portrayed as lazy, villainous thieves, their skills as proficient sailors and navigators were indispensable for river travel. Boatmen were therefore both a threat to British interests as well as a necessity for river navigation.[4] How then did colonial rule

---

4　Bacon's view on the execrable nature of indigenous boats was part of the early colonial discourse. With the increased interest in river navigation and the colonial obsession with cataloguing everything that was native, a radically different view of the river boats was

realize its goal of managing, controlling and reforming such 'unruly' groups as the boatmen? The answer lies within the broader history of British imperial expansion – one in which governmentality, with its technologies of enumeration, surveillance, and reform, along with Christian values, combined to define the project of the State, and its conception of Indian society.

## The Colonial Anthropology of India and the Civilizing Mission

From the beginning of the 19th century onwards, the shift from the economic role of the British East India Company to full British rule in India was a gradual one. It involved both a change in ideology and practice. The Company, which initially restricted its concerns to trade and commerce, became increasingly implicated in collecting taxes and land revenues. The expansion of the Company's interests also necessitated an improved ordering and managing of Indian society. Empirical knowledge gathered by the Company was therefore designed to fulfil such administrative demands. Orientalists, missionaries and British officials all collected information about Indian languages, forms of landholding, property and social structure. Initially the British based their view of the Indian social structure (caste in particular) on the Hindu religious texts. These views were influenced by the bias of their Brahmin informants, whom the British considered the actual guardians of religious knowledge in India (Amin 1989; Dirks 2001, 24, 116). As Bernard Cohn (1998) has convincingly shown, by the late 18th century and early 19th century, there evolved a (mis)conception that Brahmins were the centrepiece of Hindu social structure, with Indian society largely viewed as immutable and fixed in time, and Hindus guided by the rules and principles of the ancient religious texts. Such views were subsequently moderated, though not abandoned, as a result of the amassing of ethnographic data about Indian society from the countryside suggesting a more complex picture of India as a whole.

After the Great Rebellion of 1857, the British Crown assumed the role of governing India. The perception was that in order to avoid similar revolts the state needed to know its subjects more comprehensively. Such a rationale provided further momentum to what Nicholas Dirks (2001) has aptly called the 'Ethnographic State'. By the 19th century various missionaries, western scholars and colonial officials began to collect detailed information regarding the manners, customs and cultural practices of the Indians. These ethnographies, which reflected the anthropological theories of the time, were later published in divisional gazetteers and books and were incorporated into the enormous project of the census of British India. The colonial anthropology of India generated an abundance of information about the subcontinent – ranging from its physical features and ethnic constitution

---

developed. A report on *The Boats of the Ganges* provided a detailed analysis of the various river crafts, which it suggested were particularly suitable to the diverse physical, social and ecological characteristics of the River Ganges, see Hornell (1924).

**Figure 1.1    View in and near Benares, Charles Forrest.** *A picturesque tour along the River Ganges and Jumna.* **London. 1824**

*Source*: Toutain (1985:15)

– to the elaborate descriptions of the agricultural, industrial, religious and social life of the 'natives'.[5] Such information was methodically arranged for the purpose of serving 'as an easy reference work for colonial administrators, for the police as well as revenue agents, district magistrates, and army recruiters' (Dirks 1996, 279). This was part of the process of objectifying and normalizing the indigenous landscape (Chatterjee 1993, 19).

At the same time, such perceptions were intrinsic to the notion that the British were embarking upon a civilizing mission. As in their other colonizing missions, the British saw themselves as carrying the torch of progress and modernity to the primitive world, but their ideology and practice was also stimulated from their experience of India. By turning the Indian population and their practices into 'objects of knowledge' and placing them within the linear narrative of the Enlightenment, the British could assume authority and construct representations of the Indians and Indian society in terms starkly opposed to those of themselves (Cohn 1998; Dirks 1996; Prakash 1995). The generalizing, authoritative tone of such cultural representations arose from the anthropologists' certainty that their ethnographic narratives were based on scientific knowledge and objectivity.

The colonial perception of Indian society, however, was not a homogenous one. It evolved over time and was fraught with contradictions and opposing theories, only some of which attempted to provide a comprehensive view of the Indian

---

5    See, for example, Crooke (1974 [1876]; 1980 [1907]; Elliot 1985 [1870]; Risley 1969 [1915]; Sherring 1974 [1872]).

subjects.[6] Nonetheless, what particularly concerns me is how such representations of India functioned within colonial discourse and practice, in which a fairly distinct view of the 'other' was expounded as part of the essentializing thrust of administrative practices and policy making.

The British themselves were well aware that simple binary oppositions could not account for the heterogeneity and complexity of Indian society that confronted them. In order to control and manage this diversity, the British collected extensive information from religious texts, empirical observations and via the administrative census. 'Difference' continued to figure as an important classificatory metaphor for ordering Indian society as a whole. This 'ordering of difference' (Chatterjee 1993, 20; Metcalf 1995) was established as part of the dominant scientific paradigm embraced by the colonial regime. Within this positivistic paradigm facts were revealed by the close examination of categories, such as ethnicity, race, nature, religion and most prominently caste.[7] It was during this time that caste came to the fore as the essential ordering principle of Indian civilization. Caste was seen as the reason for and the symbol of India's backwardness, as expressing the primordial irrationality of the native, which in turn served to further legitimize British rule and dominance over its subjects.

*The Tyranny of Caste*

If the prevailing perception of many colonials was that Indian social structure was based upon and determined by the caste system, the system itself was branded as the ultimate evil. One such vociferous critique of the caste system was the missionary ethnographer, Reverend M.A Sherring. Sherring, who wrote a detailed three volume study entitled, *Hindu Tribes and Castes* (1974 [1872; 1879; 1881]), had a particular interest in Benares where he lived and conducted extensive research over several years. In the first volume of the series Sherring provides a telling account of how the British perceived their role in relation to the subject population:

> What was impossible under the former administrations is possible under English law, the fundamental principle of which is, that all men are equal. It has taken a century for this fundamental principle to be understood by the natives of India; so absolutely were they under the dominion of caste prejudice and tyranny... [British influence] is aided by that spirit of our Indian rulers... sustained and strengthened by the sound education offered to the natives of every rank... Add to this the Christian faith... which strives to elevate the depressed, to abolish

---

6    This was not a unidirectional process, as Vasudha Dalmia (1999) has convincingly shown through a close investigation of the influential writings of Harichandra of Banaras (late 19th century).

7    For an insightful exploration of the cultural politics of race and nature, see Moore et al. (2003).

ignorance, and to generate the desire for freedom in every breast... in moving
and transforming the masses of India (Sherring 1974, 248–251).

The above quote offers a unique insight into the workings of the colonial
state and its discursive principles. First, Sherring indicates how the British saw
their role as 'legitimate rulers' in India. For him, unlike previous rulers who were
either unable or unwilling to deal with the 'tyrannical' caste system, the British
were enlightened rulers who would ultimately 'transform' and free their subjects
from their primitive customs. Sherring believed this could be achieved by the
introduction of modern British values, institutions and practices, along with the
assistance of the Indian elites and the universal faith of Christianity. This, in turn,
would emancipate those souls, especially the low castes, whom Sherring saw as
shackled by the oppressive caste system. Sherring, like many other missionaries,
was frustrated by the inability to convert Hindus to the Christian faith (Dirks 2001,
47, 131). This, he was convinced, was due to the passive and gullible nature of
Hindus, who could easily be exploited by the cunning Brahmins. As he wrote:
'This credulous and servile condition of the Hindu mind has afforded a golden
opportunity to the wily Brahman, thirsting for rule and for the exercise of his
superior gifts' (Sherring 1974, vol. 3, 226).

The Orientalist construction of their colonial subjects as 'childlike', 'passive'
and 'irrational' was explained not simply as one in opposition to the enlightened
Briton, but as one resulting from the cruel indigenous system of caste. Evangelical
Christians such as Sherring, saw their mission as rescuing the poor low castes
from the abusive and hegemonic rule of Brahmins by propagating social reform.
Ironically, Sherring's detailed account of Hindu castes, which I explore in more
detail in the following section, largely relied on Brahminical texts, such as the
'Laws of Manu', to describe and understand the system. Sherring also provides
one of the earliest accounts of the fishing and boating communities in Benares.
His account was the precursor to subsequent efforts by ethnologists and census
officials to standardize, define and position the Mallah caste within the hierarchical
model of caste structure.

## Colonial Accounts and the Mallahs

Although Sherring was clearly influenced by the racial theories of his time and
drew on extensive empirical findings, he was still captivated by the ideology of
Varna (literally 'colour'), stemming from religious texts, and relied on this to
make sense of the caste system.[8] Sherring (1874: xxii) concludes that the 'existing

---

8    Here I use the term 'caste' (the Indian term *jati*) to describe the endogamous groups
that usually follow a common occupation, as opposed to Varna, which are usually depicted
as the four major caste categories set in hierarchical order: Brahmin (priest), Kshatriya
(warrior), Vaishya (merchant), Shudra (servant).

Hindu castes are of two kinds: first those of comparatively pure blood, Brahmans, Kshatriyas, and perhaps some of the Vaishyas; secondly, those of impure or mixed blood, embracing all the castes not included in the first division'. His volume of writing is divided into four parts according to this general classification of 'great Hindu castes' based on social precedence: Part I – The Brahmanical Tribes; Part II – The Kshatriya or Rajpoot Tribes; Part III – Mixed Caste and Tribes – Vaishyas, Shudras, and Others; and Part IV – Aboriginal Tribes and Inferior Castes. Each chapter examines the various sub-castes under its heading with systematic attention given to their identifying physical features, origins, geographic spread, myths and legends, ceremonies and customs.

According to Sherring's classification of castes in Benares, the boatmen belong to the overarching Mallah caste. They are placed (in Part III, sub-chapter XIII) along with weavers, dyers, self-manufacturers and others. Sherring writes: 'All boatmen are called Mallahs, no matter what caste they may belong to. Yet there is a special tribe of Mallahs, divided into several clans'.[9] A list of ten names follows, suggesting that all belong to, or are employed as boatmen and fishermen, although some follow more specific occupations: 'the Muriaris are fishermen. The Guriyas are stonemasons. The Chains are steersmen' (Sherring 1974, 246–347).[10]

Sherring himself seems confused as to the varied occupational designations found among these sub-castes. In order to establish a collective belonging under the overarching Mallah caste, he resorts to their origin myths: 'their common father, by name Nikhad' (Sherring, 347). According to Sherring the name Nikhad, also commonly known as Nishad, is a familiar one and bears important meaning for the Mallah caste. In his introduction to the first volume Sherring proposed a scientific method of identifying the 'pedigree of inferior castes' by citing the Laws of Manu, claiming that the 'Nishada' was the son of a Brahman father and Shudra mother, hence the mixed blood category (Sherring, xviii). By identifying the Mallah caste (and the various sub-castes) as originating from the same source, he endows them with a uniform identity.

*Defining the Criminal*

While recent scholarship has largely focused on colonial constructions of criminality, it is worth noting that there are numerous references to crime and punishment found in the Laws of Manu, particularly with relation to the lower orders of society. One can speculate that British perceptions of low caste Shudras as criminally predisposed was in part derived from what Sherring, and others like him, assumed were the authoritative legal texts of the Hindu tradition –

---

9    Sherring defines these clans as subdivisions 'that profess to belong to one and the same caste and tribe', but are exclusive in that they do not intermarry (1974: xxiii).

10    The various names are: 1. Mallah, 2. Muria, Muriari, 3. Pandubi, 4. Bathawa, Badhriya, 5. Chaini, Chaim or Chai, 6. Suraya, 7. Guriya, 8. Tiar, 9. Kulwant, or Kulwat, 10. Kewat.

the Dharmashastras – an equivalent to that of Sharia law found in Islam. This Brahminical and textual bias characteristic of British perceptions, was of course a problematic one, since Manu is a complex and often inconsistent text that should be regarded as a source of authority in the field of jurisprudence, rather than a rigid set of rules and laws that were enforced and followed by the ruling classes (Smith 1991).

The Laws of Manu (or Manu as the text is often referred to) are generally assumed to have been composed around the beginning of the Common Era. The laws were partly designed to establish a Brahminical hegemony, providing detailed accounts of the punishments to be meted out to those low castes that committed crimes and transgressed social and moral codes. For example, Manu stipulated the procedures to be followed by the king when punishing thieves, noting that '[o]n the first offence of pickpocket, he should have two of his fingers cut off; on the second, one hand and one foot; and on the third he should be killed' (Manu 1991, 227). Severe punishments were also given to members of the lowest orders for defaming a Brahmin, committing adultery, engaging in sexual promiscuity, and drunkenness.

In describing such legal processes, the Brahminical worldview of orthodox Hinduism was legitimized and sanctioned in the ritual and religious realms as well as the political one.[11] These transgressions of social order were conceived not only as sins, with cosmological ramifications for future lives, but were also conceptualized as crimes to be dealt with by the state power. The text thus specified the way the political authority, embodied in the king, should identify, control and respond to such acts (in accordance with ones social status, religious duties and stage of life) by delivering corporal, monetary or even capital punishment. Such constructions of crime and punishment, where the body was a primary locus of social control, and where Shudras, in particular, were subjected to the harshest penalties, far pre-date colonial views.

In other words, I want to caution here against an overly constructivist view of criminality as simply a product of European, or more specifically British, discourse and practice. To be sure, the British systematized, surveyed and conceptualized criminality in unprecedented ways and scale, articulated within the modern, bureaucratic state machinery, but there were also other actors, discourses and cultural categories that contributed to the designation of low castes, and Mallahs, specifically, as a criminally inclined.

Interestingly, the Laws of Manu also mention river travel and ferrying regulations, with details regarding the varying fees to be charged according to distance and weight of goods and people.[12] This illustrates that attempts

---

11   Here, Olivelle's (2008) recent study of 'Crime and Punishment in Ancient India: ideology of rebirth and the making of the body', informs my analysis.

12   According to Manu : '[404] At a ferry, an (empty) cart should be charged one penny, a man's (load) half a penny, a livestock animal or a woman a quarter (of a penny), and a man with no load half a quarter. [405] Carts full of goods should be charged a ferry

to standardize and regulate trade and the movement of people were a concern during the pre-modern period. It may also be indicative of the kind of practices that existed over two millennia ago and the consequent efforts by the dominant classes to control a wilful and mobile population. As we shall see, what merits but one paragraph in Manu can hardly match the bureaucratic impulse of the modern period with its proliferation of laws, institutions and disciplinary powers, designed to produce 'domesticated' subjects and an orderly landscape. Of course, we do not know whether such concerns were more central to society in the time of Manu than documented, since trade was always predominant in the Gangatic region, but we do know that these concerns assumed such prominence in the minds of the colonial authorities as to require volumes of reports, inquiries, legislations and specially designated inspectors and police officers to survey and oversee river navigation and the locals involved in it, including boatmen.

The British discourse of criminality came into prominence following the 1857 uprising and subsequent concern for establishing and maintaining law and order in the colony. The discourse of criminality, partly endorsed by local elites, was premised upon a polar view of Indian society, divided into itinerant and sedentary communities (Freitag 1991). Various marginal low status groups identified in the ethnographic register as 'wandering, itinerant tribes' were almost automatically labelled as criminally disposed and subjected to new surveillance and control methods (see, for example, Edwards 1924). Ethnographic knowledge of these itinerant groups served as the basis on which they were registered under the newly enacted Criminal Tribes Act of 1871. During this time, the Bengal authorities listed the Binds (a sub-caste of the Mallahs) as a group with criminal tendencies, committing organized dacoities (Yang 1985, 113). By 1872, the Mallah caste itself was added to the list and registered as a 'Criminal Tribe' along with other groups labelled as 'Well-Known Criminals Recently Settled in Agriculture' (quoted in Tiwary 2001, 241). Such labelling reflected the government's discomfort with wandering tribes and their non-settled occupations (Tiwary 2001).[13] As Sanjay Nigam has argued 'the urgent necessity of controlling the criminal tribes was stressed through the images and metaphors that denote their dangerous, disorderly predatory features as against the attractive, familiar, desirable virtues of settled peasants' (1990, 148). This was, in part, due to colonial commercial interests, which

---

toll according to their value, but carts empty of goods and baggage (should be charged just) a little something. [406] For a long journey, the boat toll should be in proportion to the time of the journey and the place (of destination) – but it should be understood this is just for (journeys) along the banks of rivers; there is no definite rule for (journeys) on the ocean' (Manu 1991, 195).

13    British concern with robbery, murder and smuggling on the river ways of the Gangatic region was elaborated in various publications, see for example Hutton's (1857, 74–78) section of 'River Thugs'; and Major-General R. Alexander's (1856, 15–19), fascinating account of the controversial Opium trade and smuggling and policing practices along the Ganges.

favoured settled populations from which it could more easily extract revenue. However, as several scholars have shown, the enumeration and codification of criminal tribes and caste in the colonies, was informed by the discourse on crime back in Britain (Nigam 1990; Tolen 1991).

During the mid-19th century the British developed a theory of hereditary criminality, which could explain some of the social ills plaguing 19th century Victorian Britain. Criminality, its reasons and signs, were perceived by reference to the labouring poor, identified as 'dangerous and criminal classes'. Tracing the discourse on criminal caste in administrative literature in India, Tolen (1991) observes that the British bourgeoisie had quite specific criteria with regards to what constituted the 'dangerous classes' in their own society. This included traits such as drunkenness, poverty, unsettled family life, a wandering occupation, 'poor upbringing, character defects, and hereditary predisposition', all of which were seen as both causes and signs of criminality. Such views were readily applied to the Indian context, with caste already perceived as a primary determining factor in the Indians' behaviour and occupation, which 'could be easily, if vaguely, related to racial and hereditary theories of criminality' (Tolen 1991, 108–109).

The notion that certain castes had a tendency towards a life of 'habitual crime' is readily evident in William Crooke's (1974 [1896]) four-volume encyclopaedic coverage of *The Tribes and Castes of North-Western India*. An examination of this formidable work offers further insight into how the Mallahs were relegated into a criminal caste category. [14]

*The Peculiarities of the Mallah Caste*

Crook's work is a detailed analysis of the caste system, its origins, structure and customs, and possibly the most comprehensive account of the numerous castes and tribes in North-Western India. Crooke arranged the various castes in easily accessible alphabetical order. Each caste is described using similar categories, such as marriage, death and birth ceremonies, myths, religious rituals, festivals, occupation, and social structure, to provide a comparable, standardized and holistic view of the various castes. These categories are supplemented with census figures (1891 Census) to note the general caste population and its distribution throughout the North-Western Provinces.

Crooke's account of the Mallah caste, and various associated sub-castes, is far more extensive than that of Sherring. He drew upon both textual and empirical data

---

14    In fact, the 'habitual nature' of Mallahs and their supposed predisposition to crime is given further evidence in Naidu's study (1915 [1996]) entitled, *The History of Railway Thieves*, where the Mallahs figure widely as a criminal tribe characterized by its peculiar methods of worship, drinking and dancing habits and, most importantly, as river criminals who gained 'full advantage of the railways as an auxiliary in respect of rapid retreats or as means of transporting the proceeds of their raids to their homes with security and despatch' (1915, 99).

and was conscious of the complexity of such a diverse group as the Mallah who were associated with numerous sub-castes and tribes. According to him, this made an 'ethnological analysis of them... intricate and perplexing' (Crooke 1974, vol. 3, 460). He records the various names by which the Mallah caste is known to other castes/tribes, as well as how they represent themselves. Reiterating Sherring's account he suggests that 'most Mallahs represent themselves as descended from the Nishada, a mountain tribe of the Vindhya Range' (Crooke, 461). He then goes on to note their tradition citing the mythological story in the Ramayana as an important source of the caste's identity. According to Crooke, 'their king is described in the Ramayana as having treated Ram and Sita with kindness in their wanderings'. He continues, '[t]he ancestor of the Mallahs of the Ganges valley... is said to have steered the boat in which Ram Chandra crossed the river on his way to Chitrakut during his banishment' (Crooke, 461).

Crooke goes on to systematically examine the Mallah's 'tribal organization'. In agreement with Sherring, He suggests that Mallah 'is a general term including various boating and fishing tribes... a definite social group, including a number of endogamous tribes' (Crooke, 460). He concludes with a section about 'occupation and social status' where he notes: 'The business of the caste is managing boats and fishing. Those who are well off own boats of their own and employ poorer members of the tribe to work for them' (Crooke, 466). His descriptions of their lowly ritual status seems to be reinforced by religion, where caste identity is determined by socio-economic practices and by reference to 'pollution' beliefs, attached to daily practices regarding dietary habits, ritual activities, menial labour, and marriage customs. [15]

*Inferiority, Mobility and Criminality*

Crooke's descriptions of the various associated Mallah sub-castes are listed in different entries according to alphabetical order: Bind, Chain, Dhimar, Kahar, Kewat, Muriari, Sorahiya and Tiyar. While Crooke describes the various sub-castes as being different due to their varied origins, occupational traits, rules and customs, one can conclude that all are related to the Mallah caste by virtue of their traditional occupation. That is, among the various sub-caste members, some continue to work as boatmen or fishermen, while others, as Crooke notes, practice a variety of occupational traits, for example, cultivation, palanquin carriers (Kahars) and others said to engage in building (Binds) and thieving (Chain). Furthermore, as he points out, all of these sub-castes have recorded themselves in the census under the various names included in the overarching Mallah category.

---

15    Crooke seems aware of the difficulties involved in reducing caste to essential characteristics, such as occupation/kinship, relations/social structure and so on. Nevertheless, this information is still deployed by anthropologists, administrators and officials today. Thus caste remains literally a 'timeless category'; on the new *People of India Project,* see Jenkins (2003).

In fact, Crooke seems to have realized that some of those sub-castes were socially and economically integrated into the settled village economy. Nevertheless, such considerations were conveniently overlooked by officials in their efforts to standardize and homogenize these sub-castes by reducing their diverse everyday practices to those of boating and fishing (Tiwary 2001).

Fishermen and boatmen were seen as an itinerant community, bearing the marks of ritually inferior castes, with poor dietary habits, and engaging in savage practices. Apart from eating fish and meat, some Mallahs were reported as eating rats, tortoises, crocodiles and partaking in excessive alcoholic consumption. When describing the Bind sub-caste, Crooke noted that 'the Binds eat crocodiles and field rats… They do not eat beef, and rank higher in social scale than Chamars [untouchables] for this reason' (Crooke, vol. 1, 113). In this way, colonial ethnographers categorized low social ranking according to dietary customs and rules associated with orthodox notions of purity and pollution. As Tolen (1991, 112) observes, criminality was marked by dietary habits that 'not only offended the standards of British administrators, but also were undoubtedly considered defiling by the elites from who the administrators obtained much of their information'. These dietary practices were seen as being linked to other degrading social practices, such as a lack of personal hygiene and illicit sexual behaviour, all of which were regarded as further signs of their criminality.

The behaviour of the female caste members was taken as a reflection of the characteristics of the low castes as a whole and Mallahs in particular. They were portrayed as morally unrestrained. The Tiyar sub-caste for example, is described as having 'considerable laxity of sexual intercourse' (Crooke, vol. 4, 411). In another related sub-caste, the Bind, Crooke noted that the women 'get drunk, dance, sing obscene songs, and indulge in rude debauchery' (Crooke, vol. 2, 113). When discussing the Mallah caste, Crooke explains the immorality of the women as due, in part, to the long periods of absence of the boatmen and to the community's degraded values. These value ridden accounts were reinforced by the Mallahs' reputation as thieves and gangsters.

Descriptions of the boatmen (and their associated sub-castes) and their thieving practices can be found in other passages throughout Crooke's work. According to Crooke the Chai (Chain or Chaini) are a 'cultivating, fishing and thieving caste'. He notes that their reputation precedes them as 'as thieves, impostors and swindlers' and describes them as people who pick pockets: 'They frequent fairs and bathing places, and the boys are put to steal, while the men act as "fences" and engage the attention of the victim, or facilitate the escape of the thief' (Crooke, vol. 2, 167–168). The above description suggests that thieving was a caste and family affair, whereby the children were inculcated into the trade at an early age. The profession of thieving was perceived not so much as biologically determined, but more as a hereditary occupation – part of a debased caste 'tradition' – passed on from generation to generation.

In the eyes of the British, one of the most disturbing practices was the ritual of 'human sacrifice'.[16] The infamous practices of sati and hook swinging were condemned as savage, not only by the colonial rulers but also by the native elites. These rituals were commonly perceived as the particular domain of the 'irrational', 'impulsive' and 'predatory' low tribes and castes, such as the Mallah. In 1865 the English newspaper, *The Pioneer*, provides an illuminating account of how the colonials acted upon encountering such incidents:

> It seems the Mullas [Mallahs] of Bulooa, whilst engaged in sonee pooja [propitiation of the inauspicious planet of Saturn, of Sani, it being Saturday]; got it into their heads that if blood were shed, some benefit would accrue to their community, and that the parties slain would ride again and live forever!… The throats of the wretched men were immediately cut, while their parents stood by and exhorted them to bear the pain, as they would be sure to return and live for ever. The police now interfered, and met with some rough treatment at the hands of these strange creatures, who did not approve of their orgies being interrupted (15 April 1865, quoted in Cohen 1998, 2).

As with other famous cases of human sacrifice in the subcontinent, such practices were seen as morally and physically degenerate. Crooke also describes this incident to construct the Mallahs and their sub-castes as savages; a group with evident criminal dispositions that required disciplinary measures.

It was, however, the nomadic tendencies or mobility of groups such as the Mallah that posed the most serious threat to colonial officials. As Crooke notes, 'there is good evidence that many of the river dakaities committed in Bengal are the work of Mallahs of these provinces'. He then goes on to quote a Bengal administrator by the name of Dr. Buchanan to illustrate this claim:

> "Of late years the merchants, not only of Gorakhpur, but everywhere I have observed on the Ganges and its branches, have suffered very heavy losses from the carelessness and dissipation of the boatmen who have become totally unmanageable. They have discovered the very great difficulty, if not impossibility, of obtaining legal redress against people who have nothing, who are paid in advance, and who in general escape from justice by moving from place to place with the first boat that sails. There is great reason to suspect that the owners of the boat, or at least the Manjhi who works for them, connive at the tricks of the men, and taking the full hire allow a part of the crew to desert, giving them a trifle, and keeping the remainder to themselves. The owners of the boats are totally careless about keeping the goods, and the composure with which I have seen the boatmen sitting, while the merchant was tearing his hair

---

16    For an analysis of how British rule sought to regulate such practices as *sati* and hook swinging, see Dirks (2001: chapter 8).

and his property going to ruin, was truly astonishing" (quoted in Crooke, 1974, vol. 3, 466–467).

The 'criminality' of the Mallahs was clearly established in anthropological literature. Their caste and occupation predisposed them to such criminality, and consequently the Mallah caste was listed as a criminal tribe under the Criminal Tribes Act. Notifying certain groups as criminals under the Act had important implications. As Nigam (1990, 155) has shown, it barred the caste or tribe from appealing against such notification, secondly, 'it empowered the government to resettle those notified under it, in other words, to impinge upon and actively reshape and mould the existence of the notified tribes' and finally, it amplified their social maginalization, for any interaction with such groups could be seen as breach of the law.

As Buchannan's quote illustrates, the Mallahs were considered not only a source of moral degradation, but also a potential threat to social and economic order in the colony. The overt offences against property and the overall defiant nature of the labour force posed a serious threat to the commercial interests of the rulers, challenging the maintenance of law and order. Not surprisingly, therefore, British authorities invested significant effort at curbing the mobility of boatmen and regulating river navigation along the River Ganges. Moreover, the fact that the Mallahs were already listed as a criminal tribe, empowered the government to domesticate and reform these people into obedient, disciplined and profitable labourers.

Statistical evidence gathered under the census operation provided further support for registering the Mallah as a criminal caste. The following section examines the ways in which the Mallahs were perceived and classified under the British Census of India – by far the most elaborate mechanism by which the imperial state imposed its own definition and authority on its subject population.

## The Mallahs as Defined by the Census

The systematic production of knowledge about the 'native' population reached its height with the publication of the first All India British Census in 1871. The Census provided a detailed record of Indian society, economy and polity. It extended beyond a mere utilitarian exercise, inducing the construction and cementation of certain group identities in terms of caste, race and religion.

As various studies have demonstrated, by classifying Indian society and tabulating its objective components numerically, the decennial Census imposed an order, which carried public authority (see for example, Appadurai 1996; Anderson 1998; Barrier [ed.] 1981; Cohn 1998). Anonymity and totality were the fundamental characteristics of the census institution, reinforced by the fixed categories of caste. Under the census operation certain ideas and values, such as education, literacy, egalitarianism and social progress, were prioritized, informing social classification and contributing to the normalizing and regulating of the Indian population.

Generally, information in the Census reports about the Mallah caste is scant and often imbued with contradictions and obscure information. Perhaps because the enumerators needed to standardize the caste, we find the Mallah mostly grouped with various other castes, which were broadly associated within the occupational category of fishing and boating.

By 1901 H.H. Risley's (the census commissioner at the time) controversial scheme of social precedence was approved. The scheme reinforced the abstraction of caste groups from the local (contextual) environment in which they operated and placed them in a serial group that could be measured and enumerated across India. More importantly, it created an all-India scheme that recognized the importance and validity of the religiously sanctioned social hierarchy, and its usefulness to the British administration in its endeavour to control and manage the populace. In other words, one was recognized by the bureaucratic administration of the state only as a number and part of an aggregate caste group. Individual capabilities and opportunities were measured through one's extended 'body': caste.

The reification of caste categories according to social and ritual hierarchy and the other aspects employed by the census concerning notions of social progress, education, health and law produced a new discourse of caste that had significant political and social repercussions on both the colonial state and its subjects. British officials soon realized the impact of the census and social classification on the subject population.

By the beginning of the 20th century the British received numerous petitions from newly formed caste associations (*sabhas*) claiming higher status. One explanation given by the census officials for the influx of petitions from castes claiming more respectable origins was 'the ancient tradition that the king or the government was the ultimate authority in determining questions of caste'.[17] This meant that British colonial officials had to take on the role of referees, as they approved, rejected or ignored the various claims put forward by caste associations. The census authorities discussed this process in the 1931 census:

> ...the formation of caste sabhas to advance the social status of the lower castes is not a new phenomenon, but it has become very much more common in the last decade. In most cases the procedure is more or less uniform. A new name is selected for the caste, its members are adjured to adopt the sacred thread, and various resolutions are passed dealing with such questions as food and drink, the abandonment of 'degrading' occupations, postponement of the age of marriage etc.[18]

---

17    *C of I*, 1921, *India*, vol. I, part 1. *Report*. p. 223.
18    *C of I*, 1931, *Bihar and Orissa*, vol. VII, part 1. *Report*. p. 267.

The process described above highlights the importance of symbolic collective activities amongst caste members claiming a higher caste category. Most common amongst the low castes were the claims put forward to be recognized as Kshatriya Varna (warrior caste, amongst the higher castes wearing the sacred thread).[19] The Kahars, a group often included with Mallahs, declared themselves as belonging to an all India caste association, based in Lahore claiming to be 'Kashyap Rajput' (Rajpoot): a Kshatriya Varna.[20] Such claims demonstrated the way in which the caste category became more significant for individuals than the endogamous group at the trans-local level, as it was only under these officially recognisable and uniform caste identities that various caste groups could negotiate their position with the colonial administration.[21]

It is not until the 1921 Census of United Provinces that we find evidence of an attempt by the Mallahs to improve their status in the caste hierarchy by claiming the name Nishada (often Nishad), as the overarching name of the caste.[22] This name had positive connotations for the group as it placed the caste among an honourable people who, according to the epic Ramayana, devotedly served and protected the godking Rama during his tribulations in exile. These Sanskritizing techniques were common amongst many low castes seeking to present a unified front and elevate their social position in relation to the administration and communities around them.

Nevertheless, claims for higher status were not always effective. The Mallah's criminal reputation with its exotic, unlawful and immoral behaviour as described by Crooke and others formed the basis of colonial census classification. As we have seen, under the census operation caste was further rigidified and reified as fixed in time and unchangeable. This reification of caste differences, as Metcalf notes, was most vividly 'expressed in the creation of two opposed groups of "criminal tribes" and "martial races"' (Metcalf 1995, 122). This could have serious consequences for entire communities, as being categorized as a low caste often meant exclusion from recruitment to military service, the police force or administrative jobs (Carroll 1978; Freitag 1985; Nigam 1990). Such restrictions were yet more definite for those castes like the Mallah who were identified as a

---

19    Proclaiming Kshatriya status was associated with honourable values, expressing nobility and bravery.

20    *C of I,* 1931, *United Provinces of Agra and Oudh,* vol. XVIII, part 1. *Report.* p. 530.

21    Another way to achieve higher status was to claim a different name designating a more respectable origin of descent. By assuming respectable, high sounding names these caste groups sought to 'advance claims to a position higher than usually assigned to them in the social scale' (Ahmad 1971, 168). Many caste groups claimed specific honourable names. Ahmad's example is suggestive: 'Chasi Khaibarta…caste…wanted to be known as Mahisya in order to distinguish themselves from the other section, Jalia Khaibarta, which engaged in the traditional calling of fishing and was definitely lower in status' (1971, 170).

22    *C of I,* 1921, *United Provinces and Agra and Oudh,* vol. XVI, part 1. *Report.* p. 152.

criminal group under the Criminal Tribes Act of 1871, and eventually tabulated as such in the census of 1931.[23] Mallahs were perceived as recalcitrant and unruly people in need of regulation and domestication. This was compounded by the fact that, under the census operation, the diverse occupational traits of the Mallah and their sub-castes were glossed over, in favour of a standardized view espousing an occupational uniformity delineating Mallahs or Nishads as belonging to a fishing and boating caste.

Equating caste with occupation was misleading. In fact, by the late 19th century, due to a decrease in river transport and the loss of river based resources, many Mallahs immigrated to urban centres. In Benares the new immigrant Mallahs were incorporated as labourers in the burgeoning weaving industry (Tiwary 2001), and only a minority of local Mallahs actually engaged in river based occupations. In fact, the majority of Mallahs resident in Benares were newcomers from nearby villages and had nothing to do with the river. This distinction between caste and occupation, however, mattered little to the authorities, for whom Mallahs were already perceived as criminals and in need of control and regulation.

The effects of colonial ideology and practice on the construction of the Mallah caste as a unified entity were significant and an appreciation of these processes is necessary for understanding the cultural patterns of domination and subordination that characterized the indigenous encounter with the British state. By recognizing these patterns of domination we can better understand, I believe, the way in which the British authorities sought to contain, restrict and control boats and boatmen on the River Ganges, and more specifically in Benares.


**Colonial Rule and River Navigation**

The colonial state's commercial interests in India required the improvement and regulation of communication routes in the subcontinent. One such area of investment was the control of river navigation and the use of boats for transportation of goods and people. Bernstein (1987), who documented the introduction of steamboats on the River Ganges under British rule, noted the significance of India's rivers as the 'highways of European commerce and embassy, and eventually as military routes of conquest and arteries of civil government' (1987:13). Boats were employed to carry goods and 'transport treasure-chests containing the land revenue proceeds' of the British (Bernstein 1987, 45). Ensuring the safe transport of such goods and the collection of revenue was therefore a primary concern for the British. Lt. G.F. White wrote in 1838:

> As Government despatches treasure by these boats, they are accompanied by a
> guard of soldiers…the thieves of India being exceedingly expert, and frequently

---

23    *C of I*, 1931, *United Provinces of Agra and Oudh*, vol. XVIII, part 1. *Report.*
p. 631.

committing great depredation on the river, by means of small boats, in which they glide noiselessly to any unguarded vessel, which they speedily strip of everything valuable (quoted in Mahajan 1994, 49).

As it was a major trade route in northern India, the British established trade posts along the River Ganges to control the movement of people and goods, by collecting tolls from boats navigating the river and to prevent smuggling. Cargo consisted mainly of grain, stone, timber, fuel and fodder (Nevill 1909, 80). Controlling and transporting such resources meant it was crucial for the British to ensure safe navigation from the countryside to urban centres. The British also used local boats and employed thousands of boatmen from various localities to achieve their commercial and military aims. This had social and economic implications for the boatmen, who would leave their homes for extended periods of time to work as wage labourers for the East India Company, as Lt. White continues:

Native pilots are stationed along the river, who are taken on board on different points; they receive eighteen rupees (thirty-six shillings) a month, for which they have to provide a small dingee…and crew, to sound all the depth and shoals of the river. These men are at the present period exceedingly useful in pointing out the hidden sand-banks…and in time, under the discipline of a good system, may be made invaluable (quoted in Mahajan 1994, 49).

Boatmen therefore posed a challenge for British authorities as they were both indispensable for river navigation and a threat to it. By systematically documenting all navigators and their boats, the authorities sought to control and monitor the boatmen. Subsequent additions to this were made. Each boat owner had to provide details, such as caste, patrilineal descent, place of residence and the 'length of the river under his pilotage'.[24] If boatmen did not comply accordingly they would either be fined or arrested by the local authorities (cf. Bernstein 1987, 156).

Alongside these measures, the listing of the Mallah caste under the Criminal Tribes Act had practical and beneficial ramifications for the colonials, as Tiwary (2001) points out:

In the case of the Mallahs, by enforcing curbs on their mobility and ensuring greater vigilance on waterways and rivers, the Act appears to have succeeded in facilitating transportation of revenue producing raw material and goods. It thereby provided a fillip to the growth of industries along the Ganges, ranging from Moradabad brassware, silk, and zari manufacture, furniture, etc. Bands of arrested anti-social elements could be enlisted for localised labour intensive state projects such as laying roads and railway lines (Tiwary 2001, 240).

---

24 *Rules for the Navigation of the River Ganges*, Act one of 1867, in the Regional Archives of Varanasi, Box 124, file 17, Section 6, [Henceforth RAV, 124/17, 1867].

Thus, from the ruler's perspective, categorizing boatmen as criminals justified their methods of 'discipline and punishment' (to use Foucault's words) which fused both ideological and economic concerns. Boatmen could be used as disciplined river navigators working for the empire or as manual labourers, punished by it.


## Boating in Benares

In Benares, however, boating was not only about trade. In fact, the city's centrality as a commercial post diminished from the mid 19th century due to improved alternative communication routes and the subsequent decline in river traffic (Nevill 1909, 58). A significant part of the boating industry in the city was associated with its primacy as a pilgrimage centre, drawing many pilgrims from across India as well as peddlers who traded in the city. It is therefore not surprising that a major source of revenue for the British authorities derived from taxing visitors to the city.[25] The tax was efficiently levied through the contracting of public ferries, which prior to the expansion of roads, bridges and railways, was the primary means of transport for visitors to the holy city.[26]

The management of public ferries promulgated under 'The Northern India Ferries Act' in 1878 was similar to the previous Forest Act of 1865, enabling the British to employ 'legal mechanisms to assert and safeguard state control' over resources (Gadgil & Guha 1999, 122–123). The Forest Act imposed regulations that 'curtailed the customary rights of people in the forests and made the colonial state the protector, producer and manager of forests' (Tandon & Mohanty 2000, 18). Likewise, The Ferries Act effectively restricted navigation on the river by different communities, limiting the commercial activities of boatmen and prescribing 'appropriate' and legally sanctioned operational methods for plying boats and carrying cargo. Furthermore, the Act enabled the state government and municipal authorities to directly control all ferries and legally assume control of any private boat/ferry for public use. All public and private ferries therefore had to comply with the rules and regulations set by the authorities. The Benares Gazetteer (Nevill 1909, 79) provides a list of the major ferries managed under the district board, outlining the benefits of managing the ferries on the River Ganges:

---

25    From the mid 19th century, followed by the Municipalities Act, the tax collected from imports (known as the Octroi Tax) became an essential source of revenue, As Freitag (1989) noted, the Octroi tax was 'the "backbone" of municipal income…providing more than half the revenues; other revenue derived from taxing pilgrims, as well as from assessments for water, light, and (eventually) houses; these were supplemented by income from rents and licenses' (1989, 16).

26    It is important to note that, prior to the completion of the Duphrene Bridge on 1 October 1887, the city was only accessible via a bridge of boats (Nevill 1909, 74).

> All of these [ferries] are under the control of the district board... [and] the income accruing to the [municipal] board from this source reaches a considerable amount... As far as can be ascertained no direct control was exercised over the ferries in the early days of the Government, though it is probable that the right to maintain boats for the carriage of passengers and goods was leased to private persons. All that is known is that they were owned by hereditary manjhis and were mostly in good working order.[27]

Economic interests were not the only concern of the colonial rulers. The riverscape was regarded as a public space, and as such was in need of managing and regulating, particularly due to the influx of pilgrims visiting the city. The riverbank was a place pulsing with activities that needed to be contained within British social and economic imperatives. Large scale religious festivals, such as the Burwa Mangal and Durga Puja, which took place on the riverscape, were of particular concern to the British, fearing social unrest (Kumar 1995, 126–131). It is here that an early relationship between boatmen and the local officials can be detected. The following report, dating from 10 January 1887 and addressed to the Secretary to the government of the North-Western Provinces and Oudh, is a case in point:

> The petition of one of the ghat Chaudhris [headmen] in which he represented [sic] that his boats were taken forcible possession of for the use of the Police during the fairs on the river, and that no payment was made to him for such use. I decided that the action of the Police in taking such boats without payment was illegal, and that if it was necessary for boats to be used for police patrolling the river, such boats should in future be paid for (RAV, 117/48).

From this report one can assume that at least some boatmen felt they were treated unjustly by local police; a matter that the government agreed with and sought to rectify, in accordance with its own perception of legitimate conduct. The fact that a petition was made provides a clue to the close interaction between the state and boatmen at the local level. Subsequent chapters reveal how police corruption and unsound government policies continue to figure strongly in contemporary discourse about the state. However, it is significant to note that as early as 1887 individual members of the boatman community, rather than any organized associations, were voicing their grievances to local bureaucrats. That is, some boatmen seem to have accepted the British system of law and order and used it to defend their rights. It was only later, during the early 20th century that various associations seeking to represent the urban poor began to employ the mechanism of the British judicial system to collectively voice concerns about broader issues of social and political reform (Gooptu 2001).

---

27    The name Manjhi is commonly used today by boatmen to distinguish between boat owners and workers. I discuss the precise meaning of these names as they figure within the internal socio-economic structure of the boatman community in Chapter 3.

The British were also highly apprehensive about public urban spaces such as Benares, not only because large gatherings of crowds could incite unrest amongst the unruly population, but also because of the spread of diseases. The colonial authorities in India made a direct correlation between the spread of epidemics and human mobility, especially on the major pilgrimage routes. As Arnold (1989, 256) observed, 'Banaras came to be recognized as a major turnpike along the "northern epidemic highway" [and] special measures were introduced to prevent pilgrims from introducing cholera into eastern U.P. from 1927'. As many pilgrims came to Benares by boat or employed boats during their visits, the British saw it particularly necessary to supervise and control the use of boats along the river.

*Rules and Regulations for Boats in Benares*

As the British assumed greater control over the subcontinent, they changed the communication networks with the construction of roads and railways. Such changes had a marked effect on river traffic in Benares and the operation of public ferries. The rapid expansion of the railway and the building of metalled roads, along with the construction of the Duphrene Bridge at Raj ghat in 1887, bridging the eastern and western parts of the city, diminished the use of ferries. This general improvement to transportation infrastructure lessened the overall income derived from taxes (Nevill 1909, 81). Subsequently, the British government needed an alternative way to exact tolls from the population. Eventually, in 1916, a licensing system for boats was introduced, and for the first time, boatmen had to comply with certain rules and pay fixed annual fees to ply their boats in the city.

It is important to place these developments within the wider context of urbanization in northern India. Nandini Gooptu (2001) traces the process of urbanization during early 20th century India and the effects municipal policies had on the urban poor. She describes the economic, infrastructural and territorial development of North Indian cities, such as Benares, Kanpur, Lucknow and Allahabad. Part of the rapid expansion of these urban centres was due to an influx of migrants from the countryside to the cities, which produced apprehension amongst the elites. The maginalization of the urban poor was consolidated through policy measures, such as urban planning, policing and the enforcement of taxation and regulation of economic activities. Although boatmen were not migrants, their menial occupation and low caste Shudra status meant that they were lumped together with the rest of the 'inferior classes'. As such, both the colonial rulers and the elites perceived these people as 'prone to dirty or bad habits, immoral practices and lawlessness' (Gooptu 1997, 889).

The boatmen were subjected to additional regulations for operating in public spaces and, like others who operated vehicles (e.g., horses and carriages) were forced to comply with the newly introduced laws. The implementation of licenses for boats in Benares came into effect in October 1916. It was at this point that the boatmen were drawn into a binding relationship with the colonial state; and if the state apparatus was already considered an intrusive entity by the boatmen it now directly intruded upon their livelihood.

The imposition of rules and regulations seem somewhat incongruent with the boatmen's daily work patterns, which were much more akin to the 'task oriented' work characteristic of peasant societies. As E.P. Thompson (1967, 60) has suggested, task oriented work shows little distinction between 'work' and 'life'. 'Social intercourse and labour are intermingled – the working day lengthens or contracts according to the task – and there is no great sense of conflict between labour and the 'passing the time of day'. Not surprisingly, then, for the British 'who were accustomed to labour timed by the clock, this attitude appears to be wistful and lacking in urgency' (1967, 60). Accordingly, the boatmen who were commonly portrayed as idle, drunkards and with little regard for authority were forced to go through a restructuring of work habits, under which they had to acquire new disciplines and work rules. These work rules were officially printed in a formal document, and any infringement of the rules could incur a fine, the revoking of a license or at worst the confiscation of a boat.

The issue of licenses was stipulated within what came to be known as the 'Bylaws for the Regulation and Control of Boats Plying for Hire within the Limits of the Benares Municipality' (RAV 78/102, 1916). These bylaws clearly separated municipal boats and boat owners from public ferries operating at specific ghats (called 'ferry ghats') as well as domestic river traffic from those external to the city limits. The rules saw the boatmen as responsible for obtaining licenses and abiding by the rules and regulations set out in these bylaws, and failure to do so could result in loss of license or fines. The rules were detailed, and specified such things as who could ply the boats for hire and the hiring rates according to time and distance. The licenses were in the form of a metal plate, and fixed 'to the boat in a conspicuous place'. Thus, the modern state brought the daily practices of boatmen under the strict supervision and inspection of local authorities.

A careful reading of these bylaws is striking, for it reveals the extent to which the state with its rational mechanism and policy measures sought to control the entire riverscape, and practically permeated every aspect of the boatmen's daily lives, both at the individual and collective level.

The bylaws regulated both time and space. They defined the rainy and dry seasons according to the Gregorian calendar. The indigenous seasonal nature of festivities and pilgrimage was ignored. According to the bylaws, each season had its own restrictions and prohibitions relevant to the size of boats, the maximum number of passengers that could be carried, and the number of boatmen required to man them. Local knowledge about safety and security was disregarded in favour of a new rational system of measurement. Spatial restrictions were also set in place and boatmen were required to 'keep a clear space of at least 20 yards wide in front of landing places' so as not to obstruct other approaching boats and passengers. The bylaws went to great lengths to define the various classes of boats and their hiring fees, and several tables were given to calculate fares by distance and time. One such table even specifies the *Special Fares* boatmen could charge for carrying dead bodies, with different rates for infants and adults. The colonial obsession with measurements and numbers reaches an absurd climax at the end of this four page document when it details a convoluted formula designed to give the safe load weight a boat may carry in the dry or rainy seasons. What is perhaps most remarkable is the extent the bylaws go to in providing guidelines for the individual and collective behaviour of boatmen, as the following section demonstrates (article 13):

> 5) The person in charge shall not demand a rate of hire exceeding that fixed by bylaw 17 [the rates of hire]

> 6) All disputes as to the amount of load to be carried, or as to hire due, or as to any other matter referred to in these bylaws, shall be decided by the licensing officer....

> 7) The person in charge [of the boat] shall not ply for hire when in a state of drunkenness; or make use of any insulting, abusive or obscene language or gestures, when plying for hire; or wrongly prevent, or endeavour to prevent, any other boat from being hired; or desert after being hired by time, before he has been discharged.

> 8) If any property is left in the boat, the person in charge shall take the same, unless sooner claimed by the owner, to the nearest police station within 24 hours.

Boatmen were considered prone to immoral and criminal acts and, as a visible community working in public space,[28] stringent regulations were put in place to modify such behaviour. The colonial administration attempted to rationalize, control and reconstruct the working habits of boatmen to fit within the imperatives of the colonial ideology and economy.

The penetration of the state, moreover, was accompanied by the infringement of traditional practices and community institutions. The bylaws not only stipulated how boatmen should conduct themselves with regards to other passengers and property, but also invested the local authorities with the power to interfere with intra-community affairs. These regulations were certain to have an effect on the economic and social organization of the boatman community, which had its own customary regulations on the coordination and management of boats along the riverfront.

Although there is no direct evidence suggesting that collective action was taken by the boatman community to contest the bylaws imposed by the colonial

---

28   Dipesh Chakarbarti (2001, 17) makes a similar argument in relation to the colonial regime's regulation of the bazaar: a public space which the authorities perceived as reflective of indigenous life and moral characteristics, which was imbued by 'dirt and disorder'.

authorities; it is likely that paying an annual fee, along with the forceful confiscation of boats (e.g., during festival times) and the overall state intrusion in community affairs, did generate resentment. I can only speculate as to why boatmen did not overtly contest or resist such direct impingement on their livelihood. As a minor occupational group, already labelled as 'criminals', boatmen could hardly oppose the British institutions of power and authority. Of course, the fact that boatmen were a low status, poor and illiterate community, part of the marginal urban poor, meant that they had very little recourse to official channels. In addition, as Gooptu observes, limited occupational opportunities generated 'competition and rivalries among the poor themselves, quite apart from inevitable generating tensions and antagonism against local authorities' (2001, 104).[29] Moreover, judging from the bylaws, which mention competition among boatmen over passengers, and from on my own ethnographic work, I assume that much like today, the boatman community was one fraught with conflict and rivalry, primarily due to scarce resources.

Interestingly, the municipal bylaws outlined above, unlike the 'Rules for Navigation of the River Ganges' mentioned earlier, did not specify caste, patrilineal descent, and place of residence as criteria for identifying a boatman. Similarly, the traditional work system of the boatmen, which allocated each boatman the right to operate a boat only from his residential ghat (landing place), was not mentioned. In that sense, it appears that the colonial state did not interfere with the local economic arrangements that provided (and continue to provide) the boatman community with a degree of autonomy on the riverfront. I shall further discuss the issue of 'customary rights' in subsequent chapters. The fact is, that by issuing licenses in which the name and place of residence of the boatmen were mentioned, the colonial administration provided the work system with official documents, hence institutionalizing the occupation of boating. These documents have since become important proof for subsequent generations of boatmen of their connection to individual ghats and their right to ply boats. To paraphrase E.P. Thompson (1967, 87), and anticipate what follows in this book, it seems that while the first generation of boatmen exposed to colonial rule were subjected to new orders of domination and discipline, including concepts of personhood, time and labour (Comaroff & Comaroff 1988), subsequent generations learned to live, operate within and ultimately contest them.

---

29    This is not to say that collective action from urban subaltern groups was absent. Gooptu (1997; 2001) has elaborated on the wider implications of such strict policing, subjugation and degradation of low caste Shudras by local authorities in urban centres. In part, colonial oppression heightened the awareness of these low castes to their shared predicament, thus contributing to the rise of caste uplift movements. Other factors, such as elite disapproval of the poor, internal competition amongst the low castes and resentment towards local authorities contributed in various and often unexpected ways, to the rise of militant Hinduism and its active involvement in anti Muslim campaigns. Gooptu maintains this has enabled the low castes to present themselves as the guardians of Hinduism and freedom fighters fending off colonial and communal forces.

**Conclusion**

It appears that at the local level the colonial state was determined to implement its 'rationalist program' (Kaviraj 1999, 146) through systematic attempts to regulate river navigation and formalize boating within the city limits. It is partly due to such concerns that the boatmen became closely involved with the colonial state and its administrative apparatus. Under colonial rule the boatmen were registered, enumerated, and licensed, and had strict limitations imposed on their occupation and movement within the municipal boundaries of Benares. Such restrictions remain to this day a constant reminder of the continuities between the colonial period and the present day.

This chapter highlights how colonial knowledge and new perceptions of what constituted normal, educated, modern and progressive behaviour were instrumental in constructing Indian social identities. Indeed, the colonial discourse of caste and caste numerical representation were linked to various other aspects of society. Under the new, rational, and systematic mechanism of the census and its ethnographic apparatus, the colonial power was able to follow the conduct of and change in a certain caste group in economic, social and political terms. Such were, as Foucault reminds us, the 'techniques of power', characteristic of governments from the 18th century onwards (Foucault 1998, 25). What is equally important to emphasize, however, is that such exercise of power over the 'other' also generates 'a whole field of responses, reactions, results and possible inventions' (Foucault 1982, 220). In our case, we have seen how colonial governance stimulated novel forms of trans-local caste identities, advocated through the institution of caste associations. Indeed, these caste associations were largely short lived institutions during the colonial era, established largely as a response to the census operation and other institutions of imperial governance (Bayly 1999). Nevertheless, as the following chapter demonstrates, caste associations, albeit in modified forms, have since been resurrected in postcolonial India.

Today, while many boatmen seem unaware of the 'criminal' past of their caste, others are not only aware of it, but even cast it in a positive light, referring to it as a challenge to the oppression of the British, as one boatman proudly noted:

> A long time ago, in the time of the British, one boat was carrying guns, pistols and explosives. At the time there were no trucks or good transport. The enemies of the British hired a boatman to prevent the boat from reaching its destination. At night, the boatman sneaked on to the boat and broke its wooden plates, and the boat was soon submerged underwater. Since then the British have called all boatmen big criminals. Tell me, how could they fight when all their military equipment and goods were lost in Gangaji [the River Ganges]? And all this because of one boatman.

This boatman's explanation not only disassociates the community from its 'criminal past' by denoting the bravery and skill of the boatman involved, but offers us an insight into the self-perception of the community. Rather than a community marginalized by the state control apparatus, it repositions the boatmen as central actors in the grand narrative of nationalism, and its resistance to foreign rule. Indeed, one of the main concerns of this book is to amplify the voices of the boatmen and appreciate how they perceive the world in which they are subordinated. This is not an attempt to romanticize their agency, but rather to show that they share and perpetuate many of the institutions, stratagems and practices that were meticulously recorded, and produced during the British rule. Therein lies the value of the ethnographic inquiry, for it allows us to avoid assigning British colonialism with 'pure agency', or the moment of genesis it has come to achieve in much recent scholarship. Rather, through the ethnographic lens, I hope to show how subordinate communities are creatively inhabiting, producing and at times, contesting the categories, and landscapes they operate in: enacting social and political change, and investing such landscapes (or riverscapes) with meaning. Thus, while having historical importance and resonance, such constructions do not remain static or bound by categories and concepts elucidated under the colonial regime. The rearticulation of history and myth in a way that places boatmen at the centre, rather than the margins of society, constitutes the main theme of the next chapter.

I eventually did manage to find a research assistant who would be party to my crimes. Curiously enough, he was a Brahmin, but having lived his life along the ghats of Bananas, was comfortable working among the boatmen and ghat priests. I was able to leave the world of the archives and embark upon my ethnographic work on the boatmen of Banaras.

# Chapter 2

# 'Step-sons of the State': Marginalization and the Struggle for Recognition

Nishad Samaj is a massive community, which has always made sacrifices to safeguard the Nation. History is the witness that civilisation and culture originated and developed from the valleys and rivers. This means that the Nishads have been the creators of civilisation and culture. The Nishad community has contributed to India by making it prosperous through trade, water transport and international relations. The Nishads have played an important role in the freedom struggle and continue their work of saving lives during devastating floods. They remain the vigilant guards of the Nation and true servants of society… after independence it was expected that the Nishads would receive justice and equal opportunities to develop, but this did not happen. In this democracy the agricultural farmers are secure and stable, becoming officers [of the state] while the water farmers (jal karsak), the Nishads, are deprived of their ancestral rights and traditional professions. And through the auction of these professions a handful of people are exploiting them, making money…Is this not a black spot on democracy? This black spot needs to be wiped out...

Boatman's Association, Handbill, 1979

For people who were marginalized and dispossessed under colonial rule, independence brought new hopes of occupational opportunities and restoration of their rights over natural resources. The modern Indian state was premised upon the democratic ideals of social justice, universal rule of law, and the constitutional granting of rights to all its citizens. A policy of positive discrimination was established in order to provide equal opportunities and empower the lower castes/ classes suffering social oppression and caste prejudice.[1] Nehru's vision of a modern Indian state endorsed such social programmes imbued with ideas of progress and

---

1    Under colonial rule the Mallah caste was classified as belonging to the 'Other Backward Classes' (OBC), an administrative category used by the British to demarcate Scheduled Castes (SC) from other low classes/castes. After independence the term gained momentum as the modern state's ideology of social justice and equality established protective policy measures designed to uplift those underprivileged sectors of society, such as the SC and OBC (for details, see Fuller 2003; Jain 1996; Shah 1996). Eventually, the Mallahs were registered as part of the weakest members of the OBC, now called 'Most Backward Classes' (MBC), which *supposedly* provided them with further benefits, including reservations (i.e., the allotment of places and jobs) in the education and public sectors, as well as political representation. I emphasize supposedly, because many, like boatmen, who are entitled to such benefits are unable to access them, as one needs to be well-versed in bureaucratic procedures.

scientific rationalism, alongside an emphasis on technological development and industrialization. The ushering in of a new post-independence era in which all the population would participate in and benefit from the 'nation building' project presented the state as the protector and regulator of socio-economic justice, motivated by Gandhian ideology emphasizing charity and social consciousness.

It is against this background that I explore the process of disenchantment of the boatman community with the postcolonial state. In this chapter I examine several case studies, including a development programme and other state policies, to demonstrate the contentious encounter between the state and the boatman community of Banaras, effectively contributing to its progressive marginalization. I argue that the boatman community has an ambivalent relationship with the state. This ambivalence and tension is illustrated in the way boatmen experience the Indian 'state', not as a unified entity, but through its various institutions and officials in everyday life. While it is certainly true that powerful elites have influenced and shaped state policy and actions, my main concern in this chapter is to investigate the various tactics and strategies developed by subaltern groups, such as boatmen (individually and collectively) to deal with state policies and functionaries.[2] In the process we can learn more about the values, modes of behaviour, fears and aspirations of the boatman community in contemporary Banaras. Such an examination reveals the various roles the boatmen play in the broader community and their struggle to gain recognition for these.

## Community Associations and the Forging of a Collective Voice

Community associations formed on the basis of kinship and occupational ties have long been the primary vehicle for boatmen to articulate their collective rights and resist state intervention and oppression. These contemporary associations bear certain similarities to the caste associations that operated during the colonial era. They are led by prominent members of the caste and their broad aim remains to promote caste consciousness and advance the social and political interests of the community. As such, these associations continue to be exclusive, in the sense that they represent the plight of their own caste/community members. There are,

---

2    Much of the recent literature by political economists has primarily focused on the powerful elites and their increasing influence on the modern Indian state. Studies of this approach perceive the autonomy of the Indian state as severely marred by the competing interests of the dominant classes, including industrial capitalists, rich peasants and professional elites (Bardhan 1984; Rudolph and Rudolph 1987; Vanaik 1990). While these studies have enhanced our understanding of state-society relations and the way in which certain social forces penetrate and affect state discourse and action; how such state discourse and policy is disseminated and re-interpreted at the local level is largely unexamined (Jeffrey and Lerche 2000). For a comprehensive review of the anthropology of the state in South Asia, see Fuller and Harriss (2000).

nonetheless, marked differences between the newer associations and their colonial predecessors; not least because of the fact that contemporary associations operate within a postcolonial environment, where people are no longer subjects of an empire but citizens of a democratic state. This affects their aims and strategies, which are influenced by the changes taking place around them. What is important to emphasize is that contemporary associations, such as those representing the boatmen, speak a thoroughly modern language that is anchored in the principles of social justice, equal rights and political participation. In a bid to achieve their goals of community consciousness, public recognition and to propagate the interests of the community, these associations employ a number of techniques appropriate in a democracy, including disseminating information in local newspapers, organizing community events, mobilizing members to protest government actions and the production and financing of caste journals.

In Banaras, boatman associations regularly issue press releases and handbills, such as the one quoted above. In this handbill the boatman community is inscribed into the spatial, political and symbolic structures of the nation state. The author does so by invoking ideas derived from the national discourse prevalent under colonial rule, which promoted unity, political consciousness, freedom, the eradication of poverty and subjugation of low castes, and the notion of economic and political independence. The rhetoric in the bill outlines the unique features of the community by virtue of their occupation and thus their contribution to the nation and its society (i.e., in trade, communication and diplomacy). Having established their loyalty to the nation state – as participating in a shared Indian history and the struggle against colonial oppression – the Nishad community inveighs against the failure of the state to deliver on its promises of just democratic rule. It is evident that the Nishads see their community as treated unfairly compared to the praised agriculturalists of India.

Citing the example of the agricultural farmers – the 'favoured sons of the nation' – the handbill emphasizes the uneven, 'step-motherly' approach of the state towards their community. Here the document seems to refer to certain state policies that have ultimately benefited the dominant peasant groups, such as the Ahirs/Yadavs and Jats, in the land and agricultural reforms (see Jain 1996; Tandon & Mohanty 2000, 22). Throughout my fieldwork members of the boatman community repeatedly likened the way the Indian state treats them to that of a step-mother's relationship with her step-children (*is tara ka to sautela behavar karte hai*).[3] Using the term 'step-mother' frames the relationship between the

---

3     It is important to note that the stepmother relationship is akin to the Western idea of the 'wicked' stepmother. However, according to Ramcandra Varmma's Manak Hindi Kosh (1962, 464), Sautala is defined as: 1. Child of a Saut (a husband's second wife or mistress) 2. Child of a person's father's co-wife (half brother or sister). The term seems to highlight a strong sense of rivalry with the children of the first wife or legal wife. This is slightly different from the more 'victimized' idea of 'step-son' in English. The term captures well the mingled feelings of resentment and subordinate relationship that Mallahs have with

community and the Indian state in kinship terms. As the Osellas (2000b, 138) observe, embedded in this language of kinship intimacy are ideas about 'moral responsibility, reciprocity and patronage'. Such terms describing the relationship between the 'people' and the Indian 'state' are commonly used by politicians and community leaders in various public events across India. According to the Osellas, by evoking this familiar intimacy, characteristic of patron-client relations, the state government and bureaucracy can justify 'its interventions in and demands on people's lives'. This, in turn, 'confers on people, as clients, specific moral claims, rights and degrees of political leverage sometimes denied to them as citizens of a democratic state' (Osella & Osella 2000b, 138). When boatmen use the term 'step-mother', they are suggesting that their expectations from the state have not been met. The term also indicates a feeling of being sidelined and mistreated by the mother-nation (Bharat Mata), who favours her other sons. Boatmen thus seek to differentiate themselves from these once marginalized castes, which are still considered part of the Shudra or 'backward classes', but have now become increasingly prosperous (Doron 2008).

Significantly, therefore, on the top of the bill (and many others like it) are printed the slogans, *'Victory/praise to the Nishad (Jay Nishad) – Victory/Long live the water-farmer (Jal kisan zindabad) – Victory/praise to India (Jay Bharat)'*. The saying echoes India's late Prime Minister, Lal Bahadur Shastri's famous slogan from the mid 1960s – *Jay Jawan, Jay Kisan* – Honour the Soldier, Honour the Farmer, which was coined in the wake of the 1965 war with Pakistan. The use of this slogan is designed to evoke sentiments marking the boatmen's unwavering loyalty to the modern Indian nation-state (Bharat Mata or Mother India). The slogan is not coincidental; it honours the Nishad community alongside the iconic figures of farmers and soldiers, which Jain (2004) notes, circulated widely in calendars during the late 60s and 70s, depicting them as 'men whose unstinting devotion to the state makes them worthy of emulation ('Jai') as model subjects' (Jain 2004, 226).

The handbill continues to specify a list of the boatmen's demands from the government. They ask for an immediate revoking of the ban on fishing in the city; the endowment of exclusive rights to cultivate land on the riverbanks of the Ganges; and reservations of government jobs for their community, especially in the navy, Water Police and 'flood and security departments'. It then calls on all boatmen in the city to participate in a demonstration and convention of the Nishad Samaj (society) on 9 October 1979.

Most importantly, the handbill conveys an ambivalent relationship towards the 'state'. On the one hand, the community denounces the state for failing to deliver on its promises of equal opportunity, economic growth and welfare for their community; it condemns the modern state's intrusive and meddlesome practices and policies, which it sees as detrimental to the community's economic security.

---

Yadavs, in much the same way as the child of a second or (informal) wife might have with the child of the primary or legal wife (I am indebted to Richard Barz for this comment).

On the other hand, it clearly calls for the state to intervene and provide the boatmen access to employment in the public sector and implement reservation policies. The content of this handbill is aimed at promoting community consciousness and mobilization and similar ideas are also circulated in press releases issued by various boatman community associations in Banaras. In most, the struggle for official recognition constitutes a prominent theme, which can be fully understood only when looking at the level of everyday life, where 'informal' activities render boatmen particularly vulnerable to state exploitation and persecution.

## Restrictions and Contradictions: Diving for Corpses

Boatmen are renowned for their ability to swim and dive, which brings them additional community roles, such as swimming instructors and helping in rescue operations. The best known group of boatmen called upon to rescue people are the divers (*gotakhors*) of Raj ghat, who also have the ghoulish task of retrieving corpses. This group, belonging to the Mallah caste, have traditionally worked as divers on the river and their skills derive from the many hours they spend underwater in search of coins thrown by pilgrims into the holy river (as it is considered meritorious). It is fairly common to see boatmen from all over the city diving in search of coins to supplement their income. At Raj ghat, however, this activity is particularly profitable due to its location near the Malviya Bridge, from which multitudes of pilgrims arriving by bus or train to the holy city throw coins into the sacred river.

I recall my amazement at their skills in diving deep under the bridge and their ability to retrieve considerable sums in several hours of hard work. They claim that drinking alcohol is one of the best ways of coping with such demanding work and helps them maintain their body temperature under water. When I first met the divers at Raj ghat they mistook me for a reporter and I felt quite overwhelmed by their anger towards the local authorities and police. Although these divers are a distinct group from those boatmen who regularly ferry passengers, their story reflects many of the problems and frustrations felt by boatmen in relation to harassment and exploitation by local authorities across the city.[4]

The state does not recognize 'diving for coins' as a legal occupation, so the Raj ghat divers find themselves participating in work outside the sanction of local authorities. As other studies have also shown, people operating outside the legitimacy of the state are often prone to harassment and persecution by government and local authorities (Crick 1994; Hannerz 1985). The position of the divers is therefore a precarious one, as they must maintain good relations with the local authorities and comply with their requests in order to practice their 'occupation'.

---

4    Some of the divers also ply boats to supplement their income, especially during the monsoon season when it is too dangerous to dive. However, their main source of income derives from diving under the bridge for coins.

These 'requests' generally involve the risky (and loathsome) task of retrieving corpses from the river, which boatmen rarely get paid for. At the same time, they have no redress against exploitation and harassment because their occupation is not formally recognized.

In an attempt to gain recognition and voice their complaints against government exploitation the divers from Raj ghat formed an association. By registering themselves as a formal association (with a president, secretary etc.), they have succeeded in gaining a certain degree of legitimacy as an organized group providing a service for the government and engaging in often dangerous rescue missions. In fact, the first time I met the group while drinking tea on the ghat, I was given three large registers and several framed documents attesting to their skills. The registers contained numerous letters from locals and officials commending the skills and proficiency of the divers for their efforts in retrieving corpses and other items from the river and local water sources, for example:

> It is certified that the divers Rajaram, Jhallu, Buddhan, Shivmani, Nate, Lalloo and Naggu after tireless efforts took out official files weighing more than 10 Kg from a well situated near the courthouse. Their work is greatly appreciated. The divers are residents of Naya Mahadeo, Raj ghat, Varanasi.
>
> *Seal of Police, Adampur, 1 February 1992

In Banaras people use the River Ganges and other bodies of water, such as local wells and ponds, as convenient places for disposing of unwanted items. These include incriminating items, such as guns, tax books and stolen goods. Animal carcasses and human corpses are also sometimes thrown into the river to avoid costly cremations, as it is considered both a convenient and auspicious alternative. Suicide by drowning is by far the most common method in Banaras, as death in the sacred river is thought to bring release (*moksha*). Boatmen told me that it is not uncommon for disheartened individuals, such as battered women, failing students and convicted criminals, to commit suicide by jumping from the Malviya Bridge or leaping off a boat in midstream. In such cases boatmen are summoned by the local authorities to retrieve the bodies. Many boatmen, however, try to avoid such rescue missions as they are considered risky both because of the strong water currents as well as the involvement with police. In addition, any activity associated with corpses is religiously stigmatized.

Those called upon to perform such rescue operations are generally the divers of Raj ghat. Although they gain some recognition from the authorities (in the form of letters) divers claim that the police exploit their skills. Lalu Prasad, the president of the Divers' Association described a typical incident for me:

> When the police are required to retrieve something from the river or the wells, they come to us to do the job. Sometimes they even come in the middle of the night, taking us away from our homes. They rarely give us money or recognition for our work. They say that if we complain they will stop us from diving under

the bridge and take away our boat licenses… The life of the Mallah is fruitless, even when we rescue drowning people, we remain stigmatized (*mallaho ki zindagi kitni jakam hoti hai, dubte hame ki bachaye fir bhi badnam hota hai*).

One way the divers believe they can legitimize their role as divers is by gaining a position in the Water Police (*Jal Police*). They claim that it is only natural that they, who are skilled navigators, divers and swimmers, should be granted such positions. Another diver expressed his frustration about the matter:

> If anyone needs assistance then the Mallahs are expected to rescue them, yet the Jal Police take the credit for it. The police can't even swim. They would need lifejackets if they went into the water. In reality, it is the Mallahs who should be employed as Jal Police, as should be the case in any other work related to water. We are the people who know the river (Gangaji) better than anyone else: we are Gangaputras (sons of the Ganga)! We know how to gauge the water currents, so when someone drowns we know where the body will eventually emerge; but these rights are not given to us and we don't even get a day's salary for retrieving the corpses.

Despite continued demands from both the Diver's Association (and other boatman associations, who have taken up the divers' cause as part of their own) no boatman has ever been appointed to a post in the Water Police. Their rescue work is considered unofficial and payment is largely dependent on the goodwill of the police officers involved. The boatmen themselves put this down to government discrimination against their caste, which authorities continue to see as uneducated and uncontrollable; and because they have no political representation powerful enough to lobby for their cause. I will examine these claims in more detail shortly, but for now it is important to reiterate that there are many risks involved in such rescue missions. In fact, one of the best known divers in Banaras, Sunil Manjhi, died recently while trying to retrieve items from a well for the police. Apparently, he hit his head on an iron bar while attempting to surface. His family never received compensation. For many boatmen working on the river, the divers' case, and Sunil's untimely death, are additional examples of a broader pattern of state exploitation and discrimination against their people.

## Monsoon Floods and Boating Restrictions

Similar concerns are voiced in relation to the restrictions imposed on boating during the monsoon season and to flood relief operations. The river rises markedly during the monsoon, flooding the ghats and making them inaccessible for passenger collection. This usually happens in July, August and September and during these months most boatmen are unemployed. While some seek casual jobs to support their families, others simply live off their annual savings. The major ghats, such as Dashashvamedh, Guy, Assi, and Raj ghat, however, continue to operate boats for the many pilgrims who arrive in the city at this time, mostly from the south of India. The restrictions mean that during the monsoon period the authorities can issue a blanket ban on boats from operating at any time, stating it is too dangerous to ply boats on the river. Boatmen claim that this blanket ban is detrimental to those who rely solely on the meagre income earned from ferrying passengers during the monsoon season to support their families. Furthermore, they argue that the ban is unfair and unlawful as boatmen are required to pay the licence fees to ply boats during both wet and dry seasons. The bylaws specify that, during the monsoon period, several boatmen must man a boat when carrying passengers as it is too difficult and risky to single-handedly navigate a boat in the fast and dangerous currents. Provided boatmen comply with these conditions, they are in fact licensed to operate their boats during this time. What is important to emphasize here is that boatmen see this as a contradictory and inconsistent state policy, insofar as different levels of state bureaucracy issue different policy directives at different times.

The extensive restrictions imposed on boating during the monsoon season have caused frustration and anger amongst boatmen, who argue that their community is excluded from the decision making process, even when it directly relates to their livelihood. Moreover, as is the case with divers, boatmen argue that local authorities have double standards, and exploit their skills when needed, as Krishna a boatman from Dashsavamedh ghat explained:

> During the floods we go from village to village to rescue people. This is done by order of the District Magistrate [DM] who informs us through the boatman associations. We load our boats onto trucks and go to rescue people stranded in flooded villages. When we return, if we don't get cash-in-hand we have to go again and again to the DM's office to receive our pay. It is dangerous work and we play with our lives to save other people (*jan par khel ke logo ko bachte hai*). There are also other dangers we fear in floods like poisonous snakes and scorpions, yet the government does not even offer us life insurance.

Krishna also suggested that despite such exploitation, as well as the supposed job reservations in the public sector, the government is dismissive of their aspirations to be recognized officially. If Krishna and many others like him were to be recognized as official government employees, they would gain much security and peace of mind; providing them with social and economic benefits throughout the year and alleviating the problem of police harassment.

Having a government job in India is attractive for a number of reasons. First, it provides a stable income, along with social benefits, such as medical care, pensions, holidays and more. In addition, government employees have easier access to resources, such as loans and public housing. As part of the Mallah caste, which has been classified as belonging to the Most Backward Classes (MBC), boatmen are aware of those government benefits that they are entitled to receive.

Indeed, boatmen I have spoken with often pointed to the benefits other castes, such as Yadavs (buffalo herders) and Chamars (sweepers) have accrued from various government positive discrimination schemes. More specifically, they highlight the way in which other underprivileged groups, such as the sweepers, are incorporated into the formal public sector (see Searle-Chatterjee 1979). Boatmen believe that by having members from their own community in key positions, such as the Water Police, and the departments in charge of agriculture, fisheries and transport, they would be able to influence the state and local policy making that directly affects their livelihood. However, such jobs are extremely hard to come by and it is widely known that government sector employment demands more than simply being an MBC or, for that matter, having the right qualifications. Political clout, along with the means to pay off the hierarchies of power is even more important (Jeffrey & Lerche 2000). For members of the boatman community in Banaras, being as they are socially, politically and economically marginalized, attaining a job in the government sector is an almost impossible goal. The divers' case and the restrictions imposed on motorboats during the monsoons demonstrate the inconsistencies and double standards of state policies and actions, contributing to what boatmen claim is the systematic marginalization of their community. At the same time, the way in which boatmen and their community associations articulate their plight suggests that they are perfectly aware of their rights as citizens of a democratic state. Hence, a tension emerges, whereby state policies are seen as discriminatory and harmful, yet the only way to rectify these is by increased state intervention and official recognition of the boatman community's valuable role in India, and Banaras more specifically.

However, if such appeals for state intervention indicate a view of the state as the guarantor of social justice and rights of the oppressed, these perceptions have continuously been dispelled. Ironically, it is because of increased state intervention, in the form of an ambitious development plan to clean the River Ganges, that boatmen have suffered the most.

## The Ganga Action Plan and the Marginalization of the Boatmen of Banaras

Since precolonial times boatmen have worked in various, river related occupations. In Banaras, their work has included fishing, sandmining (i.e., extracting sand from the riverbank), cultivating the fertile land on the riverbank, primarily on the eastern bank, and ferrying passengers on boats. Over the past three decades these occupations have all come under threat with some, such as fishing and sandmining, being completely banned and others, such as agricultural cultivation, markedly reduced. The loss of their livelihood, boatmen argue, is a direct result of the Ganga Action Plan (GAP), a waste management scheme designed by the central government to clean the polluted river. A close examination of the GAP serves to illustrate the disjuncture that exists between the rhetoric of the state, as an entity concerned for the welfare of its people, and the harsh reality of exclusion, corruption and dispossession, especially for the weakest sectors of society. [5]

*The Historical Background of the Ganga Action Plan*

Following Independence, the government of India aimed to provide healthcare and economic security for its poverty stricken citizens. By the late 1970s, however, many citizens had lost faith in the various development schemes devised to alleviate their poverty and misery. Corruption and bureaucratic mismanagement created frustration and anger when the vision of a better future did not materialize. The 1980s brought a period of instability and danger in India. Indira Gandhi's assassination, the killings in the Punjab and the sensitive situation in Sri Lanka contributed to the turbulent feeling in the country. In addition, the environmental disaster in Bhopal, where thousands of people died and many more were poisoned and permanently impaired had 'left the nation in a sombre mood' (*Times of India* 24 December 1984).

The gas disaster in Bhopal drastically highlighted the feelings of discontent held by the people towards government policies and subsequent actions. In Bhopal, the nation witnessed the devastating effects of untethered industrialization, modern technology and environmental pollution. The appalling conditions of the workers there, blatant corruption and mismanagement, were all exposed. This corruption ran through all levels of government, from Congress politicians down to the local law enforcement agencies. The central government was unable to deal with this acute situation in any comprehensive manner.[6] Many people lost faith in the government and its politicians for they were revealed to be self-seeking and constrained by bureaucratic chains and administrative red tape. This political and social uncertainty led to many becoming disenchanted.

The tragedy of Bhopal prompted the newly elected Prime Minster, Rajiv Gandhi to redress these issues by promoting the Ganga Action Plan (GAP) as a grand development scheme designed to reinforce the vision of a strong modern Indian State. A good example of Gandhi's awareness of the difficult issues that confronted the nation can be seen in his address made to the Rajya Sabha (Upper House) on 23 January 1985:

> We have seen the tragic incident in Bhopal... [We] are looking at how to stop any
> factories from polluting our rivers and our air... The first river we are attempting
> to clean is the Ganges. I will not say purify because nobody can purify the

---

5    For an in-depth discussion tracing the social, political and legal reasons behind the failure of the GAP, see Ahmed (1991); Alley (1994; 2002).

6    The extent of corruption and mismanagement was very widespread. Officials ignored the company's tainted safety records and provided the industrial licence needed. For more details, see *The State of India's Environment 1984–1985: The Second Citizens' Report* (Agarwal & Narain 1985, 216).

Ganga. But we will try and clean it... To do these things, we will need a fast administration, a clean administration... To do this, we need technology. We need a new education and we need to look after the health of our people (Gandhi 1987, 20).

The GAP symbolized the Indian government's commitment to protecting the environment by utilizing advanced modern means, as well as demonstrating national concern for the health of its people. But it had another important feature: it was a plan to save the holy Mother Ganga. The symbolic meaning of such an act captured the imagination of the Hindus in India, especially those in the holy city of Banaras. The GAP was officially launched in Banaras on June 1986, with much ritual display. However, since its celebrated inauguration, the plan has been widely criticized both in the media and among state and local officials. Overall it has failed in its attempts to clean the Ganges; a result of poor planning, technological mismanagement and corruption at the various levels of administration.[7]

On a more technical level one of the primary reasons for the failure of the GAP was the adoption of a Western model to clean the river, which was based on one developed by the Thames Water Authority. In a blind attempt to imitate Western countries, the government overlooked the obvious fact that the European model was not designed with India's climate, geography and ecosystem in mind (see Kumara 1995). Another similar example of bad planning was the building of electric sewage pumps, which have been thoroughly ineffective due to the continuous power cuts that occur in Banaras throughout the day; hence much of the sewage flows back into the river.

The discrepancy between rhetoric and reality becomes more evident when we examine how the GAP was deployed in Banaras. Praised by Gandhi as the 'Peoples Programme' the GAP partly failed because it neither involved the people nor did it bring environmental awareness to the lower classes. Rather than unifying India's population, the implementation of the Plan actually accentuated the division between government officials and locals in Banaras.

*Fishing, Cultivation and Sandmining*

When the GAP was launched the local authorities in the city were under pressure to produce fast results in cleaning the river. This focused primarily on the local level, where the people with a living relationship with the river soon experienced a top-down development approach. It is important to understand that, directly or indirectly, the majority of the population in Banaras depends on pilgrimage and tourism as its major source of income. *Pandas* (priests), Doms (an untouchable group working in the cremation ghats), merchants, dhobis (washermen), Yadavs

---

7    Such claims surrounding the GAP affirm Gupta's (1995, 276) contention about the way in which the discourse of corruption 'turns out to be a key arena through which the state, citizens and other organizations and aggregations come to be imagined'.

(buffalo herders) and boatmen, are all groups especially reliant on the river and its banks for their economic livelihood.

At the local level, the implementation of the GAP proved most detrimental to the boatmen's livelihood. New policies were introduced, including a ban on fishing, restrictions on cultivating land, and the eradication of sandmining from the riverbed on the eastern side of the river. The government claimed that fish help in the decomposition of corpses and other organic material thrown into the river and thereby help to reduce pollution. Boatmen argued that such perceptions are misleading, and that the real cause of pollution is the continual flow of factory effluent and urban sewage into the river. Once more the boatman associations provided the mouthpiece for boatmen to express their voice in public, articulating the collective plight of the community, and mobilizing people for collective action against the state, as the following excerpt from a meeting illustrates:

> It was unanimously decided that a massive demonstration be organized at the office of the Divisional Commissioner on 2 August 1993, with a boat and a net to protest the ban on fishing in the Ganges, and in relation to other demands it was decided to submit all the details related to the demonstration to local officials as well as in a press release to the local newspaper (1 August 1993).

The above quote is a resolution taken from a meeting of the Mallah Samuday Sanghars Samity (the Mass Association for the Struggle of Mallahs, Varanasi, hereafter MSSS). These meetings were systematically documented and their minutes given to me by one of its leading members, Chotilal Nishad. The proper conduct of these meetings and painstaking documentation demonstrates the level of awareness, organization and sophistication of such caste associations. A short excerpt from a newspaper report shows the avenues they pursue to achieve their goals and voice their grievances in the public sphere: 'The government has banned fishing in the name of cleaning the Ganga … The boatmen who depend on fishing for their economic survival have been brought to the verge of starvation'.[8]

In Banaras, fishing has long been a controversial activity. Crucially, the boatmen's complaints about the fishing ban are not only directed at the state, but also reflect an ongoing concern regarding their own place in the social fabric of Indian society. A common view amongst boatmen is that the current ban on fishing is a result of lobbying by *pandas* (Brahmin priests who operate on the riverfront) who say that fishing should be illegal in the holy precincts of the city. Brahmins generally regard the practice of fishing and consuming fish as defiling and immoral. According to the Brahminical orthodoxy (however different in practice) killing animals and consuming meat is considered a sinful act. In recent years,

---

8    The quote is taken from a local paper clipping, dated 1 August 1993. However, because he does not keep records regarding the page and often the name of the newspaper, I am not able to identify it as such. A copy of the newspaper report is available from the author.

**Figure 2.1      Boatmen fishing under the Malviya Bridge, Raj ghat**

due to increasing attention to the severe problems associated with pollution in the River Ganges, the *pandas* have found allies in environmentalists and government officials, the latter claiming that fishing contributes to an increase in river pollution, as fish eat organic material, such as sewage and decomposing dead bodies. Early in my field research the matter of river pollution and the ban on fishing was raised in an interview with a boatman named Ramprasad:[9]

> There is a ban on fishing in the river on the pretext of cleaning the Ganga (*Ganga pradushan ke nam par*). Religious leaders and local *pandas* want to ban fishing because they consider it as killing animals (*jiv hatya*) in a holy place. For us, the Nishads, it is our birth right (*hamara janm sid adhikar hai*) to fish and we will continue to do so as our ancestors did.[10]

---

9      Interview, Ramprasad Nishad, 6 April 2002.

10      My research assistant later noted that the pathos with which the boatman said the words, 'It is our birth right!', reminded him of the famous freedom fighter and patriot, Bal Gangadhar Tilak (also known as Lokmanya), who famously said 'Freedom (Swaraj) is my birthright' (see Cashman 1975; Hay 1991, 140–148). Once again, this boatman seems to be drawing on the national discourse of independence, which instead of promoting resistance

Ramprasad continued by accusing the *pandas* of double standards, corruption and religious misconduct:

> They ban fishing in the name of religion. The *pandas* say that Kashi is a religious and pious (*dharmic*) place and that no animals should be slaughtered here, but what about killing buffalo? Is that not a problem? In the past my father had a contract to fish in the local pond and he gave the *pandas* 50 percent of his earnings. That killing was no problem for the *pandas*. And what about sacrificing goats? Both god and the *pandas* are happy with this. The *pandas* commit a double sin. First, they stop our families from earning our livelihood and then they sacrifice goats inside temples, which is also animal slaughter.

As a result of the ban on fishing many boatmen have resorted to secretly fishing at night. As one boatman explained: 'Since about two years ago it has been illegal to fish in the Ganga, so we fish at night and bribe the police to avoid harassment. I usually give them some of the catch and during festivals we give them either cash or whisky'. So while bribery and corruption is fed by the ban, boatmen do not consider paying off the police as immoral, rather it is the only way to deal with local officials: the pragmatics of everyday life. In this sense, fishing reminds us of what Scott (1989) refers to as 'everyday forms of resistance', a practice which technically does not require a high degree of co-operation. Moreover, such practice is seen as ideologically justifiable because it is derived from the common belief that fishing is the Mallahs' traditional right, something denied to them by the state and local Brahmins. However, resistance by the subordinate boatmen to the ban on fishing is not exclusively confined to 'everyday forms' or expressed within the boundaries of 'hidden transcripts', where boatmen subvert the authority and morality of Brahminical ideology and practice. Boatman associations continue to engage in more open political action, circulating petitions, press releases and performing occasional protests, where they coherently articulate their moral and political objections to government policies.

Still, regardless of the strategies used when dealing with the police and local authorities, boatmen continue to be viewed as undisciplined people who engage in criminal acts. As such, they remain vulnerable to the whims of the local police, which at best amount to unpleasant harassment and at worst to prosecution and jailing.

---

against the oppressive colonial regime and the uplift of low castes, has in fact reinforced the violation of people's rights by bowing to dominant sectors in Indian society.

*Cultivation*

> The Nishads must have their traditional rights back so they can continue to
> cultivate on the banks of the Ganga, producing water melons, musk melons,
> cucumbers, and other vegetables...[11]

Boatmen have been cultivating the fertile land along the riverbanks for generations. In Banaras, cultivation occurs on the eastern side of the river. Ploughing the land generally begins as the water level recedes around December and continues until harvesting, which, depending on the crop, occurs in the months March to April. However, with the implementation of the GAP in Banaras, these cultivation practices have also come under threat, as one boatman explained:

> The Nagar Nigam [Municipal Authority] believes that if they collect rubbish
> in boats and dump it on the other side of the river they are cleaning the river.
> Is Ganga not on the other side also? Nowadays, Banaras and Ganga pollution
> have become synonymous, but what about other areas along the Ganga which
> are polluted? One cannot just clean the Ganga in Banaras; the flow of sewage
> also arrives from other cities. Ultimately, the Mallahs are the ones who bear the
> brunt. For example, the Department of Forestry has tried to prevent us from
> fishing and cultivating in the name of Ganga pollution. They banned fishing and
> then released *lakh* (100,000) turtles to eat the dead bodies floating in the river.
> Afterwards, they told us we could not continue to cultivate the land on the other
> side of the river because the turtles must come up there for resting and nesting.
> Now the government blames us for the death of the turtles, saying we poach
> them. Yes, it is true that some boatmen hunt turtles, say a maximum of 10,000
> turtles, so where are the other 90,000? The authorities seem to forget that Ganga
> is a flowing river and with the floods the turtles also flow down the river.[12]

The boatman cited above cogently accuses the government of failing to deal with the true causes of pollution. Apart from pointing to the ineffectiveness of state government policy, he suggests that the whole project ultimately serves to displace those boatmen who rely on the river for their subsistence. Over the past decade the 'scavenger turtle scheme' has come under much criticism, not least because 'there is no way to monitor how many turtles there are in the Ganga or to keep record of their progress' (Ahmed 1991, 246; Menon 1997). Once again, the boatmen are seen as criminals engaged in illegal poaching and jeopardizing the waste management scheme. It seems that the media affirms this view, but also, more importantly, affirms the inefficiency of the GAP. A leading journal, *India Today* (1997), noted:

---

11    Interview, Ramdas Nishad, December 2002, Banaras.
12    Interview, Lakshman Nishad, 6 April 2002.

Around 28,820 turtles were released into the Ganga at Varanasi in the hope they would feed on corpses. Most of them were poached... In a bid to keep it out of the public, the sewage was diverted and discharged into the Varuna river in Varanasi, which ultimately empties into the Ganga. Villagers along its point are suffering from water-born diseases like jaundice, skin infection and malaria. They are known as GAP victims.

The journal report goes on to mention that many of these 'GAP victims' come from the village of Sarai Mohana, located at the southern edge of the city, with the majority of the population belonging to the Nishad/Mallah caste. While not many boatmen practice cultivation on the scale practiced in the past, around 50 families of boatmen continue to cultivate the fields on the margins of the city. As with fishing, every now and again a local official comes to warn them against cultivating, and leaves again with a small bribe. When speaking with Gangaram, a boatman who regularly cultivates the riverbank, about the future prospects of cultivation, he was doubtful, and expressed his agitation with the government policy, saying, 'they think turtles are more important than human beings'. Stretching his arm forward, he added, 'our blood is just as red as theirs [government people]'.

Frustrations over local authority efforts to clean the river were often expressed in interviews I had with various boatmen. They suggested that methods used by the authorities to clean the river were purely cosmetic, as one boatman said, 'the government is putting lipstick on a woman wearing a dirty sari'. Meanwhile, one

**Figure 2.2    Cultivating on the other side of the Ganges**

of the real causes of pollution, namely, the constant flow of sewage from the city into the river, continues unabated.[13] The end result is that the poor and dispossessed are those who pay the price for the government's ineffective waste management plan. The resentment towards the state is all the more evident when boatmen recall the banning of sand transportation by boat.

## Sandmining

The River Ganges carries vast amounts of alluvial soil and sand, which accumulates and is exposed when the river recedes in the dry season. In the past dozens of barges were used for sand transportation and could be seen anchored on both sides of the river.[14] Thousands of boatmen mined the sand on the other side of the river and transported it to the city for use in construction. In addition, they worked as wage labourers loading and offloading sand from the boats:

> ...prior to Independence our society was considered the backbone of the national economy. The Nishads worked in transportation. The Nishad boatmen had the monopoly on water farming and sandmining...but after Independence... India began destroying their traditional rights with the help of capitalists and Mafiosi...as a result the Fisherman's Society came to the verge of starvation.[15]

In the past, boatmen claim, government contracts for extracting sand from the riverbeds across India were given exclusively to the Nishads, as it was considered an aspect of their traditional occupation. However, with increasing private ownership, economic reforms and rapid urban development, sandmining has become a lucrative business, and various other stakeholders have begun to impinge on the Nishads' monopoly. Banaras presents a similar case; thousands of members of the Nishad/Mallah caste were once employed in the business of sandmining for generations, which provided them with a stable and relatively good source of income. This has subsequently changed and one family from the Yadav caste now has monopoly over the sandmining business.[16]

---

13    Boatmen willingly show the curious passenger the source of pollution–the urban sewage gushing down the river next to Sarai Mohana and Shivala ghat. The unabated flow of sewage, which constitutes more than 85% of pollution in the river, is no secret.

14    In the film *Forest of Bliss* by Robert Gardner (1985), the prominence of sand barges and the scale of activity involved in sandmining can be seen.

15    *Nishad Jyothi*, March–April (2001, 6).

16    This has caused much anger amongst boatmen, because in line with reservation policy it is the Nishads who have the prerogative for sandmining. According to many boatmen, the Yadav managed to obtain the contract by using a Nishad as the chief applicant. These claims were often followed by boatmen castigating their own caste members for selling out and betraying their own kind.

**Figure 2.3    Sandcarrying barges on the main ghat, Banaras (pre-ban)**

*Source*: Photograph © Pierre Toutain-Dorbec

With the implementation of the GAP in Banaras, the transport of sand via the river to the main ghat was banned. Sandmining was considered an eyesore, grouped with other 'untidy' practices, such as laundering clothes on the ghats by washermen (dhobis).[17] Many boatmen not only lost their livelihood without compensation, but were also left with huge and useless boats. The boats decayed and the boatmen were forced to look for alternative sources of income. Sand still continues to be mined, but is transported to the city outskirts via the Malviya Bridge by trucks. More than 15 years later, the frustration and bitterness of the boatmen is still apparent. They consider Rajiv Gandhi's injunction and the GAP to be a blunt act of economic dispossession of their community.

Indeed, the GAP, like other state development programmes, designed to legitimize its rule, appears to have produced an adverse reaction among those considered its primary beneficiaries – the people at the grassroots. For boatmen, the 'myth of the state' has been shattered (Hansen 2000). In the eyes of boatmen the state remains distant, biased and non-responsive, and the everyday experience

---

17    Once again it is the low caste/class people, such as the washermen (dhobis), who serve as easy targets for GAP officials to demonstrate their efficiency in controlling pollution. Under the GAP, laundering clothes is also deemed polluting and unsightly. For more details on the case of the dhobis and their protests against the government, see Ahmed (1991, 248–254).

is that of further marginalization, loss of income and persecution by the local police.


## Mythic Tradition, Collective Memory and the Politics of Resistance

To fully appreciate the way in which boatmen perceive and imagine the Indian state, we must also consider older constructions of the state, derived from indigenous thought and cultural structures and practices. Hansen (2000, 26) calls this the 'longue durée perspective', which in the Indian context refers to various institutions and moral values, including 'older registers of kinship and the Brahman-Kshatriya relations'. Unfortunately, in his insightful analysis of the 1992/3 Mumbai riots, Hansen focuses on Western political thought as the primary element underscoring contemporary discourses on the state. In my view, however, the cultural perspective is equally necessary and instructive when investigating the significance of the state for people in everyday life, specific forms of domination, and for recognizing culturally valued strategies for dealing with the state.

I have already addressed the cultural dimension in terms of how boatman associations evoke notions of kinship, patronage and family ethos to position themselves within the narrative of the nation-state, make claims and gain recognition. This dimension is also evident in the way that boatmen perceive Brahminical influence on state policy, such as fishing. Boatmen insist that their economic marginalization is intrinsically related to broader patterns of caste prejudice and ideological domination. More generally such sentiments, along with the perception of an unsavoury allegiance between the bureaucratic and cultural elites have been systematically promoted in the Nishad caste journals and popular discourse. Throughout my fieldwork I encountered a number of key mythical stories which boatmen related to me as 'evidence' of their dignified status and the injustices they have suffered by high castes, particularly Brahmins.

The Eklavya story, in particular, is one in which the link between the political and the social constitutes a prominent theme. This myth is a branch story within the Hindu epic Mahabharata, and is essentially about a young prince, called Eklavya Nishad, and his ardent devotion to his guru.

The story tells of the young Eklavya who wanted to learn archery from Drona, a Brahmin who taught warrior princes the mastery of weaponry. The latter refused to accept him as his student since he was a low caste Shudra. Motivated by supreme devotion and determination Eklavya installed a clay figure of his guru Drona to worship and practise archery before it. Before too long he became an unrivalled archer. Meanwhile, Drona was determined to make his favoured disciple, Arjuna, the most competent archer in the land. However, following an incident on a hunting trip, Drona and Arjuna became aware that there existed an archer even more accomplished than Arjuna. To their surprise this was the low caste Eklavya, who attributed his skilled archery to Drona. As his guru, Drona demanded the disciple pay his customary fee (*dakshina*) in the form of his right-hand thumb. Undaunted, and with due humility and devotion, Eklavya cut off his thumb and placed it at the feet of his guru. Thus, Eklavya could no longer remain the best archer in the land.

The story of Eklavya is subject to various interpretations, according to one's ideology. From an 'orthodox' Hindu perspective, one could argue that Drona's refusal to take Eklavya as his disciple is consistent with the principle of dharma and karma. That is, because of Eklavya's low caste status, he is barred from engaging in the art of war, which is restricted to the Kshatriya (warrior) caste, to which Arjuna belongs. His attempts to become an archer are therefore a breach of the social hierarchy of the caste system (*Varnadharma*). However, other elements in the story, especially Eklavya's inferior status and his virtuous qualities of diligence, bravery and unflinching devotion, have made this story very popular amongst low caste groups across India.

For the Nishads, Eklavya is a hero, whose devotion and sacrifice must be celebrated and commemorated. Once, when discussing the story with a leading member of the community Bhayalal Nishad, I was handed a caste journal, the *Nishad Jyothi*. Bhayalal said, 'you see, the Brahmins who hold the knowledge of the *puranas* try to cover up such good stories about the Mallahs, because they want to continue to exploit us and treat us like dirt, but now the truth is being revealed'. Indeed, it is in caste journals where one can find overt challenges to Brahminical power, where traditional texts are being reinterpreted by the Nishads. These journals serve as a platform for members of the community to raise their fears about their current position and to voice their long standing grievances and mistrust of Brahminical ideology and the state.

In one issue of the *Nishad Jyothi* I found a commentary interwoven within the Eklavya story, authenticated by direct Sanskrit quotes from the epic. In this narration, Eklavya is extolled for his bravery, devotion and moral integrity as opposed to the cowardly and selfish nature of Drona and Arjuna. In addition, the article highlights that in the Mahabharata itself it is said that Drona's demand from his disciple should not be seen as that of guru-*dakshina* but rather as a salary or wage (*vetan*).[18] The implication is that it is Eklavya, rather than Drona, who upheld the 'true' principles of dharma and reciprocity by unquestionably allowing his guru to have his thumb. Such interpretations of the story suggest that even within the framework of guru-devotee, where the act of giving *dakshina* is sanctioned, Drona's behaviour cannot be justified. His motivations were flawed and his request unjust.

The narrator goes on to retell and interpret this myth and the source text in a way consistent with indigenous tradition and in doing so convincingly and authoritatively presents views echoing contemporary low caste sentiments. For example, he laments that despite Drona and Arjuna's contemptible behaviour, '… politicians and bureaucrats continue to honour Dronacharya and Arjuna for their heroism and courage, rather than admire the true devotee (*guru-bhakt*), son of the

---

18	*Nishad Jyothi*, 28, March–27 April, 2001. p. 9.

Nishads, Eklavya, who they feel ashamed of'.[19] The author continues to argue that it is because of 'Brahminical domination (*Brahmanvadi*) that the ordinary man (the son of the Nishads) can not achieve greatness'. He states 'that if he [Eklavya] had been born into a family of Brahmins, he would be able to attain the status of a great man (*Mahapurush*)'.

The narrator highlights the existing hierarchical order and the social political structure as represented by the Brahmin (Drona) and the Kshatriya (Arjuna) respectively, while Eklavya, the Shudra, is the repressed within it.[20] As such, the story is employed to emphasize the marginalization of the community, both in the past and today. The text is reappropriated to serve as a 'cultural weapon', to use de Certeau's term (1984, 171), providing a vehicle for the author to expose the hypocrisy and violence of elite ideology and its oppression of the low castes. Interestingly, the piece concludes with a rebuke of the Nishads themselves, followed by a petition for a conscious effort by members of the community to reclaim their heroes from both high and low castes. By interpreting the Eklavya myth in light of contemporary fears, ambitions and aspirations of the Nishads, the narrator invites his audience to 'remember anew' past deeds, and construct their social and political identity accordingly.

It is important to emphasize that highlighting the 'true' nature and achievements of low castes as part of India's history and culture is a common feature in caste uplift discourse, reflective of the contemporary political climate of North India. Since the early 1980s low castes have steadily increased their presence in the political arena of India's most populated state of Uttar Pradesh. Badri Narayan (2001) reports of an increasing amount of literature (i.e., booklets, folktales, songs and myths) produced and circulated in North India, shaping and demonstrating the newly found confidence and assertiveness amongst low castes, especially untouchables (Dalits). In a recent interview, the leader of the low caste Bahujan Samaj Party (BSP), Mayawati is quoted as saying:

The people who write our history wiped out all traces of Dalit Raja-maharajahs. For a long time our history has been wiped out. The social system is such that someone like Bijli Pasi found no mention in our history books while there is evidence that the Pasis [an untouchable caste] at one time were ruling this area... So I am not history, I am only highlighting history that has been consciously suppressed (*India Today*, August 1997, quoted in Jafferlot 1998, 39).

---

19    *Nishad Jyothi*, pp. 9–10.

20    Shankar (1994) makes a similar point in an insightful analysis of the story and its allegorical application to postcolonial scholarship.

The story of Eklavya has also been central to the political discourse of lower castes in Northern India in general.[21] Phoolan Devi, herself a member of the Nishad caste, used the story and its powerful symbolism throughout her years in politics. As a member of the federal parliament (MP) until her murder in July 2001, Phoolan Devi was a vocal campaigner against Brahminical oppression and a strong advocate for the rights of the poor and marginalized sectors of India society.[22] Clearly, the meaning and potential power of the Eklavya story did not escape Phoolan Devi. When released from jail in 1993, Phoolan Devi launched a group by the name of 'Eklavya Sena'. This group, which was initially formed to teach self-defence to low caste people, soon became a leading organization protecting and fighting for the rights of backward castes all over North India.[23] The following excerpt from a local newspaper indicates how she used the myth to promote her cause:[24]

> The story of the legendary tribal hero of the Mahabharat, Eklavya, plays a pivotal role in all her election meetings. "Eklavya was our king. Now, we shall establish 'Eklavya raaj' [Eklavya's rule] and ensure that the poor get justice and honour," is her message to the downtrodden before they go to the polls (quoted in Kumar 1999, 16).

By using the term 'Eklavya raaj', Devi was consciously invoking and reversing the utopian ideal of Ramraj – the righteous reign of the divine prince Rama – which in this context refers to Brahmin-Kshatriya dominant socio-political order. Her call to establish 'Eklavya raaj' was thus an overt challenge to the ideology of social hierarchy propounded by the dominant elites. What is important to emphasize is the way in which such cultural frameworks, based on shared symbols, terms and references (Hansen 2000, 24), inform contemporary popular discourse on the state. The Eklavya myth offers a meaningful device for members of the Nishad caste, to articulate and justify their perceptions of and practices relating to the state.

---

21    During her first term in power (1996), Mayawati named a stadium in Agra, Eklavya stadium (Jafferlot 1998, 47). Interestingly, in the *Nishad Jyothi* I found a commentary noting the danger of Eklavya Nishad being appropriated by other low castes as their own hero.

22    Originally the famous 'Bandit queen', Phoolan Devi became a powerful symbol for low castes in India. Devi was an MP for Samjvadi Party (SP). The SP draws its support mainly from members Backward Classes. It is also based in the North Indian state of Uttar Pradesh (UP).

23    The term *sena*, 'army', also has religious connotations for many Hindi speakers due to homophony with the verb *sena*, 'to serve or worship'. I am indebted to Torsten Tschacher for this comment.

24    One could draw a parallel between Devi and Eklavya. Both appeared as anti heroes within a larger story. Despite being marginal characters, they gained popularity because of their heroic qualities and motivations.

Such perceptions of distrust and questioning of hegemonic Brahminical culture and state discourse and action are further stimulated by the rise of caste politics in the Northern state of Uttar Pradesh. The message of dissent echoes strongly amongst subordinate populations who are increasingly demonstrating confidence and assertiveness as an oppositional order, with strong political representation (see Jeffrey and Lerche 2000; Narayan 2001). For the boatman community in Banaras and the Nishad community more generally, political figures like Phoolan Devi and the current Chief Minister, Mayawati offer access to state power and new hopes for being heard as a group severely impaired by caste structures and state policies (see Gupta 2001).

In July 1997 Phoolan Devi was invited by members of the boatman community of Banaras to participate in the annual celebrations of the *Nishad Jyanti*. The celebrations marked the 20th anniversary of the building of a local temple dedicated to Guha Raj Nishad: a revered mythical figure of the Nishad community.[25] The celebration had a distinctly political angle.[26] Prior to this much publicized event numerous pamphlets, handbills and press releases were distributed, hailing Phoolan Devi, as a daughter of the Nishads, president of the Eklavya *sena*, and a celebrated MP. The event was orchestrated by the local Mallah Association (MSSS) with the National Backward Class Development Finance and Development Cooperation (NBCDFDC). In this way the cause of the Nishad/Mallah community to restore their traditional rights (e.g., fishing and sandmining from the riverbeds) was placed in the wider context of government policies and social and economic displacement of the backward and disadvantaged sections of the population in India.[27] As such, the associations aligned themselves with political leaders drawing on the broader issues of displacement of low caste/classes in Indian society. It appears, however, that this political rallying has been relatively ineffective. The central government's policies are more enduring than one off events such as this. It is not surprising that the majority of boatmen who previously relied on fishing, cultivation and sandmining have since opted for alternative sources of income.

It is difficult to gauge the precise number of boatmen who have lost their livelihood as a result of the restrictions imposed on sandmining, fishing and cultivation. Boatmen I have spoken to say it amounts to several thousands. Some

---

25    The temple, dedicated to Nishad Raj, was built by members of the community and is located on Nishad Raj ghat overlooking the Ganga. The temple has various functions: it is a venue for community events, including weddings, religious rituals, meetings of the community caste association and other cultural celebrations, as well as an afternoon school for children of the neighbourhood.

26    Such celebrations of caste identity generally combine worship of the caste deity (in this case Nishad Raj), a number of speeches made by local and regional community leaders and a cultural programme. This pattern is followed with certain variations by other castes across India. For a similar case amongst the Izhavas of Kerala see Osella & Osella (2000a, 160–167).

27    The details of the event were reported in the local newspaper, *Dianik Jagran* (12 July 1997).

boatmen were clearly devastated by such restrictions with many accruing heavy debt, and subsequently destroying their families. One boatman, Sanjay Manjhi, whom I came to know well was gravely affected by the ban on sandmining. He had previously been well-off, owning three sand barges. After the restrictions were imposed, he was unable to make a living and became a heavy drinker, an addiction that eventually destroyed him and consequently his family. Sadly, he recently committed suicide. This boatman's tragic story sheds light on the predicament faced by those boatmen who relied on sandmining for their livelihood. Some boatmen, however, have been able to adapt to the new circumstances by converting their barges into passenger boats and entering the highly competitive and lucrative pilgrimage and tourist business. The result is that the occupational diversity of boatmen working on the riverscape has been reduced to that of ferrying passengers. This, in turn, has affected the way in which the boatman community perceives itself and the challenges it faces as it tries to adapt and respond to the changes taking place in Banaras, India and the world around it. As such, boatman associations have developed new strategies of engaging with the state, stressing cooperation and collaboration.

**Collaborating with the State**

Boatmen who continue to work on the river have become increasingly aware that the problem of pollution in the Ganges is now a high profile issue at both a national and international level. Such awareness largely derives from their daily encounters with foreign tourists, as well as local and international politicians and activists who frequent the river. Recently it appears that members of the community have also been responsive to the pressing issues of pollution, as the following press release issued by the All Embracing National Nishad Awareness Assembly (Ranshtriya Nisdhad Jagran Mahasabha) shows:

> ...On July 4th 1999, as previously scheduled, the members of the Nishad community assembled at 8 am on Assi ghat and cleaned the banks of the Ganga until Dashashvamedh ghat [the main ghat].... In this first phase of this campaign to clean the river, the community joined hands and raised their voices calling slogans, like: Ma Ganga ki Seva, Mallah Karega (Mallahs will perform the service for Mother Ganga), Ganga Seva, Bharat Seva (Service to Ganga is service to the Nation)...Nishad Ekata Zindabad (the Nishads stand firm and united). In addition, members of the community used their boats and motorboats to collect rubbish from the river... Concluding the programme in Dashashvamedh ghat, a senior member of the community said: 'Whoever cleans Ganga Ma clearly deserves to be called Gangaputra'...Mr. Nishad then appealed to sanitation workers and members of the community to take a pledge to clean

the bank of the Ganges on their ghats… prominent members of the community
participated in the event…(Reg 6, 23)

This press release neatly sums up the way in which boatman associations seek
to gain broad recognition and visibility in the public realm as a community working
for the greater good of society. By organizing such events boatman associations are
also able to engage with the state and local authorities in a collaborative fashion,
joining forces with the administration to clean the river, not least by using their
boats and motorboats for the task. By presenting their campaign as a grassroots
one, instigated by purely devotional motives, boatmen are subverting what James
Scott (1990) calls the 'public transcript'. At one level, boatmen demonstrate
compliance and conformity with 'how the dominant groups would wish to have
things appear' (1990, 4). At another level, they are able to 'infiltrate the public
transcript with dissent and self-assertion' (1990, 138) Rather than be viewed as
breeching the law (e.g., by fishing and contributing to the pollution in the river) or
overtly contesting Brahminical power by declaring themselves Gangaputra – a term
commonly associated with Brahmin priests – boatmen employ devotional idiom
and practice in a sufficiently ambiguous fashion to express their dissatisfaction
with government policies and infuse it with their own message.


## Motorboats, Pollution and Collective Action

The recent introduction of motorboats on the river is a response to the changing
nature of the pilgrimage industry in India, and in Banaras in particular. Although,
the majority of boats (90%) are still manually handled, an increasing number of
boatmen have invested in converting their rowboats into motorboats (see Figure
2.4). This is because pilgrimage is nowadays organized as 'packaged pilgrimage'
where pilgrims may visit various sacred destinations across the subcontinent in
less than a month (see Gold 1988; Fuller 1992). Motorboats provide a quick and
efficient way for pilgrims to complete their visit to the city in time. However,
the issue of river pollution continues to haunt the boatman community, as the
authorities intermittently ban the operation of motorboats, arguing that they
constitute a major source of noise and air pollution.

Boatmen complain that the authorities harass them for operating motorboats
on the river even though they are officially licensed to do so. There is a measure
of bureaucratic inconsistency in relation to the legality of operating motorboats.
Officially, the municipal authorities have approved the introduction of motorboats
on the river, gaining considerable income from licence fees. Gaining an operating
licence for a motorboat costs seven times more than that for a rowboat (i.e., Rs.350
per annum). However, as the issue of river pollution remains on the agenda, the
need to produce quick and visible results at the lower level of the state is pertinent,
as the following article from *Dainik Jagran*, reports:

> The chairman of the National Environment Protection Council...Dr. B.D. Tripathi has said that approximately 62 diesel run motorboats...cause smoke and hydro-carbons in the entire river area. This compels the lovers of boating and tourists to breath in polluted air. Dr. Tripathi, who has been nominated by the Allahabad High Court, for the central committee formed to examine the issue of pollution control schemes, said that he has urged the Chief Secretary of Uttar Pradesh in a letter...that all diesel engine private boats be banned immediately....He added that boats should also be painted for the beautification of the river area (18 December 1998, 5).

Amita Baviskar (2002) recently argued that India is witnessing the rise of what she calls 'bourgeoisie environmentalism', where middle class 'concerns around aesthetic, leisure, safety and health have come to significantly shape the disposition of urban spaces'. These concerns are expressed in various 'beautification schemes' that seek to retrieve 'green spaces' and 'clean air' in urban spaces, often by displacing whole populations and at the expense of 'food and shelter for the poor'.[28] The chairman of the National Environmental Council quoted above strongly echoes these sentiments, when he declares the riverscape to be a space for tourist consumption, free of pollution and unsavoury sights and smells.

Ensuring spatial control and order over the riverscape is a contentious issue, both historically and politically. Unlike the national level administrators and agencies, the municipal authorities are more aware of these historical and political river dynamics, and especially of the indispensable services boatmen provide for the ritual and tourist economy of the city. The resulting confusion forms the background to the haphazard implementation of restrictions by the local authorities. A fine example of this is the impending decision by the High Court on whether to ban motorboats creating confusion amongst officials and boatmen alike and producing a state of bureaucratic limbo. During 1999, the local authorities wrote several formal letters to the Ganges Pollution Control Unit in order to clarify whether licences should be issued for motorboats or the ban imposed.[29] A period of uncertainty ensued and the boatmen were harassed by the Water Police (*Jal Police*) for operating motorboats. At times, the decision to ban motorboats was upheld by the authorities, at other times it was ignored. The boatman community, on the other hand, has been consistent in its vehement opposition to the ban, once again, using its associations to try and fend off state interventions. In a letter sent by the *Ardash Matsyog Sahakari Samity* (the Exemplar Fisherman's Cooperative Association) to

---

28    For a comprehensive review of the literature pertaining to middle class sensibilities and their relation to the environment, see Mawdsley 2004.

29    I hold photocopies of the documents given to me by members of the Mallah community in Banaras, which I cite as Reg. (Author's Register). In this case, a number of letters were sent to the General Manager, Ganges Pollution Control Unit, from the Office In charge of licensing, Municipal Authority, Varanasi from January until August 1999, asking to clarify the issue of licences for motorboats. (Reg 6, 46–47).

the District Commissioner the association requested that the 'unthoughtful order of the Municipal Authorities of stopping motorboats' be revoked.[30] As the following excerpt details in point form:

> 1. The boatmen are *poor* labourers who have been practising their occupation for generations. 2. As such we have been serving the government and the public in many ways….3. The pride and identity of Varanasi is associated with Ganga and the pride of Ganga is related to the boats of the *poor* Mallah. 4. From all around the world tourists arrive…to get a glimpse of the ghats of Kashi from our boats, which are in the lap of Ganga Ma (my italics).[31]

Thereafter the author lists the reasons why a ban on motorboats is unfair to the boatman community and will ultimately harm the city and its reputation. It is argued in the letter that tourists who come to the city for a short stay are in haste to complete the 'world famous morning tour of Varanasi, comprising a boat ride from Raj ghat to Assi ghat. Therefore, it is only with the service of "small motorboats" (*chote chote steamers*) that tourists may depart from the city with the "pride of Kashi in their minds" (section 10). It reverses the claim made by the authorities that motorboats disturb tourist activities and argues instead that boatmen provide a much needed service for tourists, who have but little time to enjoy the marvels the city has to offer. Throughout this section of the letter the boatmen are presented as the custodians of local knowledge in Banaras, as well as serving as life guards for local bathers and as tour guides for foreign visitors. The first part of the letter concludes by praising the boatmen as a devoted community contributing to the greater public good and tourist industry.

Having established the credentials of the community, the second part of the letter goes on to address the issue of pollution and the ruling motorboat ban. It convincingly argues that across the city there are thousands of generators, motorcycles and buses emitting smoke, carbon dioxide and pollution, which go unnoticed or at least unchecked by the authorities. It is, it claims, because the boatmen are *poor* labourers that the government and police find them easy targets to harass with regards to motorboats and pollution. The letter addresses the District Commissioner in the final paragraph:

> Therefore, you are humbly requested to extend your contribution to the welfare of the *poor* boatmen, so that we can continue to serve the government and public effectively. You are requested to ask the Chief City Official to stop torturing us

---

30   Letter dated 11 June 1999 (Reg 7, 10).

31   The term 'lap of Mother Ganga' (*god bharna*) refers to the way in which newly married women have their laps filled with sacred articles so that they may be blessed with child. Here the term implies that the boatmen are the blessed children of Ganga Ma (see also Chapter 4).

and issue us licences for small motorboats. We will be highly obliged to you
(my emphasis).

It is interesting to note the sophistication with which the letter draws on several
distinct notions of community. The first of these appears in the letterhead which
features the name 'the Exemplar Fisherman's Cooperative Association'. Although
the letter is addressing the problems of boatmen, and even more specifically those
who operate motorboats, it is written in the name of the fisherman community,
thereby lending it an authoritative and broad foundation.[32] The content of the letter
clearly elaborates on a second, locally bound notion of community: the boatmen
of Banaras. By virtue of their traditional occupation, the boatmen are portrayed
as the guardians of local knowledge and it is claimed that they are particularly
suitable to impart such knowledge to tourists. In fact, it is their duty, privilege,
and responsibility to serve and mediate Banaras for the foreign visitors (an issue
I discuss further in Chapter 5). Thus, the authorities are asked to recognize the
boatmen's significant contribution to the local industry of pilgrimage and tourism
and the greater public good.[33]

Boatmen continuously emphasize that they are a poor and oppressed
community, despite the fact that in recent years some members of their community
have become increasingly wealthy, as a result of the burgeoning pilgrim and tourist
industry. This is reflected in letters and handbills where the term *garib* (poor)
features widely both as a noun and adjective. Apart from expressing a state of
being, or appealing to the state to realize its declared aim to protect the poor, the
term also seems to indicate a distinct interpretation and experience of modernity,

---

32    Of the many associations, I could only trace the MSSS, with nominal consistency
to the mid 1970s. What became increasingly apparent is that these different associations
emerge rather on an ad-hock basis, whereby new initiatives continuously emerge,
representing particular interests or being geared towards specific issues of struggle. It does
appear that these associations do unify and are able to mobilize Mallahs in situations when
acute measures have been taken against the boatmen community. This is the partly because
of a sense of kinship; many Mallahs continue to have someone in their extended family
working on boats. In addition, there is certainly a sense among Mallahs of all occupational
designations in Banaras that plying boats represents a kind of archetypical or traditional
Mallah occupation.

33    This rhetoric of a hierarchically ordered territory and its evocative vocabulary
of place, authenticity, meaning and embodiment, echoes Massey's (2004, 9) notion
of 'Russian doll geography', with its 'persistent focus on parent-child relations of care
and responsibility'. In our case, while the relations between locality, the nation and its
people certainly evoke notions of loyalty, care and responsibly; boatmen are also careful
to highlight their own contribution (and cultural practices) to this relational construction
of place. This is expressed in the celebration of Banaras as a pilgrimage and tourist centre,
which necessarily involves responsibilities emanating from the links between identity,
place and culture: produced and reproduced through the flow of a transient population of
tourists and pilgrims.

**Figure 2.4     Motorboat with Pilgrims**

shared by many marginalized communities across India. According to Linkenbach (2000, 50) who writes about a village community in the Himalayas, the term poor 'serves to denote the lack of respect and social recognition one [has] to bear', with the powerful groups in society benefiting from the exploitation of local resources, while 'denying the local inhabitants the chance to share in modern developments'. A similar point can be made in our case, where boatmen claim Ganga has been exploited by corrupt politicians, local officials and powerful Brahmins who siphon ('eat') money on the pretext of cleaning the river. In the process, it is the poor, ordinary citizens who suffer, through loss of customary rights, police harassment and caste prejudice.

These letters as well as other efforts such as demonstrations and protests proved effective and in 1999 the ban on motorboats was revoked. As I have highlighted, there are sharp inconsistencies and contradictions within the administrative process, whereby the authorities issue licences for motorboats and then revoke them at will. This precarious situation in which boatmen find themselves is perhaps best exemplified by the recent decision in 2006 by the U.P. Forestry Department to implement its decisions forcefully and declare the whole area of Banaras 'a turtle sanctuary'. For boatmen this meant a blanket ban on fishing, cultivation and motorboats and staunch enforcement of this by local police. Boatmen are all too familiar with such whimsical actions designed to satisfy the upper echelons of bureaucracy. This latest ban prompted members of the community to take strong action and on 1 August 2006 the various boatman associations instigated a mass demonstration against it. Halting city traffic as they defiantly marched through the streets of Banaras, the protesters shouted slogans, such as *The nets and the boats are our weapons – we have rights over the water; Ban the turtle sanctuary – do not harass the Mallahs; As long as the Nishads are alive – Ganga will remain free; Whoever clashes with us – will not be able to cross the river.*

Local reportage of the demonstration noted the aggressive nature of the procession and the local authorities' inability to control the crowd. It also highlighted that the striking boatmen denied tourists the famous boat ride at sunrise that day. In all likelihood, the newspaper reports were based on press releases that the boatman associations were canny enough to circulate in advance.[34]

The protest culminated at the Collector's office, where leaders of the MSSS met with the District Magistrate (DM) and Collector presenting their demands for the removal of the ban on motorboats and the turtle sanctuary restrictions. During the meeting with the local officials an agreement was reached with the DM to allow boatmen to continue operating motorboats. According to my informants, the DM could not provide any written assurance since it was the State Forest Department that had instigated the ban as a result of declaring the Ganga in Banaras 'a turtle sanctuary'. Nevertheless the DM informally guaranteed that the boatmen could continue to operate motorboats without any police persecution. Ironically, boatmen can still run their motorboats on the river but because the ban officially remains in place, motorboat licences are no longer issued and the local government is subsequently losing revenue.

This case is a good illustration of the various levels and functionaries implicated in what is commonly perceived as the unified body of the 'state'. Drawing on Herzfeld's work, Sivaramakrishnan (2005) rightly points out that 'the state itself must be seen as the product of ongoing strategies and tactics rather than a reified entity that both its proponents and detractors, for their respective and contingent purposes, hold it to be' (2005, 228). Boatmen are mostly aware of the multiple agencies of the state involved in their economic marginalization, from the localized ones, embodied in the police and upper level municipal officials, up to the State (Forestry Department), and National levels (GAP). While boatmen may refer to the government (*sarkar*) as a cohesive entity, bent on stripping them of their traditional livelihood, their modes of action reveal a mix of everyday forms of resistance and more open political action, so that resistance becomes 'customized' to the needs of the users, while simultaneously addressing the particular form of domination, be it political, material, ideological or social.

---

34    See, for example, *Hindustan* 30 August 2006, p. 6.

## Conclusion

The modern Indian state has extended its reach into Indian society far more than its colonial predecessor. Development discourse and practice continue to be primary vehicles for the state to establish its legitimacy (Chatterjee 1997; Gupta 1995). The GAP advocated progress and development based on the foundations of science, whilst Rajiv Gandhi used it to show that India was a state that cared for its poor, thereby continuing the social and moral legacy of his grandfather, Nehru.

Nevertheless, as a close examination of the GAP clearly reveals the Indian state has become alienated from the ordinary people by failing to appreciate local practices, sentiments and cultural values. The lack of communication and understanding demonstrated by policy makers reflects a social division within Indian society; between the disadvantaged lower classes and the dominant strata of society who dictate state policy. This view may reinforce Kaviraj's (1997) argument of a fundamental disjuncture that exists between the elites and the mass population. His assertion that the ideas of liberal democracy, held by the middle class elites, remain unintelligible to the masses must be questioned. At the level of everyday life, the way in which boatmen express their plight and act to fend off state domination, demonstrates that they understand and are well aware of the inner workings of liberal democracy, including ideas of citizenship, public accountability, rational legal authority and democratic rule (see also Gupta 1995; Parry 2000).

Kaviraj (1991, 85) does acknowledge the possibility of subaltern resistance, but only insofar as it is subversive, echoing what James Scott (1985) calls the 'weapons of the weak'. Accordingly, elite and state discourse is seen as ideologically coherent and powerful, constantly propagated and circulated in the public realm, while subaltern ideas are viewed as 'less structured' and as such good as 'defensive weapons' only. The problem with such a dichotomous view, as Reed-Danahay (1993, 223) aptly observes, is that it 'depends upon an overdrawn view of ideology (official or unofficial) as a coherent message'. As we have seen, state ideology and action is itself inconsistent and ambiguous, involving multiple institutions at different levels. Moreover, subordinate populations, like the boatmen, deploy an array of weapons, ranging from basic to highly sophisticated. Indeed, the increasing assertiveness among low castes in general and boatmen more specifically, derives its strength from a systematic and articulate ideology designed to challenge state-elite domination. While such ideology may appeal to 'traditional' institutions or particularistic interests, it is firmly embedded in and thrives on modernist state discourse, with its notions of citizenship rights, social justice and a universal set of norms and values.

The resulting marginalization of the boatmen through haphazard policies is one case study among many, in which subaltern groups subjected to state development programmes have lost their traditional rights and control over their subsistence resources. Donald Moore (1992) has stressed that 'struggles over land and environmental resources are simultaneously struggles over cultural meanings'. For the boatmen, control, access to, and exclusion from the Ganga and its resources is couched in cultural idioms of rights and entitlements. The various strategies and approaches employed by boatmen (lobbying, handbills, mobilization, press releases, and coalitions) echo what Somers (1994) calls the 'narrative construction of identity'. In this case, boatman associations frame their contemporary experiences of marginalization and dispossession through narratives and memories that are designed to naturalize links between 'people', 'culture' and 'place' (Gupta & Ferguson 1992; Malikki 1992). By employing a repertoire of public, social and cultural narratives that are available to them, boatmen seek to define the parameters of their current space and entitlements regarding the riverscape, and more broadly their position in society. Such narratives encourage an identification of boatmen with the nation, Banaras and Ganga through a process of creative 'fixing' of cultural essences/identities onto both the physical and symbolic geography of the city. These 'subaltern strategies of localization' derive from both local and non-local processes (Escobar 2001), and are articulated through everyday practices and meanings, concepts of citizenship, devotion, loyalty and kinship terms (Mother India/Mother Ganga), so that the knowledge of and attachment to the Ganga and Banaras assumes a multilayered and moral quality, 'shot through with the histories of interaction with state and other "external" agents' (Moore 1997, 92).[35]

Boatmen have an ambivalent relationship with the state, whereby resistance, negotiation and cooperation are equally important strategies of engagement in everyday life. In some ways it is only in organized conflict with the state that the community momentarily assumes a measure of homogeneity, both in the sense of shared identity and common political projects. It would be misleading to suggest that the boatmen are a homogenous community, for not only is the notion of 'community' historically and socially constructed but, as the following chapter demonstrates, the boatman community itself has fractures and internal conflicts; it is rife with power struggles and internal rivalries.

---

35    Escobar's essay, 'Culture sits in places', is a powerful reminder that the recent literature driven by an anti-essentialist critique of place, culture and identity is only one side of the story and one which remains incomplete if it means we 'lose sight of the continued importance of place-based practices and modes of consciousness for the production of culture' (2001, 147).

Chapter 3

# The Moral Economy of Boating: Territorial Clashes and Internal Struggles

We have been living in the regal court of Ganga since time immemorial (Hum log anant kaal se Ganga ka darbar mei rhete hai).

Shambu Manjhi

## Hello! Boat?

*'Hello! Boat? Hello! Boat? Hello! Boat?'* These are the words that echo around, spoken from ten, twenty mouths as you step onto the ghats of Banaras. *'Hello! Boat? Hello! Boat?'* After continuous repetitions, the words have a lingering effect, much like an insidious jingle that refuses to fade, puncturing the spiritual ambience of the riverfront (one tourist I met even suggested I title this book, *'Hello! Boat?'*). As customers what we fail to understand is why, after so many rebuttals the boatmen continue to beseech us with the same nagging question. Indeed, the unfavourable initial encounter between boatmen and tourists seems at odds with what we would commonly expect from service providers, in terms of the courtesy and responsiveness to market and consumer needs, characteristic of the tourist service industry in the West.

But there is more to the story than that. The two words *Hello! Boat?* encompass the complexity of the informal institution of boating: a work system used by boatmen operating along the ghats of Banaras and based on customary rules and regulations – something I describe as a moral economy. It is unlikely that the following account of the boatmen's work system will offer any consolation to those tourists visiting Banaras. However, I do suggest that there is a certain logic underpinning this pestering practice, derived from the boatmen's own unique social and spatial arrangements on the riverfront.

The notion of 'moral economy' owes a great deal to the influential works E.P. Thompson (1971) and James Scott (1976) published over three decades ago. Both theorists identified the transition from embedded economies (pre-capitalist/ peasant) to free market economies as a traumatic one for the poor. Under the aegis of the moral economy subsistence for the poor was socially guaranteed. Norms of reciprocity and redistribution meant that the poor could rely on the ruling and more prosperous classes to ensure minimum income during desperate times. Subsistence was seen as a social right, and it was the notion of social justice and moral obligations, rather than strict rational economic reasoning, that directed and regulated economic action and goals. According to this view, the rupture of the older moral economies, a result of expanding capitalist markets and the increased demands made by the colonial state, spurred riots and resistance amongst the poor.

In the South Asian context, the notion of a moral economy has been used to highlight the detrimental effects of Western economy and colonial rule on peasant society. In a series of illuminating studies of famine and food riots in India during the late 19th and early 20th century, Arnold (1979, 1984) and Hardiman (1996), both founding members of the Subaltern Studies School, suggested that famines were never simply a result of climatic factors. Rather, the dearth and hunger experienced by the subordinate classes were largely due to a combination of technological advancements, state legalisation, land reforms and the imposition of *laissez-faire* policies. Such changes precipitated shortage and destabilized the older moral economies, propelling the rich and powerful to exploit the poor and engage in unethical practices. The result was moral outrage fuelled by hunger, which in some cases manifested itself in incidents of theft, arson and looting, and in other instances, as large scale food riots, both of which constituted a subaltern response to a breach of their customary rights and practices.

The notion of a 'moral economy' can also explain much of what I have discussed in the previous chapter, involving the boatmen's own definition of justice, norms and rights. The state's intervention into the lives and practices of boatmen and its expropriation of their most valued resource – the Ganga – is a case in point. By severely restricting access to the river, fishing and the agricultural land along the riverbanks, the state has come to be seen as violating the boatmen's age old customary practices and their shared moral rights. Indeed, such breaches of their customary rights have prompted boatmen to stage mass protests against what they perceive as their systematic exploitation and economic marginalization.

In the following the moral economic approach one should be cautious not to simply highlight resistance and conflict as the only recognized mode of engaging with the state and market economy (T. Arnold 2001). As I argued in the previous chapter the boatmen's response to such intrusions is a more ambivalent one. Still, the moral economic model remains useful for describing and analysing the social values and practices underlying the boatmen's informal work system. A detailed exploration of this work system reveals a unique set of social, technical and economic arrangements underpinned by subjective notions of social justice and moral expectations, largely designed to protect the community from the potential threats of market economy and state intervention. At the most abstract level this means that all boatmen, regardless of socio-economic status, are entitled to a living from the river economy. But the empirical reality is always more complex, for this is a 'living and breathing' moral economy, and as such it is constantly debated and contested within the community itself. My concern in this chapter is, therefore, to explore processes involved in the reproduction or change of such moral economies as they function in everyday life.

Focusing on a concrete manifestation of a moral economy means that we must shift attentions from the realm of values and ideals to that of behaviour and practice. Once behaviour comes under investigation, the difference between formal rationality (the maximizing of material self-gain) and substantive rationality (where economic transactions cannot be reduced to 'rational' modes of economic calculations) becomes less definite (Parry 1974, 106; Bernal 1994). The ethnographic vantage point enables me to examine the boatmen's moral economy, not only to reveal its social mores, but also for what it can tell us about relations of domination and subordination within the community itself.[1]

My examination here of the river economy reveals the ambiguities and contradictions inherent to a moral economic system in 21st century urban India, where market forces, state intervention, and political changes necessarily alter the needs, wants and aspirations of the poor. As Marc Edelman (2005, 232), recently observed 'subsistence standards' are changing rapidly across the world, where 'rising expectations, fuelled in many cases by government programmes and politicians' rhetoric, have meant that landlord-, market-, or state-based threats to economic opportunity, accumulation, or improved welfare are now at least as important as challenges to village autonomy or historical patterns of reciprocity'. How boatmen face these challenges, I argue, is by carefully managing a moral economic order that seeks to minimize the threats and risks, while at the same time tapping into the new opportunities associated with market economy and state interventions. The success of this endeavour remains an open ended question.

## The General Attributes of the Work System of the Boatmen

The work system used by the boatmen on the riverfront comprises two interrelated systems. The first and more general level spans the entire riverfront, where customary rules and regulations prescribe economic behaviour for all the boatmen. The second is more specific, at the ghat level and offers a parallel but more nuanced moral economic order, whereby the normative ideas underpinning it are embraced in differing degrees, depending on the specific social and material conditions of the various ghats. The two systems are intrinsically connected as some of the rules and regulations, technical arrangements and social relations are similar and to a degree dependent on one another. The working system that applies to the riverfront is uniform. Similar rules apply to all boatman communities regardless of their ghat and socio-economic status. These rules define economic and social conduct along the riverfront and their overarching framework is based on territorial arrangements specifying the boundaries of the various ghats and the corresponding jurisdiction of each individual ghat community.

---

1     Thomas Arnold (2001, 90) makes a similar point when observing that, by using the 'diffuse language of shared universes or traditional norms and obligations', moral economists 'too often suppress rather than reveal the various sources of communal legitimacy available at any one time; they inhibit a clear understanding of why communities choose one set of legitimatizing rules and principles over another'.

The majority of the ghats along the riverfront accommodate a distinct boatman community. Within these communities there is a clear socio-economic division between resident boatmen, known as *ghatwars* and non-resident boatmen. As resident boatmen, these *ghatwars* have sole jurisdiction over their defined space, and this entitles them to (a) park their boats on that ghat and (b) derive their income from the ghat economy. By ghat economy, I mainly refer to the practice of taking passengers on boats. Other ghat related jobs often differ according to the specific ghats and may include loading boats, diving, fishing (discreetly), performing rituals, operating tea stalls and teaching people to swim in the summer.

The general work system rule across the riverfront is simple: passengers entering a specific ghat territory can only be taken on the boats of those boatmen (*ghatwars*) who have exclusive jurisdiction over that ghat. This is the rule of thumb that governs all economic transactions between the respective ghats in Banaras. This rule (necessarily) prevents non-resident boatmen from picking up passengers outside their designated territory. For example, a boatman from ghat (a) who takes passengers from his territory (ghat a) on his boat to another ghat (ghat b), is barred from taking new passengers from ghat (b). In other words, unless the passengers want a return trip, the boatman must return empty to his own ghat (a). This rule is maintained across the entire riverfront and it is part of a simple and efficient system that enables the smooth running of boats along the Ganges and prevents potential conflict between communities.

Throughout my fieldwork, boatmen maintained that the work system of boating was an ancient one, which originated long ago and has been passed down orally over generations. A common reply to my inquiries about the origins of the system was that 'it has always been practiced' (*dada par dada ka samay se*), 'it is a matter of custom, an age old custom that originates from the time of our ancestors (*purvaj*)'. A closer examination reveals, however, that the system has evolved over time to meet the needs and changing fortunes of boatmen across the riverfront. In other words, the rules regulating passenger distribution along the riverfront are deeply embedded in historical and social processes that affect the wider riverscape economy.

The most evident social distinction within a ghat is between resident boatmen and non-resident boatmen. Both belong to the same caste (Mallah), but their social and occupational position and status within the community (i.e., either a specific ghat community or the whole riverfront) is markedly different. The resident boatmen (*ghatwars*) have the right to operate boats on a ghat, while the non-resident boatmen (*mallahis*/drivers) work as casual labourers for the latter and have no residential rights on the ghat. According to customary practice, one can only be a resident boatman of a ghat by virtue of patrilineal descent. Generally, the *mallahis* work as oarsmen for the resident/rightful boatmen for 50 percent of their earnings.

The majority of boatmen who work on the river are able to recognize *ghatwars* and their respective ghats simply because they were brought up on the riverscape environment and the community is relatively small in number. According to customary law, a *ghatwar* is not allowed to either sell or rent his residential rights on a ghat to another boatman.[2] In fact, boatmen are so familiar with their working environment that the majority are able to recite by heart the names of all 70 odd ghats in successive order. This mutual recognition that boatmen have of territory, rights and property makes the system transparent, and provides a means for holding one another to account.[3] In schematic terms the work system across the riverfront reveals certain aspects that we can identify as uniformity, equality and mutuality. Uniformity means that the same rules apply along the entire riverfront and it also implies equality among all resident boatmen who share the same rights and privileges as their counterparts, regardless of their socio-economic status. In return, these rights are mutually recognized as binding upon all members of the community. The adherence to the rules and regulations governing the system is not forced through any single coercive authority imposing its will on the weaker members of the community. It results from an economic system based on customary practices and enforced by institutional restrictions, social relations and traditional values. Although state law allows anyone with a licence, regardless of caste or status, to operate a boating business, the work system, integrated by local norms and customs, prevents outsiders from entering the boating business. For boatmen, it is hardly necessary to enforce such institutional restrictions or formalize them in writing. As we shall see, in everyday life traditions are often contested and negotiated and there is a degree of flexibility within the work system to adapt to change.

Generally, the boatmen view their work system as part of their ancestral heritage and highlight its benefits and functions as mitigating conflict and ensuring order is maintained across the riverfront (cf. Parry 1994, 112–3). They claim that the work system prevents potential competition over passengers between the respective ghat communities. According to the *ghatwars* I spoke with, it is rare for anyone within the community to transgress these rules. They claim that these customary practices were set in place by their ancestors for the benefit of everyone to ensure the rights of *ghatwars* across the riverfront are maintained. The following example of how the work system operates on the riverfront level is indicative of the efficiency of the system. It also demonstrates that, despite the apparent uniformity and equality among *ghatwars* in terms of rights and privileges, there are stark socio-economic differences amongst *ghatwars* across the respective ghats. These differences are underpinned by the historical and geographical variations that exist across the riverfront ghats.

---

2     As opposed to the ghat priests, who can sell and lease their rights to fellow priests. See Parry (1994).

3     In this respect I follow Trawick's (2001) formulation, which he applies to the context of an agrarian community in Peru. For Trawick the principle of transparency means that 'everyone knows the rules and has the ability to confirm, with their own eyes, whether or not those rules are being generally obeyed, to detect and denounce any violation that occurs' (2001, 267).

## The Territorial Organization of the Riverfront

The working system of the boatmen of Banaras is intrinsically connected with the spatial organization of the riverfront and its ghats. The ghats, most of which are made of stone and concrete (*pakka*), form a lengthy chain that extends in a crescent shape along the western bank of the River Ganges. The distance between the southernmost ghat of the city (Assi ghat) and the northernmost one (Raj ghat) is approximately seven kilometres. The ghats are generally named after a place, a mythological figure or the patron/s who built them. The buildings and temples on the various ghats bear witness to the city's legacy as a place of princely patronage during the British raj, in which donations by Maharajas (princes from across India) for the building of such magnificent structures publicly expressed and asserted their royal legitimacy in India (Parry 1994, 43). At the time, many of the ghats were owned and maintained by devout Hindu princes and princesses (Rajas and Ranis) and wealthy noblemen (Thakurs).[4] Unfortunately, these majestic buildings are in a growing state of neglect due to the withdrawal of princely patronage since the early 20th century. Currently the majority of the ghats are under the jurisdiction of the Municipal Authority. The names of the ghats, however, still testify to their past glories and are clearly visible as they are painted in English and Hindi on the walls of the various buildings, temples, and ghat walls along the riverfront.

There are no physical barriers restricting passage from one ghat to another across the riverfront, and during the dry season one can walk the length of the riverfront in under two hours. The boatmen's territorial mapping of the riverfront, however, differs from what is visible to the lay person. For the boatmen, the ghats have clear boundaries called *hads*, which indicate the precise place where each individual ghat territory begins and ends. Such territorial identification is the basis for the system of passenger distribution across the riverfront. The ghat boundaries marked by the boatmen are very different to those painted on the walls. For example, under the boatmen's territorial organization, Assi ghat encompasses the territory of the adjacent three ghats: Ganga Mahal, Rivan and Tulsi ghats. The northern border of Assi ghat is marked by a large water pump tower, built during the British time (known by the locals as *pampua ghat*).[5] On Assi ghat there are four families of *ghatwars* who have sole rights to earn their livelihood in the territory under their jurisdiction. The territory north of the pump becomes the jurisdiction of the Bhadaini ghat boatman community, and covers the territory from the pump up to the steps leading down to Bhadaini ghat (see map of ghats). Similarly, boundaries exist along the entire chain of ghats to mark the distinct territories of each respective boatman community. Moreover, according to my informants, these boundaries are sanctioned by local protective ghat deities known as Ghatwarin Ma, worshipped

---

4    In fact, in 1930 only a minority of the ghats were owned by the Municipal Board of Benares (Motichand 1931, Appendix F).

5    The water pump was built in the 1890s by the British primarily to supply Banaras with suitable drinking water (Nevill 1909, 262–263).

by the ghat community on specific occasions considered auspicious or risky, such as diving or going on a long trip.[6]

The customary rules regulating the passenger distribution across the riverfront must be understood in concrete terms. Let me briefly return to the experience of the 'ordinary tourist' to illustrate the point. A tourist arriving at Assi ghat, either from the road or the alleys leading to the ghat, enters the area under the authority of the Assi ghat boatman community. The tourist is then approached by a boatman inquiring whether s/he would like to take a boat ride. Sometimes, though, the potential customer is clearly uninterested in boating, preferring to take a pleasant walk north along the ghats. As the person proceeds north, walking up the stairs, s/he crosses the 'invisible' ghat boundary and enters the jurisdiction of another ghat – Bhadaini ghat. Having entered the territory of a different ghat, the tourist would then be approached once more by boatmen asking: '*Hello boat? Madam/Sir do you want a boat?*'. So, by the time they reach the main ghat (covering the three kilometre stretch from Assi ghat) s/he would have been asked this same question, '*Hello boat?*', at least a dozen times.[7] Ironically, the only escape from this frankly annoying pestering is to take a boat ride. The *ghatwars* from smaller ghats, such as Nishad Raj ghat, are well aware of their disadvantage, as one boatman noted: 'Nishad ghat boatmen are poor because they don't get many customers, except the "irritated passengers" or "used customers" who come from the other ghats. We have no road access to our ghat, so nobody comes'. This also means that the prices of boating are generally less when one takes a boat from the smaller ghats, as they are often desperate to take tourists for almost any price.

Apart from raising issues related to the tourist-host interaction, which I discuss in detail in Chapter 5, this example illustrates the way in which the work system appears to limit the development of a market economy based on free competition. That is, the customary law underpinning the work system prevents the wealthier and powerful boatmen from transgressing their boundaries to dominate other ghats and so cannot maximize their profits. Surely, the *ghatwars* from smaller ghats are also held back and their prices have to stay low. In other words, the fact that such rules and practices apply to all *ghatwars* in a uniform and roughly equal fashion does not necessarily entail an even distribution of wealth and power. As the cited boatman above notes, a boatman's wealth is largely dependent on the ghat in which he works.

Different ghats have different earning potentials. A ghat may be considered commercially lucrative for historical, cultural and architectural reasons. For

---

6     Ghatwarin Ma deities function in a similar manner to neighbourhood protective deities, known as Bir Babas, insofar as they are said to control and protect a specific space and are believed to be especially responsive to human fears and desires (Coccary 1989, 134).

7     Tourists find this incredibly annoying and recently some local merchants have been able to tap into these tourist sentiments, producing and selling T-shirts in the market with the pre-emptive reply printed in bold letters: *No Boat, No Rickshaw, No Hashish.*

**Figure 3.1     View of Assi ghat**

example the major ghats, such as Assi, Dashashvamedh and Manikarnika, are religiously significant places where ritual activities are continuously performed; these ghats draw large numbers both of pilgrims and tourists who participate in various ways in the cultural and economic activities that take place there. Other ghats, such as Gai ghat and Raj ghat, although less religiously significant, have an advantage because of their physical location and proximity to pilgrim hostels and train stations, and therefore obtain a high flow of passengers. Moreover, most of the major ghats have road access from the city facilitating easy access to the ghats. It is on such ghats that the boatmen's services are considerable. These services range from purely functional, taking people from one place to another, to more comprehensive services, such as assistance in rituals or organizing a hotel for the foreign visitor (see Chapters 4 and 5).

On smaller ghats, ferrying passengers is considered a bonus rather than a reliable source of income. For example, Nishad Raj ghat, named after Nishad Raj, the celebrated king of the Nishads from the epic Ramayana mainly serves the daily needs of members of the boatman community who live in its proximity. Above Nishad Raj ghat the second largest Mallah/Nishad community in Banaras resides. The ghat space is used both for ritual purposes and community gatherings, as well as practices such as bathing, washing utensils, repairing boats and fishing equipment, and as a playground for their children. This ghat, although close to Assi ghat, lacks the physical and cultural advantages that render Assi ghat such an attractive destination for locals, pilgrims and tourists. Other smaller or community ghats are in a similar situation. In non-central ghats, such as Nishad Raj ghat, the boatman communities living there must resort to other means of earning, the most common being fishing, cultivating the fields on the other side of the river and other jobs not directly related to the river economy, such as sari weaving and white washing houses.

What is important to emphasize, however, is that under the work system of the riverfront, poorer *ghatwars* are still entitled to earn from the river economy; and boatmen from the less lucrative ghats exercise their rights to do so. These rights include: using the land on the eastern side of the river for agriculture, retrieving valuable artefacts from the river, and other provisional rights, which enable the weaker boatmen to secure their subsistence needs. It is because of their inability to earn from passengers that the boatmen of minor ghats, such as Nishad Raj, have the prerogative to practice cultivation. This provides them with a minimal subsistence and ensures that they can survive the difficult summer (monsoon) months. Thereafter, they may engage in other types of work to survive the rest of the year. Interestingly, the poorer members of the riverfront community do not see such actions as charity on the part of the wealthier and more powerful ones. On the contrary, these rights are theirs by virtue of belonging to the wider boatman community: all boatmen have the right to earn something from the riverscape. This claim about morality, obligations, and justice embedded in the economic system will be established and examined more fully in the latter part of this chapter. For the moment, it is sufficient to note that the work system does provide certain measures to ensure subsistence for all members of the community.

It is plainly obvious to all boatmen that taking passengers on boats is the most profitable activity. All other work done by boatmen demands more time and labour and is ultimately less profitable and reliable than ferrying passengers. It is not surprising that some boatmen who work on the smaller ghats still wait for the stray tourist to enter their territory in the hope that they may be convinced to take a boat. As mentioned earlier, the majority of boatmen I spoke to named an age old tradition as the primary source of the legitimacy of the rules related to passenger distribution and the inherited right to work on a particular ghat. A few boatmen, however, clearly expressed their misgivings about the system and its inherent inequalities, as one boatman from Panchganga ghat told me:

> Only four ghats have really good earnings throughout the year: Assi, Dashashvamedh, Gai ghat and Raj ghat and the rest of us have very little income (*aur ghato par koi kamay nehi hai*). The *ghatwars* from the big ghats overcharge the pilgrims and tourists, but if a *ghatwar* from another ghat tries to take a passenger, they [the other *ghatwars*] will fight with him. I think the government should interfere and break up this system so that all the boatmen can earn their livelihood equally. All these ancestral rules should change.

What this statement suggests is that the work system is not only biased towards those who inherit a place on the more lucrative ghats, but also that this is an autonomous system in which the community, rather than an external authority, determines the rules. Some boatmen are clearly frustrated and request the intervention of the state, which may be perceived as an unbiased authority capable of wielding authority over the powerful members of their community. Nevertheless, members of the community rarely seek state intervention and the boatmen have succeeded in retaining relative autonomy in managing their affairs. This, I would suggest, is because the local authorities are unable and unwilling to protect rebellious boatmen from their peers. The only intervention by state authorities is when it is under pressure to provide fast results (e.g., the Ganga Action Plan), or when local conflicts result in violence and death.

The above boatman's desire for government interference also suggests that the system is essentially unfair and is enforced by the powerful boatmen from the major ghats; any challenge to the system is met with physical punishment imposed by the powerful and wealthy members of the community. Customary laws and traditional practices therefore mask power and inequality as well as limit conflict and unbridled competition. Furthermore, with the increase of tourism over the past few decades, subsistence standards have also changed; the weaker *ghatwars* are therefore seeking state intervention that would redress an imbalance through allowing them more access to resources (tourists/pilgrims).

The demarcation of the riverscape as outlined above is an important illustration of the ideological and political dimensions of such spatial organization. A critical geographer's perspective may emphasize 'how relations of power and discipline are inscribed into the apparently innocent spatiality of social life, [and] how human geographies become filled with politics and ideology' (Soja 1989, 6). Equally important, however, is to note the appropriation process involved in the construction of this lived space, what de Certeau (1984, 95–6) described as the poetic manipulation of urban space, where ordinary people are engaged in multiform acts of everyday resistance that elude the panoptic administration of the city. In our case, another dimension of agency becomes apparent; one which is not necessarily reducible to that of resistance: the flip side of domination. Rather, it is the agency of production and reproduction of space thorough meaningful social practice. For boatmen the spatial relations and social inequalities which are mapped onto the riverscape represent and define not only the experience of marginalization, exclusion and domination (e.g., by the state or local elites), but also the moral and practical concerns and social inequalities within the boatman community itself. A closer look at the social construction of space along the riverfront must therefore examine the complexities involved in the politics of lived spaces, for as Pile (1997, 27) aptly observes, 'resistance in one direction can be oppression in another'. From this perspective then acts of resistance are rendered more ambiguous, multiple and fractured. In the following section I explore several case studies from three distinct ghats: Assi ghat, Dashashvamedh ghat and Raj ghat. These examples will illustrate the internal ghat dynamics that exist on each ghat, from which we can gain insight into the social arrangements and power struggles involved on specific ghats and across the riverfront as a whole.

## Assi Ghat

*Territorial Jurisdiction and Inherited Rights*

Disputes and conflict between ghats are a rarity on the riverfront. The *ghatwars* on the major ghats jealously guard their territory and protect their rights. However, as Scott (2000, 198) observes, when disputes do occur it is a good way of 'finding out how strongly a particularly strong custom is adhered to… [and] what happens when it is violated'. The Assi ghat boatmen gave me an example of how such disputes are settled. Several years ago a drunken boatman from Gai ghat came to Assi ghat, along with ten other members of his family, shouting and claiming to have legitimate rights to operate his boats on Assi ghat. He argued that his paternal grandfather had operated boats on the said ghat and therefore he was entitled to reclaim his rights. The *ghatwars* of Assi ghat told him that he must provide written proof of his entitlement. The boatman from Gai ghat was unable to prove his rights and eventually the *ghatwars* of Assi ghat violently drove him and his companions off their territory. Such disputes generally occur in the more lucrative ghats, and in some cases conflicts over ghat space are debated in the courts.

The above case never made it to court; it was settled between the respective groups. The story, passionately narrated to me by several boatmen from Assi ghat, illustrates two important aspects of the work system. The first is that, regardless of any internal divisions, the *ghatwars* of an individual ghat will unite and exhibit group solidarity when fighting off any outside intervention and infringement on their rights and territory. Any take-over bid on a ghat is always couched in terms of ancestral rights and tradition: the ultimate source of legitimacy (cf. Fuller 2004). According to the Assi ghat boatmen, one must be able to prove one's rights on the ghat. However, such proof is extremely difficult to obtain; mainly for practical reasons: the majority of boatmen were (and still are) illiterate. Moreover, there is an inherent contradiction to procuring such proof as the system itself is said to be based on oral tradition, which can only be verified through customary practice enforced by social sanctions. All boatmen know the rules and conventions and are able to physically monitor and supervise any violations, thus protecting their own rights from intruders. Although the *ghatwars* of Assi ghat employ force, they say such actions are sanctioned by the institutions and values set in place by the community. As such, they are protecting their own individual rights and reaffirming their social identity as *ghatwars*, which in turn serves to endorse the sanctioned overall work system and social arrangements of the boatmen.

What I later realized, however, is that although patrilineal descent is a necessary condition for claiming one's status as a *ghatwar*, it is insufficient when a new claim arises. As the informants explained to me, even if the boatman from Gai ghat could have proved his claims, either in writing or by confirmation from other members of the community and neighbourhood, the fact that he was absent from the ghat for a long period of time deprives him of such rights. The need to be an active boatman is essential for maintaining one's rights over time, as the following example clearly demonstrates.

*Internal Ghat Politics: The Case of Lakshman*

The following reconstruction of Assi ghat's history is based on many conversations I had with both boatmen and other locals from the Assi neighbourhood. My initial data about the families of Assi ghat was based on family trees, which I constructed during the initial stages of my research. Afterwards, I confirmed this data by cross referencing it with material gained from subsequent conversations and interviews.

Four families of *ghatwars* occupy Assi ghat. Among these four families, two are more powerful and prosperous than the others, the reason for which I shall return to later in the chapter. All *ghatwars* claim that their forefathers have been working on the ghat since time immemorial, but in more concrete terms they link their respective families to their grandfathers – the four patriarchs (Lalu, Raju, Varun, Vinod). One of the patriarchs (Lalu Manjhi) had four sons, all of whom were entitled to ply boats on the ghat by virtue of patrilineal descent. Two of the four sons were earning from the ghat as *ghatwars*. The third son was fortunate enough to get a stable government job and decided to leave the boating business altogether. The fourth son (Gopal) died more than fifteen years ago leaving a wife and son with no source of income. Gopal's son (Lakshman) grew up with his cousins on the ghat and began earning a minimum income by plying boats for others at an early age. Since he had no boat he worked for other boatmen (mainly his cousins) on the ghat for 50 percent of the earnings. Recently, he managed to save enough money (Rs.25,000) to purchase a medium sized rowboat. As a boat owner, Lakshman was able to reclaim his title and full rights as a *ghatwar*.

Although some of the boatmen from Assi ghat (descendants of the other three patriarchs) were clearly dismayed at the prospect of another boatman encroaching on their livelihood, they did not prevent Lakshman from operating his boat on the ghat. In other words, despite the fact that it is probably against their interests and they will inevitably lose some income as a result of Lakshman's new status, his rights have been acknowledged and ratified by the *ghatwar* community. There are many reasons why Lakshman was accepted into the fold; the most obvious is that he answers the necessary requirement of patrilineal descent. In addition, having spent his childhood on the ghat and being involved in its economy, his status and family relations are recognized by everyone there. His family, which includes two uncles who are *ghatwars*, ensured that he had the backing (physical and familial) to support his claim. Although there are tense relations between the family factions on Assi ghat, the other *ghatwars* recognized Lakshman's entitlement and violent conflict was avoided. By permitting Lakshman to enter the *ghatwar* community, the Assi *ghatwars* reinforced their social identity and the traditional rules of the ghats. Such accommodation not only reaffirms their own position and mitigates possible conflict, but also justifies their actions in terms that are widely acceptable across the riverfront. These assertions of status and customary practices are further enforced in cases when boatmen are rejected from the *ghatwar* community, as the following story reveals.

*The Case of Vishnu*

One of the first boatmen I met was Vishnu, an unassuming soft spoken middle aged man without *ghatwar* status. Vishnu and his wife operate a small tea stall on Assi ghat. His wife Lakshmi makes pakora (snacks) and tea for the locals and tourists who come to the ghat to enjoy the peaceful atmosphere, far from the busy and polluted city streets. Lakshmi is a lively woman, and her tea stall was a central place for me throughout much of my fieldwork. The other tea stalls on the ghat were owned by one of the *ghatwar* families from the ghat, whereas Lakshmi's stall provided a relatively neutral space for interaction, where I could invite any boatman to sit and have tea with me without rocking the boat(!). Although Vishnu owns a rowboat, because he is not a *ghatwar* he is barred from participating in the local work system, operating on the ghat.

The *ghatwars* of Assi ghat operate a system of passenger distribution based on bidding. All *ghatwars* are located at a strategic point overlooking ghat space where they can sight and bid for potential passengers. When a visitor enters the ghat territory, boatmen immediately stake their claim on the person as they emerge (i.e., the bookshop, the temple, the road etc). By making a call (*boli*) the *ghatwar* has

**Figure 3.2    Assi *ghatwars* scouting for passengers**

the right to approach the potential passenger and inquire whether they would like a boat ride and negotiate a price. The intricacies of the *boli* system are discussed in further detail in Chapter 5. For now it is important to note, that only *ghatwars* are allowed to participate in this bidding system. For this reason Vishnu was never present on the cliff.

When I asked Vishnu why he was barred from participating in the bidding his reply was harsh. Like his father (Kenaya), Vishnu claimed, he is not one to fight and prefers to remain outside the competitive and dirty (*ganda*) passenger (*savari*) business. According to him the *ghatwars* are always fighting over passengers, making dodgy deals and sometimes gambling. By gambling he referred to those cases when two or more *ghatwars* toss a coin to decide who had first bid/call (*boli*) for a passenger. Vishnu then went into his stall and returned with a crumpled letter. He slowly stretched out the letter declaring that this was his proof and entitlement to operate a boat like the other boatmen. The letter was signed by the District Magistrate:

> An inquiry was conducted into the complaint made by Vishnu Manjhi about the fact that certain boatmen were stopping him from sailing his boat on Assi ghat…According to the manual of the Municipal Authority (Nagar Nigam) 1997, anyone can receive a licence to ply a boat. These licences are issued for persons from a specific ghat to pick up passengers and to drop them at the same ghat after the boating. Under the jurisdiction of the Municipal Authority, neither a person nor a particular family have monopoly (*ekadhikar*) [over the boating business]. Similarly, no tradition has any legal authority [apart from the Municipal one]. Therefore, if Vishnu Manjhi is willing to ply a boat on the River Ganges by receiving the legal licence to do so from the Municipal Authority, he may be extended the help [of the authorities] and stern action should be initiated against the man who tries to create hurdles… In any case such case he may contact the Imprecator in charge of Bhelapur [local] Police station.
>
> Signed: Alok Kumar,
> District Magistrate, Varanasi 28 August 2000

Although Vishnu holds a licence to ply boats, he prefers not to exercise his legal right to take passengers as the rest of the *ghatwars* do. In order to get police protection, he claims, he would need to pay a lot of bribe money to the police, money that he does not have. Nonetheless, Vishnu has other means of supporting his family. Apart from the tea stall, Vishnu has managed to forge several intermittent ties with locals who employ his services that are outside the *ghatwar* system of passenger distribution. For example, he works for a local bookshop distributing advertising pamphlets on the river during the early hours of the morning to the numerous tourists taking a boat ride at sunrise. He also receives a small but stable daily income by ferrying a holy man and his disciples, who reside in a nearby ashram, across the river and back. There is, therefore, a grey area in which a boatman who is not entitled to bid for passengers is nonetheless able to earn from the ghat economy. Vishnu and his wife have also managed to establish personal relationships with long term tourists, who return annually to Assi ghat. Several of these Western tourists have contributed to the family's subsistence over the years by buying them home appliances, such as a fan, cooking utilities and more Moreover, thanks to one such tourist, Vishnu was able to repair his ageing boat. Thus, Vishnu and his family have been able to remain marginally above the subsistence level. The *ghatwars* who operate on the ghat do not object to Vishnu's strategies for gaining an income, as long as he does not transgress the boundaries. Their resources and rights are guarded and they do not feel threatened by Vishnu in any way.

Vishnu's story reveals more than just concerns about economic self-interest and his explanation and letter of endorsement enables him to at least to represent himself as one who has the legal and moral high ground over the, in Vishnu's words, 'self-interested and greedy' *ghatwars*. As for the *ghatwars*, excluding Vishnu from the working system serves to delineate themselves from other non-resident boatmen, and thereby assert their position as legitimate *ghatwars*. Thus, despite the authorities' support for Vishnu's claim, the *ghatwars* continue to be judge and jury, as it were, over the affairs of the ghat. Such disregard for the official line affirms the independence that boatmen seek to maintain in relation to their own ghat and river economy. The exclusion of Vishnu from the ghat's work system could be explained as a mixture of utilitarian self-interested behaviour, but also as an action that follows the obligations and expectations of the *ghatwars* under the rules of customary law and the overall work system.

The government plays a significant role in the equation. As the letter shows, the official line (the decree of the state) overrides that of any ghat community.[8] Under this law anyone, regardless of caste or traditional occupation, may ply a boat provided he has the licence to do so. As we have seen in the previous chapter, however, while the rhetoric is forceful, enforcing it is hardly conclusive. Although, the government is powerful and decisive in certain cases, such as in its implementation of restrictions under the federal government's Ganga Action Plan. At the same time, as Vishnu's case demonstrates, in matters concerning internal affairs of the boatmen, the government is not under any pressure to enforce its declared laws. What is arguably an autonomous working system operated by the boatmen on the riverfront, partly results from the lack of state incentive to impose its will and authority on the boatman community. One question remains, however: why did Vishnu bother acquiring the letter if he realized that the authorities would not back him up? It seems to me that such action on his part indicates disapproval of the dominating power relations of the ghat – a sign of insubordination. Furthermore, Vishnu's appeal for state intervention, similar to the boatman from

---

8     When I spoke to the licence officers regarding the issue of *ghatwars*, they told me that they do not interfere with Mallah affairs. They added, however, that anyone could ply a boat and take passengers regardless of his caste, provided he obtained the licence from the Municipal Authorities (interview, Shitla Prasad Singh, 20 March 2002).

Panchganga ghat, is indicative of the moral economic discourse, whereby the practices of the powerful *ghatwars* are perceived as unethical and exploitative. It may well be that Vishnu continues to keep the letter in the hope that in the future the police may back him up if circumstances change.

As I started probing more deeply into family histories through my conversations with various members of the dominant *ghatwars* families, I began to pierce what initially seemed to be an impenetrable wall of silence. The presentation of the *ghatwars'* entitlements as deriving from 'time immemorial', in fact, revealed itself as going back only two generations. Therefore, it could be argued that the patrilineal system of descent hailed by the *ghatwars* as legitimizing their social identity and consequent rights and privileges is based on questionable historical reality. Such a proposition, however, would overlook the significance of oral tradition, and mnemonic systems (i.e., songs, stories, poem and rituals) as important sources of authority and legitimacy amongst boatmen in certain contexts. It may well be that, apart from a litero-centric anthropologist; everyone knows that a long line of patrilineal descent is a negotiated tradition, used to legitimize decisions and practices within the community and outside it. A close examination of their oral history shows this to be the case.


## Power, Patronage and Ancestral Rights

Throughout my stay at Assi ghat I had many conversations with Ganesh Babu, the oldest *ghatwar* on Assi ghat. During these conversations Ganesh related a story about the three other patriarchs who established themselves as the *ghatwars* of Assi ghat. I was able to cross reference many of his claims by talking to other *ghatwars* and ghat functionaries (i.e., barbers and priests) on Assi ghat and the neighbouring ghats. What follows is a narrative constructed from these conversations and from other information I gathered during my fieldwork about the history of Assi ghat, to give a sense of the historical changes that are pertinent to contemporary ghat dynamics.

Ganesh's story begins in the early 1900s. During that time his father (Vinod Manjhi) was the only *ghatwar* on Assi ghat. Under the British rule the riverscape was markedly different. Assi ghat was made of clay (*kachcha*) and there were no roads leading to the ghat.[9] The southern boundary of the city was marked by the Assi *nala* (stream) dividing Assi ghat from the fields of Naguwa (today Naguwa is an upcoming residential neighbourhood) south of Assi. Being the southern boundary of the city the British administration set up a taxing station on Assi ghat, where they levied the Octroi tax on imported goods, such as grains and stone, coming to Benares by boats from Chunnar and Mirzapur.

---

9    Assi ghat only became a *pakka* ghat (built of stone) in the mid 1980s with a spacious platform and quiet atmosphere. This is partly the reason for its rising popularity amongst locals and foreigners alike and to its becoming a lucrative ghat.

> At the time there were no motorcars or roads and everything was transported by boat. We had much bigger boats that could hold truckloads of sand and goods. When food grains and other goods arrived they would be unloaded on Assi ghat where there was a market. From the market the goods were distributed around the neighbourhoods and the city on bullock carts. Unlike today, [laughing] there were hardly any pilgrims or foreigners coming to Assi ghat, most of the pilgrimage activities occurred on the main ghat. [March 2002]

The issue of how the three patriarch *ghatwars* established themselves on the ghat was an especially thorny topic. Ganesh's replies were often laced with profanities describing the chicanery and 'brown-nosing' of the 'so-called *ghatwars*'. According to Ganesh, none of the patriarchs except his father were originally from the Assi ghat neighbourhood. 'They just drifted here from other neighbourhoods, establishing themselves by buttering up powerful people and exploiting the generosity of my father, who let them earn now and then from plying boats'. I asked Ganesh to relate the process of how the respective patriarchs established themselves on the ghat.

> Vinod and his younger brother Raju did not even own boats. They used to report to the Octroi Tax collector the amounts of grain unloaded on the ghat. In return the collector gave them grain in payment. In the evening the brothers used to go around the villages behind Banaras Hindu University (BHU) via Naguwa. Everywhere they went they carried a *katiya* (hook) with which they retrieved articles lost in the village wells, like pots and pans etc. This is how they made their living. Sometimes when they were desperate they would plead to my father: 'Brother let us work [to ply a boat] as we only managed to earn 10 paisa today'. So my father gave them some work once in a while as *mallahis*. [March 2002]

As for the other *ghatwars*, Ganesh explained that the second one, Varun, was the adopted son of a widow who sold flower garlands and ritual paraphernalia on the ghat. As she was childless she adopted one of her nephews and brought him up on the ghat. Such adoption practices are not unusual in Indian society.

As mentioned earlier, at that time Assi *nala* (stream) separated Naguwa from Assi ghat. According to boatmen, one of the most powerful figures on Assi ghat was a landowner called Singh Sahib, who owned the *nala* and the land in Naguwa. Ganesh and his father would park their boats in the *nala* as it provided a safe and secure mooring, especially in times of flooding. During the floods (July to September) they ferried the many people from around the neighbourhood across the *nala* to defecate in the Naguwa fields (the only 'latrine' available to them, much like today!). At other times of the year there was a makeshift bridge enabling safe crossing to the Naguwa fields.

According to Ganesh, Vinod and Raju managed to get a small boat and implored Singh Sahib to allow them to ferry passengers across the nala during the flood season. They argued that since they had no rights as *ghatwars*, this would enable them to make a minimum income. Having consulted Ganesh's father, Singh permitted them to ferry passengers across the *nala*. Vinod and Raju began plying boats across the *nala* during the floods and continued to work for the Octroi boats and in the villages in other seasons. However, over time, as they won the support of Singh, they began pushing to ply boats on the river as well, claiming, 'We have the right! We have become *ghatwars* now'. According to Ganesh, his father tried to stop them, but he was one against many. Later Raju and Vinod also gained the support of another powerful patron who provided them with a steady flow of passengers. Thus, concluded Ganesh bitterly: 'First they buttered us up for a long time, now they eat our butter!'.

The story of the third patriarch Lalu follows a similar pattern. Lalu was a boatman employed by the British Water Works. His job was to retrieve dead bodies from the river with his small boat and to take out animal carcasses sucked into the Bhadaini water pump. Lalu would also take his employer, Gendria Sahib, and his friends on his boat to the *reta* (sandbars or shoals that surface when the river recedes after the monsoons) for pleasure and thus began to establish a clientele. Over time, Lalu and his family also began working for the local priest (panda) who resided at Assi ghat. According to Ganesh, they performed all the demeaning menial labour, like cleaning out cow dung from the pen and various other errands for the panda's family. Thus, they were able to win the favour of the priest, who in return let them take his clients (*jajmans*) on their boat. Ganesh explained that his father never disgraced himself by trying to ingratiate himself with powerful people.

> Lalu and the others ingratiated themselves by performing menial tasks and flattering the panda, to win his support. This is how they managed to worm themselves onto the ghat. Initially, my father tried to stop them but my family was small. They bullied us and eventually established their position by force. Nowadays they have many descendants and continue to intimidate people around here. But my family hasn't discarded our politeness even though the rest of the world may do so. We won't bully others. We won't give up our tradition as long as we are alive. [March 2002]

When I inquired about Vishnu's father and his status on the ghat, Ganesh explained that Vishnu's father was an honest man, who never got involved in such deceitful and dishonourable practices. Ganesh backed up his authoritative account of the ghat history by noting that even today, people living in the neighbourhood can vouch for his authentic status as a *ghatwar*, while none of the others would be able to do so. His story clearly indicates how ghat dynamics are implicated within a wider set of social relations among the boatmen, between boatmen and patrons and boatmen and their peers.

As I mentioned earlier, when inquiring into their status as *ghatwars* of Assi ghat, the boatmen generally referred to ancestral rights passed down through generations.[10] Over time, however, as members of the ghat community realized that I already possessed some pieces of the historical puzzle, many sought, in private, to put matters straight. Ganesh's version was confirmed. Nevertheless, while the history that they are referring to is much more recent than implied, the concept of ancestral rights (and 'time immemorial') is still intrinsic for their notion of identity and legitimizing status, rights and everyday practice. What is more surprising, however, is that the same claim is employed by boatmen when contesting their rights in a court of law, as the following example from Dashashvamedh ghat demonstrates.

## Dashashvamedh Ghat: Contesting Ghat Space

Competing over rights and space is a sensitive issue in Banaras, not only for boatmen but also among competing Brahmin priests operating on the riverfront.[11] The contentious issue of who has rights to ply a boat, and on which ghat, is perhaps best represented on the main ghat, known as Dashashvamedh ghat. This ghat has long been the centre of ritual and business activity in Banaras. An account from the early 20th century illustrates the historical significance of Dashashvamedh ghat:

> We now come to the central and the most frequented spot in Benares, the Dasashwamedh Ghat which is directly connected with the city by a wide road, and to which almost all important streets in the main part of the town lead. Compared to other ghats it is the most spacious and can hold a large crowd of pilgrims. It is one of the five great 'Tirthas' (sacred spots) of Benares, and the place simply abounds with temples... The whole place has a busy look with attractive stalls, for it has not only a religious but also commercial importance. One also notices a crowd of boats loading and unloading cargo, now mostly consisting of Chunar stones, which are stacked in an open space between Dasashwamedh and the Man Mandir Ghats (Motichand 1931:51–52).

---

10    One family claims to have been plying boats for Saint Tulsi Das, the author of the popular version of the Ramayana (*Ramcharitmanas*) who lived in Varanasi during the 16th century. This connection, they proudly note, is still maintained through the continuous connection with Tulsi Das' descendant: the revered Brahmin priest from Tulsi ghat, Veer Bhadra Mishra. The family is also actively involved in the local *Ramlila* (a month long dramatisation of the Ramayana in the Assi neighbourhood). In the *Ramlila* episode in which the boatman (khevat) ferries Lord Rama across the River Ganga, it is their family who regularly provides a boat for this purpose, with a member of the family acting the part of the khevat.

11    These issues have been discussed by colonial administrators, see Nevill (1909), as well as contemporary anthropologists, see Parry (1994). For a discussion on the Gangaputras in Ayodhya, see van der Veer (1988).

Dashashvamedh ghat still retains its supremacy over all other ghats. Its central geographical location along with its religious significance render it a pivotal point in the city. In fact, it is somewhat misleading to speak of Dashashvamedh ghat as one ghat (see map of ghats), as its territory actually consists of several distinct ghats. The main road leading to the ghat area branches out into several lanes, each leading to a different set of steps descending to the ghats. The ghat names are painted on the walls of each ghat. To avoid confusion I shall refer to the entire area, as it is commonly known, the 'main ghat' (on most tourist maps it is called Dashashvamedh ghat). The main ghat consists of four ghats: Shitla; Dashashvamedh; Prayag; and Prachin Dashashvamedh ghat. The southern part of the main ghat is called Dashashvamedh ghat (painted on the wall). The southern extension is known as Shitla ghat because of the popular temple located there dedicated to Shitla Ma – the goddess of small pox. The southern part of Shitla ghat overlaps with Ahilyabai ghat and the boundaries, as we will shortly see, have been subject to considerable contestation in the courts.

The fact that the ghat is a central place for pilgrimage makes it a particularly attractive and competitive space for boatmen servicing the pilgrims. The earlier quote from 1931 attests to the significance of the ghat during that time. It is not surprising therefore that boatmen have been coveting the lucrative space of the main ghat for many decades. The following excerpts from a court document from

**Figure 3.3    View of Dashashvamedh (main) ghat from the river, with Brahmin priests sitting on platforms (under umbrellas) providing ritual services for pilgrims and locals**

1949 provide a good example of how such disputes over the ghat space were represented in court. In 1949 a major dispute between two boatmen over space and rights to ply boats on the main ghat took place. The dispute was eventually taken to court. The following document is worth quoting at length for it reveals as much about British law and how custom was debated and affirmed then and now, as it does about the plaintiff's claims concerning the infringement of other boatmen on his territory and customary rights.

> The plaintiff begs to submit as follows:[12]
> That the town of Banaras is situated on the western side of the Ganga and is divided into various ghats which are named separately and most of which are pakka (stone) ghats.
> 1. That for public facility: a number of boatmen from the Mallah community keep boats and render their services by plying them to the general needs.
> 2. That in order to ply such boats a license has to be obtained from the municipal board and fee to be paid.
> 3. That since time immemorial by virtue of consistent course of events the following custom has evolved and has been given judicial recognition every now and then.
> 4a. A particular group of boatmen, or a particular family of boatmen have the right of parking its boats on particular ghats to the exclusion of others.
> b. The particular family or group of boatmen are not liable to pay any fee or toll to anybody claiming to own the ghat.
> c. The particular group or family of boatmen alone is entitled as of right to render its services on its particular ghat and it alone is entitled to take passengers for short or long trips at a particular time to the exclusion of others.
> d. Under the said right of monopoly the particular group or family has the obligation to offer its services to those who are willing to pay for it.
> e. None has the right to interfere or encroach on the exclusive right or jurisdiction of the particular group or family and such an interference or encroachment is deemed to be an act of trespass.
> 5. The aforesaid custom is immemorial, continuous open and accepted.
> 6. The ghat enlisted below is in the exclusive jurisdiction of the plaintiff and his family and has been so since time immemorial and in practise nobody else but the plaintiff and his ancestors have been exercised in the said customary right forever and any attempts to interfere therewith has always been successfully replied by the plaintiff and his ancestors…
> 7. That the plaintiff in order to meet public demand possesses a number of boats duly licensed and has engaged servants for the purpose of plying them and has always been parking his boats on the said ghats as a matter of right and this has been going on since the time of his ancestors.

---

12    Court of Additional Civil Judge, Banaras: suit no. 146 of 1949. Note: the text itself was not altered, despite some grammatical errors.

8. That about 19 years ago [i.e., 1930] the father of the plaintiff died... the plaintiff was 4 years old at the time and was the sole heir and successor of his father. As a result his mother had to engage the services of a different person to ply boats for wages.

9. That about 10 years ago the services of the defendant were engaged by the plaintiff through his mother...until the year 1948 when turning dishonest the defendant left the services of the plaintiff and attempted to park his own boats on the said ghat within the plaintiff's territory and to take passengers on the said ghat without rights and by show of force.

10. That the plaintiff thereupon made representation to the leading members of the community against the unlawful act of the defendant and the defendant also agreed to abide by their decision. However, when the said person decided in favour of the plaintiff, he [the defendant] slipped away and did not ascribe his signature to the award thus arrived at but it is fully binding on him.

11. That since then the defendant continues to park his boat on Ahilyabhai ghat and by sheer use of force attempts to take passengers on the said ghat and the plaintiff has therefore no course open to him except to file a suit for the declaration of his right and for the injunction against the defendant...

In subsequent articles a list of the ghats under the plaintiff's jurisdiction is given. The complexities and ambiguities concerning the application of modern law in British India have been elaborately discussed by various scholars who point out the transformative effects that British law had on communities and individuals concerning the manner in which disputes were settled and articulated (see, for example, Appadurai 1981; Cohn 1996; Das 1995; Fuller 1988; Galanter 1992). The claims by the plaintiff demonstrate the systematic fashion by which the plaintiff presents his claims in the court of law in the prescribed manner. Such disputes, which were once resolved within the community council (*panchayat*) were adapted to fit the legal system and there are several implications to this. To begin with, merely translating from Hindi into English legal terminology necessarily changes the meaning and values of such customary rules and practices. What was once sanctioned on the basis of caste/community and debated within the local community councils must now be articulated and justified within the universal and impersonal terms prescribed under the British legal system.

As the plaintiff himself noted, the traditional manner of solving such disputes by resorting to the community council proved ineffective. He therefore opted for the modern legal system. In the court, however, the plaintiff had to argue in the terms that had to be substantiated vis-à-vis the defendant and the state legal mechanism: hence the recurring assertions of customary rights since time immemorial. The following statement made on behalf of the defendant shows the manner in which he, in turn, sought to refute the allegation made by the plaintiff:

> That the existence of the custom relied on by the plaintiff is emphatically denied. The alleged custom is vague, inconvenient, uncertain and unreasonable. The plaintiff has not cause for action.

> That there is no custom or monopoly of any man, boatman of particular family of Banaras to ply and park boats on any particular ghat…

Ultimately, the case was decided in the defendant's favour. The latter was able to prove his claims in line with the requirements of the law and thus override the plaintiff's assertions of ancient customary rights. Under the modern legal system establishing customary rights, based on hereditary rights and status, is difficult to achieve. This is simply because the modern legal system, as Galanter (1992, 15) points out, relies primarily on 'uniform territorial rules, based on universalistic norms, which apportion rights and obligations as incidents of specific transactions, rather than fixed statuses'.

Fifty years later the plaintiff, who recently passed away, religiously retained all documents testifying to his rights and territory. Over time, the territory of this old man who previously had jurisdiction over five ghats shrunk to one. Nonetheless, because of the central location of the ghat the plaintiff's two sons are very wealthy. They own more than 25 boats and employ over a dozen *mallahis*. As we shall see in the next chapter, such conflicts and a long history of disputes and litigation (amongst boatmen themselves, as well as between boatmen and priests) seem to have taught them the significance of written documentation. As the previous account shows, appealing to the formula of 'time immemorial' will not always be enough for the boatmen to retain their monopoly over the boating business of Banaras.

Boatmen nowadays speak of the need to retain written proof of their rights on the riverfront. Attaining written proof of one's rights as a *ghatwar* is considered valuable as it reinforces one's rights over space in relation to other boatmen who may pose a threat, for example, when a non-*ghatwar* boatman or boatmen from other ghats attempt to claim ownership of a ghat. In addition, the changing commercial and touristic environment of the riverscape, and the imminent threat of commercial boats and members of other castes encroaching on their traditional occupation also motivates some boatmen to have their rights formally established. Such recognition, many boatmen feel, would place the members of their community in a better position to defend their rights against potential threats from external factors.

## Cementing Tradition and Hereditary Rights: Enumerating the *Ghatwars*

Efforts were recently made to assemble, for the first time in history, a full list of all the *ghatwars* in Banaras. The list was compiled by a newly formed association called 'The Young Boatman's Association' (*Naw Yuvak Manjhi Samity*). The title

'Manjhi' indicates that the association is mainly committed to advancing the specific interests of boatmen. Although Manjhi is primarily a title used by *ghatwars* who own boats, the association presents itself as inclusive and representative of all boatmen regardless of their socio-economic status. Their declared reason for compiling the list of *ghatwars* was to avoid potential disputes between respective *ghatwars*.[13] The press release stated that: 'A discussion on the problems of boatmen was held in the meeting of the Manjhi society'. Its content, however, did not reveal all that occurred in the meeting or their full motivations to compile a list of *ghatwars*. I initially heard about the meeting from a boatman who brought me the notice announcing it was taking place. On the day, about 50 boatmen arrived at the meeting, which was held on the large platform at Chauki ghat, positioned close to Nishad Raj temple and ghat. The meeting was well organized and the participants were seated on a red mat and given tea and pan (betel leaf containing various condiments).

As the meeting commenced the committee secretary raised several matters to be discussed. The president urged the people to assist the committee in compiling a list of the *ghatwars* and their respective ghat boundaries. He claimed that recently several members of the Yadav caste (traditionally milkman) had begun plying boats on Manikarnika ghat, taking passengers for profit. 'Although these people are powerful, we must not let them set a precedent; we must demonstrate and prove our rights to the government'. The secretary then added:

> We don't have any proof except our boat licences that we are *ghatwars*. If we compile a list, the committee will forward it to the government. The commissioner has assured us that he will put his stamp of approval on it. Doing so through this committee will be cheaper than doing it individually. Thus, we can have our rights properly recognized by the authorities.[14]

The secretary then suggested that a list of *ghatwars* and boundaries would also help solve disputes within the community and people would not need to resort to costly court procedures or pay bribe money to corrupt policemen. In the following months the committee managed to compile this valuable list. As I learned, however, the task was far from easy. Certain ghat boundaries which were not clearly marked, but rather subject to local arrangements between adjacent ghats, had to be fixed; this was met by opposition from some *ghatwars*. In addition, the issue of legitimacy regarding rightful *ghatwars* is often a contested matter, one that some boatmen are highly reluctant to investigate or formalize. This reluctance reveals the power relations and struggles within the community itself. Weaker *ghatwars* are subverting efforts by the more dominant and well-off *ghatwars* to impose a formal codification of their practices and rights. In other words, formally documenting their hitherto informal customs may have some

---

13  Press release, dated 21 July 2002.
14  These quotes are taken from a meeting which occurred on 20 January 2002.

benefits for the more powerful members of the boatman community, but it also entails loss. As Thompson argued in his brilliant investigation of custom in 18th century England, 'uncodified custom – and even codified – was in continual flux. So far from having a steady permanence suggested by the word "tradition", custom was a field of change and of contest, an arena in which opposing interests made conflicting claims' (Thompson 1991, 6). In this instance, subordinated *ghatwars* refused to relinquish the 'power of custom', (which would favour the powerful) and traditional jurisdiction to official state jurisdiction. The irony is that state intervention was actually sought out by weaker members of the community (as we have seen), but only insofar as it appealed to their conception of 'justice' and moral economic sensibilities.

The full implications of such a list for the boatman community are yet to be seen. As far as I know, the list has not been completed or officially recognized by the authorities. However, the continuous push by the association to compile such a list is also indicative of what boatmen perceive as an impending threat to their livelihood. The need to cement their rights and territorial jurisdiction is essential in the current environment. The stigma associated with the caste's hereditary occupation – ritually low, degrading manual labour – remains operative. However, what was once a low income profession is rapidly becoming commercially viable for the boatmen who operate on the major ghats. These boatmen are aware of the looming threat from outside capitalist ventures and of the urgency to protect their property and rights from the claims of the state and other potential non-state actors. Recently, the Taj Ganges hotel (partly owned by the Maharaja of Banaras) converted an old sand barge into a houseboat and began offering its mostly foreign clients the luxuries associated with princely travel. In addition a commercial motorboat by the name of Ganga Darshan (literally meaning Auspicious View of Ganga) has begun taking mostly wealthy Indians for river cruises.[15] Although the two boats do not pose an immediate threat to the boatmen, many are already talking of a change for the worse and are seeking to retain their independence and establish a firm monopoly over the boating industry in the city. However, in order to fend off external challenges, the *ghatwar* community must generate support from the entire community. It is therefore crucial that the *ghatwars* maintain good working relations with *mallahis*, who comprise the majority of boatmen on the riverfront. In the following section I examine more closely the complex relationship between the *ghatwars* and *mallahis* on Raj ghat, revealing more about the socio-economic relationships and power relations amongst the boatmen of Banaras.

---

15     The owner of Ganga Darshan is a wealthy and well connected lawyer in Banaras. For the (symbolic) inauguration of the boat he invited the Superintendent of Police to attend, signifying to all boatmen that any sabotage to his boat would entail serious consequences.

## Raj ghat: the Relationship between *Ghatwars* and *Mallahis*

There are certain provisions and measures built into the work system, which not only protect the interests of the *ghatwars* but also of the *mallahis*, ensuring they are also able to benefit from the river economy. The *mallahis* have certain rights enshrined in the customary laws across the riverfront. This is especially evident on the major ghats where *ghatwars* employ *mallahis* on a regular basis. On most of the major ghats it is the *mallahis* who ply and maintain the boats of the *ghatwars*, usually for 50 percent of the earnings. There is no binding contract between them and indeed some of the *mallahis* shift from one ghat to another according to demand. The *mallahis* can be relatives of the *ghatwars* who come from the nearby villages to earn ready cash during the high season. The majority of these workers, however, have no close kinship relations with the *ghatwars* and are often employed during the busy times of the year on the major ghats where there is a large flow of passengers and a need for more working hands.

Because of the temporary nature of this working relationship, it seems *mallahis* on the main ghat do not pose a threat to the hegemony of the *ghatwars*, despite, cases where individual *mallahis* have succeeded in establishing themselves as *ghatwars*. I have not heard, however, of any collective action by *mallahis* working on the major ghats against their employers. Raj ghat is a striking example where the working relations between *ghatwars* and *mallahis* are clearly embedded in a wider set of social relations and ethical considerations. The *mallahis'* rights and privileges in the ghat work system appear to defy what one would call rational maximizing behaviour.

Raj ghat is located in (what is considered) the oldest part of the city. According to historical and archaeological accounts, the original settlers of the city first inhabited the Raj ghat plateau more than 2500 years ago (Eck 1983). The area was strategically advantageous for the original inhabitants as it was well situated on a high plateau bordering the River Ganges. Today, due to the ghat's proximity to the Kashi train station and the Grand Trunk Road; Raj ghat serves as the central terminus for pilgrim groups. It has a large flow of pilgrims arriving in Banaras from various parts of the continent, particularly Bihar (Gaya) in the southeast and Ayodhya in the northwest. Nowadays, a road leads directly to the ghat, and there are spaces where both trucks and buses can park and unload. The convenient setting of the ghat, the parking and adjacent facilities, such as pilgrim hostels (*dharamsalas*), make the place especially attractive for the many pilgrim groups arriving via road or train.

The centrality of the Raj ghat as a port of call for visitors throughout the centuries is probably why the largest concentration of the Mallah community resides in the vicinity of. According to boatmen, it is inhabited by the oldest and largest boatman community in Banaras – there are approximately 350 Mallah households. The community has several structures and temples marking its long standing presence in the area. Over the ghat stands a well maintained *akahra* (wrestling ground) patronized by the Nishad community of Raj ghat. On the inside walls of the *akhara* episodes from the Ramayana are colourfully depicted; similarly, at the pilgrim drop-off point (bus park) there is a much larger painting of Lord Rama, Sita and Lakshman being ferried across the River Ganga by Khevat. At the top of this mural is the phrase: 'sometimes even the Lord depends on the services of devotees'. I shall discuss the meaning of the episode in detail in the following chapter, but for the moment, it is worth noting that the episode figures in devotional songs, film and TV productions. As one boatman said: 'Everybody is familiar with this episode in the Ramayana, and the painting reminds the pilgrims that they are taking a boat ride on Ganga Ma, just like Lord Ram, Sita and Lakshman did. This is good for business'.

The social organization of the community is largely based on occupational activities. There is a functioning *panchayat* (community council) that operates on Raj ghat. The matters discussed in the *panchayat* are mostly to do with social affairs and it also organizes community events and discusses local issues regarding work relations and family disputes, ranging from marital problems to petty property claims. In some cases, boatmen prefer the *panchayat's* assistance rather than approaching legal institutions, which are often costly and time consuming. The problem as everyone seems to agree, is that the *panchayat* cannot sufficiently enforce its decisions. Therefore, when serious disputes arise over property and rights, members of the community generally favour using the legal system. It should be noted, however, that of the Mallah communities living on the riverfront, only Raj ghat and Nishad Raj ghat have a *panchayat* currently operating. At Raj ghat this is a result both of the antiquity of the community and the large number of its members living in the neighbourhood, the majority of whom still derive their livelihood from the river economy. Indeed, it is a community largely sustained by the pilgrimage industry and ghat related work readily available to most of its members.

The pilgrimage industry across Banaras offers unskilled work to a large number of people. The majority of the male members of the Mallah community living on Raj ghat derive their livelihood directly or indirectly from it and from ghat related jobs. Such work involves carrying wood, operating tea stalls, selling religious paraphernalia to pilgrims, diving for money or working on boats as *mallahis*. Some boatmen work as wage labourers, unloading trucks full of wood onto huge boats, which are then ferried to Manikarnika ghat: the main cremation ghat.[16] The majority of boatmen, however, rely on the boating business and ferrying pilgrims as their main source of income.

Most pilgrims arriving in the city come on package tours and follow a similar itinerary. This involves *darshan* (the auspicious sight of god) and worship at the central sacred sites; and most groups take boats to these sacred places. Travel by boat is both pleasant and practical as it is much easier to access the sacred places by water. Over the years, the boatmen have established a system to accommodate

---

16　The approximate salary for a worker unloading one truck is between Rs.20–30.

the large numbers of pilgrims arriving in Raj ghat. Under the overall system of passenger distribution, the territorial jurisdiction of Raj ghat covers the area from the north of the ghat where steps descend from near the train station to Prahlad ghat on the south (see map of ghats). The system follows a rotation known as *pari* (turns, or shifts). There are eight families of *ghatwars* called *paridars* (*pari*-owners) who take successive turns operating a twelve hour shift (i.e., from 6pm until 6am the next day). During this shift, the assigned *paridar* has the right over passengers arriving at the ghat. If, for any reason, he is unable to take the passengers, then the next *paridar* in line has the right to do so.[17] The matter is somewhat complicated as the ghat territory is divided into two parts. The northern part is occupied by four different *ghatwar* families (I shall call them a cluster) that have the right to take passengers arriving from the train station area, while those working on the southern part have rights to passengers arriving from the road. The two clusters alternate between the locations when all (within each cluster) have had their respective turns.

As on other major ghats, the *ghatwars* of Raj ghat also employ *mallahis* to ply and maintain their boats. Generally, between one and three workers are sufficient for manning the boat and catering for the needs of the pilgrims. There are around 300 hundred *mallahis* working on Raj ghat as part-time casual labourers. Due to the large number of *mallahis*, a rule was established specifying that only those people who are present on the bottom platform of the ghat at the time the passengers board the boat can serve as *mallahis* for that specific boat ride. If, for example, workers are late or decide to leave the area momentarily while the pilgrims perform ablutions and are not back by the time the boat departs, they are barred from working as *mallahis*. Only those *mallahis* present will earn and divide between them the 50 percent share of the boat ride, while the other 50 percent remains that of the *paridar*.

What is remarkable in this system, however, is that even in instances when a boat is full of pilgrims (i.e., there is no room for the *mallahis*), the *mallahis* present can still earn their share of the allotted 50 percent by simply *walking* the parallel distance along the ghat that the boat will cover. Thus, a *mallahi* will calculate according to the number of passengers on board and his subsequent earnings, whether it is profitable for him to walk the distance or not. These calculations have become more complex over the past decade with the introduction of motorboats by *paridars*. The benefits of motorboats are clear. A motorboat can perform the same task as a rowboat in less than half the time, meaning that the *paridar* can work many more rounds than with a rowboat. However, motorboats do not require *mallahis* (as oarsmen) and this

---

17     On Raj ghat there are a number of cases when the next *paridar* (*pari*-owner) will take passengers: 1. if the assigned *paridar* has all of his boats engaged with other groups; 2. if the *paridar* is momentarily absent from the ghat, then another boatman can quickly and discreetly load his boat with passengers. In this case the original *paridar* subsequently has no claim to these passengers (cf. Parry 1994, 95).

has implications on how the boatmen perceive themselves, since previously, as workers, their source of production was their hard physical labour. Receiving 50 percent of the earnings for the trip was seen as a *decent* wage for the hard labour performed by the workers. Nowadays, however, with the introduction of motorboats, we are witnessing the decreasing value of physical labour along with an increase in population and demand for work.

On Raj ghat the *mallahis* still retain their traditional rights as workers to earn their livelihood from the boating business. They continue to work on the boats, even though their labour is less needed and valued because of the increased use of motorboats. Some workers serve as guides to pilgrims around the sacred sites. For many others, however, tagging along for the ride in order to receive their share is the only alternative. The following example will illustrate just how this system operates in daily life. Two buses full of pilgrims arrived at the ghat. One hundred and four pilgrims were scheduled to visit the Vishvanath temple (considered to be the most sacred in Banaras) near the main ghat and each of the passengers paid Rs.10 for the return trip. The overall amount received was Rs.1040 out of which Rs.75 was deducted for fuel and the remaining Rs.965 was divided between the *mallahis* and *paridar*, leaving the *mallahis* a sum of Rs.482 to share among themselves. In this case only six *mallahis* boarded the boats and 21 others walked the distance so they could receive their share, which eventually amounted to Rs.17.8. Those *mallahis* on board were mainly concerned with directing and guiding pilgrims to the temples and safeguarding the pilgrims' belongings. The

**Figure 3.4     Pilgrims alighting at Shivala ghat**

other workers who arrived on foot much later were only there as token workers so they could receive their due share.

When I asked why those workers who do nothing still receive money, the common answer was that it is traditional. The logic behind this was explained later by one of my main informants from the ghat, himself a *mallahi*: 'Anyone willing to work should be able to earn something. In this way we manage to earn Rs.40–50 a day to buy basic food (*dal roti chaal jata hai*). Everyone should eat, but for us this means we need to dig the well daily to drink the water; this is what I call poverty'. Thus, regardless of the underemployment that exists on the ghat, the *mallahis* are able to earn minimum subsistence from the boating industry. It is this notion of justice articulated in the idiom of rights which I examine in the concluding section of this chapter.


**Rights and the Notion of Haq**

One of the most common words I heard when discussing the rights of boatmen in the city was the term *haq* (right/property). When used by the boatmen it often refers to their right to work in any water related activity. Boatmen claim that as members of the Mallah/Nishad caste, they should have the prerogative over river related jobs, such as fishing, boating, sandmining, swimming instruction and working in the Water Police. The term is also employed when asserting their ancestral rights to officiate rituals on the riverbank, a matter contested by Brahmin priests working on the ghats (see Chapter 4). Such usage of the term is directed towards an external audience, such as when pushing for acknowledgment by state authorities or other castes of the community's rights, deriving from their hereditary caste occupation. However, the rights boatmen derive from being members of the community are also directed internally, revealing shared ties and reciprocal relationships between members of the community.

It is in this context that the term *haq* is also used to justify the fact that *mallahis* continue to earn from the ghat economy, though they may not work as oarsmen. The *mallahis* often use the term *haq* to indicate their moral rights to work as boatmen on the riverfront, regardless of the fact that they are not *ghatwars* and do not own a boat. This commonly used term originates from the Urdu language and is in common usage in Arabic.[18] It may be instructive to compare it to the term *haqq* in the Islamic context, as Clifford Geertz (1979) writes in the context of Moroccan society:

---

18    According to the Hindi-English Oxford Dictionary the word *haq* carries several meanings: 1. just, 2. right, 3. justice, 4. a claim, privilege, franchise, 5. due share, due claim, 6. duty, obligation, 7. behalf, benefit, (McGregor 1993, 1054).

> ...haqq means "right," "correct," "authentic," and therefore "a right, title or claim to something," rightful possession," "property," "one's due," one's duty, responsibility," "accountability,"... legitimate share in something... Clearly, haqq is a rather extreme example of the tendency we have been tracing of Arabic to link a set of disparate ideas into a single morphologically marked off conceptual field no one lexeme can even begin to sum up (Geertz 1979, 210).

The way in which the boatmen use the term suggests certain similarities between *haq* and the Arabic *haqq*. Such usage denotes the entitlements and possession one has by simply being born into the Mallah caste. Here the term *haq* implies equality and uniformity shared by all members of the community. Boatmen often speak of *Mallah ka haq* (the rights/entitlements of Mallahs) when referring to their inherited rights to practice activities associated with the River Ganga. Another example of how the term *haq* is applied in the discourse of social justice is found in the context of festivals and during rituals. In festivals, regardless of whether a boatman works as a fisherman or in any other job, he is equally entitled to retrieve artefacts from the river: it is his *haq* (right). This is particularly evident during certain festivals, such as Durga Puja and Saraswathi Puja, when thousands of worshipers from all over the city and the surrounding villages come to Banaras carrying big and small wooden statues of the goddesses. The festivals are marked by long processions that come to a stop on the major ghats. Thereafter, the worshipers take the statues of the goddesses (*murti*) onto boats midstream where they are ritually immersed (*viscrjan*) and released into the holy river. Such occasions are a good source of income for the boatmen, especially *ghatwars*, as thousands worshipers perform the ritual immersions. After the sacred idols are released, many boatmen set out and retrieve the idols from the water; once released into the river, the idols are considered the boatmen's *haq* (possession/property). They then strip the idols of their adornments (sometimes including gold jewellery) and clothing in order to use them and to resell the wood at markets. Interestingly, however, those who retrieve the sunken idols are not the wealthy *ghatwars*, but rather the poorer members of the community. The reason behind this is twofold. The *ghatwars* have already benefited substantially from the festival by carrying passengers. In addition, there is a moral expectation that they let other members of the community have their legitimate share of the earnings derived from the river economy. This relates to the fact that there is no territorial jurisdiction barring boatmen from taking anything out of the river. As one boatman told me, 'Mother Ganga does not care if you are a *ghatwar* or not, all boatmen are her devoted children'.

At Raj ghat, however, the term *haq* is incorporated into everyday life, that is, it refers not only to a right practised during festival times, but also to daily activities. At Raj ghat such rights constitute part of the broader socio-economic relations between *mallahis* and *ghatwars*. *Mallahis* use the term to articulate their expectation of getting their fair share of the economic activities on the ghat from the wealthier *ghatwars*. At the same time, the *ghatwars*, as the wealthier members of the community, are expected to provide a minimum subsistence to the less privileged members of the community. The *ghatwars* comply with such expectations for a number of reasons. Firstly, if the needs of the *mallahis* are not met, the *ghatwars* face the real risk of social unrest, which could result in violence and damage to property. Secondly, the *ghatwars* have an interest in securing the support of the *mallahis* in order to mobilize them in times of crisis. I saw this myself during an organized demonstration against police harassment. *Mallahis* provide the numbers needed to stage impressive demonstrations against the government. In addition, *ghatwars* want to maintain good relationships with the rest of the community and having wide support from within the community during major social events demonstrates their generosity, wealth, power and popularity. Finally, manpower is also important in cases of conflict between *ghatwars* or between *ghatwars* and other ghat functionaries. It is in the *ghatwars'* best interest to retain broad support from the *mallahis* as it ensures a more secure and favourable environment to operate in.

The case of Raj ghat certainly demonstrates an explicit moral economy. The specific historical, geographical and social conditions at Raj ghat preserve strong elements of kinship, neighbourhood, and other forms of social relations characteristic of an integrated community. Economic behaviour is embedded in a wider set of social relations and modes of communication, including mutual obligation, reciprocity, justice and moral rights, all of which inform daily interaction in the course of everyday life.

## Conclusion

I started this chapter describing the *'Hello! Boat?'* phenomenon as the bane of all tourists visiting the ghats. To us it seems astonishing that the boatmen do not respond to the market and act in a manner more pleasing to their prospective customers. What I have shown, however, is that when you enter the ghats of Banaras, you are entering a cultural world, where certain personal ties, customary rules and moral expectations form human interaction and inform economic activity.[19]

While my primary concern in this book is to examine the multiple ways in which agency is exercised within structures of domination, the system of passenger distribution on the riverscape cannot be fully captured by reference to the agency of power alone. Sherry Ortner (2001) argues this point when she makes a heuristic distinction between two modalities of agency. According to Ortner, the first modality is 'the agency of (unequal) power', which is defined and takes shape within wider relations of domination and resistance. The second modality, described as the 'agency of intentions – of projects, purposes, desires' (2001, 79), accounts for the relative autonomy in the exercise of agency of marginalized people, emerging out of their own needs, wants and aspirations and articulated in

---

19    This is similar to Geertz's (1979, 137) idea of a trader entering the cultural world of the tribal society in Morocco.

culturally meaningful ways. For boatmen, the latter form of agency is located in the spatial order of the riverscape: produced and reproduced as a result of an ongoing project to improve one's social and economic position in relation to one's peers in the riverscape economy. Such desires and actions *are* culturally constituted, insofar as they only make sense within a specific, historically grounded, value system and cultural logic. This is not to say that such cultural logic determines the boatmen's behavior or the unfolding of events; nor is it beyond the reach of power, suffusing all social systems. On the contrary, boatmen, like most people, revise and reshape their intentions and desires, identities and spaces throughout the course of their ordinary lives. The moral economic order of the riverfront, too, remains subject to competing and culturally meaningful interpretations, which reflect and spatially embody the struggle over access to resources.

Banaras is certainly a far cry from the precolonial peasant societies, and one must be cautious in applying Scott's original concept of moral economy to different socio-historical circumstances (Adas 1980). Indeed, Scott's (1985) subsequent study detailing the micro-politics of the moral economy in rural Malaysia is in some ways more germane to my examination of the boatman community in Banaras, where I emphasize relations of domination and intra-community conflict and friction. In this later study, Scott traces the increasing economic inequalities amongst villages to exogenous forces, such as the green revolution, technological innovation and market economy. But while these new circumstances meant that rich farmers could and did renounce many of their past practices of material and symbolic social concern, the moral economy continued to operate as a moderating framework under which the weaker members of the community sought security, by appealing to the rich to restore traditional customs and practices.

My own examination of the work system in Banaras deals with similar issues. State interventions, the changing nature of the tourist/pilgrimage industry and introduction of motorboats have all affected the river economy. Such changes are pivotal to an understanding of the working system and the changing relationships within the community as well as the increasing economic disparities within the *ghatwar* community and between *ghatwars* and *mallahis*.

While *ghatwar*s from the major ghats have found new fortunes by tapping into the burgeoning tourist industry, this has also generated new concerns about state and commercial interventions into the boatmen's livelihood, which by now is almost exclusively limited to that of ferrying passengers. To retain their monopoly on the boating industry and preserve their autonomy, prosperous *ghatwars* have a vested interest in maintaining, at least to some degree, certain elements of the moral economic order. Consequently, the socio-economic arrangements and customary regulations of reciprocity, mutual obligation and the guarantee of minimum subsistence for all boatmen across the riverfront continue to be the basis of a common, if contested, tradition.

At the ghat level we find a 'living' moral economy that is embraced to differing degrees, largely contingent upon the socio-economic circumstances and histories of the specific ghats. While the system certainly favours the more powerful *ghatwars*, both weaker *ghatwars* and the *mallahis* seem to accept their inferior status as long as they are ensured a right to subsistence. It seems also true that *ghatwars* increasingly view their obligations towards the *mallahis* as those of employer to employee (i.e., contractual and impersonal), as at Assi and the main ghats, whereas the precepts of the moral economy remain strongly embedded in the social and economic relationship and *pari* institution at Raj ghat; here the *mallahis* are able to exert influence over the local *ghatwars* and invoke a broader intra-*mallahi* norm of reciprocity (*haq*) to support those without work.

Unlike Scott's peasants, boatmen are part of a market-structured community, and most households do not live by boating alone, at least one family member will work in temporary unskilled jobs elsewhere, thus reducing the family's dependence on the river economy. Nevertheless, subsistence security remains a central concern for the majority of households and for that reason, I would argue, the work system remains an important ideological and economic institution for ensuring the stability and security of the community. At the same time, by highlighting the material concerns as informing shared cultural norms and values of boatmen, I do not wish to dismiss equally pertinent aspects of the boatmen's lives and worldviews, including their religious beliefs and desire for higher social status and dignity, a subject I turn to in the following chapter.[20]

---

20 Cf. Adas (1980, 527) who argues that the materialist bias in Scott's work is problematic as it 'obscures other vitally important aspects of peasant life and outlook, these include their religious beliefs, personal attachments to particular leaders or groups, aspirations for higher social status and prestige'.

# Chapter 4

# River Crossings: Boatmen, Priests and the Ritual Economy of Banaras

The boat is like a god, and only with a boat can you cross the river.

Deepak Manjhi

As a pilgrimage centre for Hindus, Banaras is known as a *tirtha*: a spiritual 'ford' where the boundaries between the physical world and the sacred one are permeable. A *tirtha*, as Diane Eck (1983, 24) describes it, is a powerful place, where one can easily and safely cross over 'the river of *samsara* – this round of repeated birth and death – to reach the far shore of liberation'.[1] Nonetheless, such powerful 'crossing places' must be negotiated for the worshipper with the help of meaningful symbols, ritual assistants and organizational structures – they cannot be negotiated alone. The organizational structures, including a variety of institutions, ceremonial practices and ritual transactions form the basis of the Banaras ritual economy; and central to this economy are the ritual specialists, facilitating and instructing worshippers in matters of ritual and belief.

---

1    It is interesting to note the contrast between the plethora of literature about Banaras as a "crossing place" (*tirtha*) and that of Kumar's illuminating study of the low class artisans of Banaras and their use and conceptualization of space, unmarred by mythological or religious meanings and practice. For Kumar, the act of crossing the river (*Ganga par*) is a recreational activity, part of a popular practice known as *bahari alang* or outdoor trips, which locals take to the outskirts of the city in search of a carefree environment. Kumar highlights the aesthetic and affective dimensions of such outings, which generate a shared ideology of leisure among artisans, marked by a sense of freedom to control their own time–'a crucial facet of their identity' (1988, 92). As such, she seems to suggest that these beliefs, practices and alternative spaces harbour the possibility of politics, where the riverscape becomes integral to the mediation of subaltern identities and where artisans are able to produce their own sense of community, away from the surveying gaze of the elites. What is unclear, and Kumar does not push the point further, is the potential for and extent to which such spaces and practices are expressing subaltern 'resistance to the values of dominant groups' (Haynes 1989, 417). Jonathan Parry (1994) is much more explicit about the political dimensions of the sacred space of the city's riverfront, examining how historical contingencies and conflicts amongst ritual specialists (especially Brahmins) have contributed to the spatial organization of Banaras' ritual economy. But like Kumar, Parry too stops short of examining the multiplicity of culturally valued strategies and perspectives involved in the construction and production of the riverscape as an arena of appropriation and popular resistance.

Recent studies examining the sociology of the ritual specialists (or sacred specialists as they are sometimes referred to) operating in Hindu pilgrimage centres have greatly enhanced our understanding of the dynamics of religious belief in Hindu society and power relations involved in the ritual domain, gift exchange, and temple organization (e.g., Fuller 1984; Parry 1994; van der Veer 1988; Vidyarthi et al. 1979). However, in focusing on the primary ritual specialists, and in particular the most dominant group – Brahmin priests – little mention is given to the weaker ritual specialists or to the worshippers themselves, as actors who are equally implicated in the production and negotiation of and, in fact, contestation over the ritual economies of the sacred centres in India.

In the case of the Banaras boatmen and priests, the relation of domination and subordination is clearly visible. The lives and everyday practices of both groups are shaped in relation to the sacred River Ganga and the ritual economy surrounding it. Within this ritual economy the Brahmins, as Parry (1994, 23) observes, 'set the dominant religious tone of the city'. These priests, a highly heterogeneous group, constitute the most numerous and powerful group of sacred specialists in Banaras, catering for the needs of both visiting pilgrims and the local inhabitants of the city. There are also other groups of ritual specialists, who are positioned as ritually inferior according to Brahminical orthodoxy, but who nonetheless play an important role in the ritual economy of the city. The question if and how these subordinate specialists, including barbers, boatmen and untouchable doms (caste of funeral attendants), defy Brahminical domination of the ritual sphere and protest caste prejudice is rarely examined.

According to Brahminical orthodoxy, these ritual specialists are religiously, morally and socially inferior to them. The boatmen, for example, while seen as actors in the ritual economy of the city, are positioned as people of low ritual status. This is due to the defiling (even sinful) nature of aspects of their work, including carrying corpses and fishing, and because they engage in manual labour.

Boatmen, however, situate themselves very differently within the ritual economy of Banaras. Boatmen refuse the degradation accorded to them by Brahminical orthodoxy, and are careful to emphasize their crucial role in the economic, social and religious life of the city. Boatmen pride themselves as being the ultimate devotees of Lord Rama and the River Ganga, flagging the episode from the popular Hindu epic, the Ramayana and the propitious encounter between the divine king, Rama, and the boatman, Khevat, as evidence of their distinguished position within Hindu hierarchy and tradition.

In this chapter I explore the way in which boatmen use myths, rituals and other symbols as vehicles for asserting their role as valued ritual specialists, operating within the ritual economy of Banaras. More specifically, I look at rituals that accompany life cycle events, in which the River Ganga is worshipped as the mother goddess, Ganga Ma. At these times, the everyday riverboat turns into a sacred deity; and the boatman becomes an essential ritual specialist assisting the locals in the conduct of life cycle rituals. In the first part of the chapter I focus on a post-wedding river ritual wherein a seemingly mundane activity like boating is turned seamlessly into a sacral event. In the second part I analyse it, seeking to re-examine the influential organizing ideas of domination and hierarchy with attention to how the subaltern boatmen ingeniously subvert their assigned position as 'the dominated', thereby interrupting the traditional priestly order. In addition, my analysis of a foundational myth of the boatman community, with its devotional overtones, reveals the performative and meaningful aspects of myth – as a way of knowing and being – conferring privileges and rights and informing social practice. I draw attention to how hard dichotomies of great/little tradition, subaltern/elite, dominant/dominated, contestation/cooperation, become more fluid when examined in the context of daily interactions at the grass roots level.

My aim is to suggest a more dynamic view than those offered by the conventional approaches for understanding caste claims on lucrative ritual practices and the allocation of valued sacred space in Banaras. I do so by showing how the boatmen's appropriation of Hindu textual tradition and symbols of domination enables them to construct a cohesive identity for themselves and a meaningful place in the Hindu social hierarchy – one that reinforces their role as ritual specialists and furthers their social and economic interests. I ground this argument in a searching examination of indigenous categories and a careful analysis of the views of people who have engaged in post-wedding rituals, known as Ganga Pujaiya, as well as in myth and its exegesis as it was related to me by boatmen. Finally, I consider the strategies employed by the boatmen, which enable them to maintain their monopoly over the ever-growing business of boating on the river.


**Myth, Ritual and Resistance**


The meaning and function of myth and ritual has long been central to anthropological literature. Generations of scholars have analyzed myths and rituals in terms of their capacity to generate meaning and maintain, strengthen and reproduce social order. More recently, however, with the increasing attention given to theories of practice and power, myths and rituals are also being investigated as part of the arsenal deployed by the weak in their everyday struggle within systems of domination (e.g., Comaroff 1985; Contrusi 1989; Dirks 1991; Mines 2002). I have already discussed the problems and possibilities of the Subaltern Studies approach in the introduction of this book. Several scholars have questioned whether the constant preoccupation of this approach with the concept of resistance advances our understanding of the multifaceted nature of resistance and the ambiguities of agency found in subordinate populations (Kaplan & Kelly 1994; Reed-Danahay 1993). In a penetrating critique of recent studies, Ortner (1995: 177) evokes the notion of 'thick description' as an antidote to the 'air of romanticism' characteristic of much of the literature on resistance. Accordingly, she argues that in highlighting resistance these studies tend to gloss over the 'prior and ongoing politics among the subalterns'. Such considerations inform my own analysis, and form the background against which I examine the social ecology of the riverfront in Banaras and the ongoing politics of the boatman community itself, to provide a more holistic rendition of the ethnographic present and subaltern struggles. Only this way, I believe, can we fully appreciate the social complexities and ambiguities inherent to the practice of resistance.

*Hinduism and Rituals*

Hinduism is often described as a way of life. Not only do rituals and ceremonies underpin important periods in life, such as marriage, birth, childhood and death, they permeate daily routines like eating and bathing. The most common daily rituals, *puja* (worship of deities), are often performed with practical aims in mind, such as achieving economic success, recovering from illness, purging pollution, removing one's sins and avoiding harmful elements that afflict people. Many of these daily rituals are performed more elaborately during important life-cycle events such as the transition from childhood to adulthood and – often closely connected with the latter – marriage.

In Hindu culture marriage is a cherished sacrament. Appropriately, it is celebrated by an elaborate series of rituals that may occur over a long period of time. In Banaras most wedding ceremonies are followed by a post-wedding ritual called Ganga Pujaiya, which generally occurs a day after the main festivities and culminates on the riverscape.

The latter ceremony begins with a procession in which the newlyweds and members of their family stop at various local shrines to worship local protector deities of the neighbourhood. On reaching the riverfront, the party performs a *puja* to the holy river to receive Ganga Ma's blessing for the newlyweds. This ritual is generally conducted by a resident Brahmin priest (*panda*) from the ghat. The priest instructs the mother of the groom in the performance of the ritual and then utters a series of Sanskrit mantras to sanctify it. On completion, the priest receives a *dakshina* or fee for his services.

Sometimes Ganga Pujaiya rituals in Banaras are followed by another for Ganga Ma. This happens when a *manauti* or vow of propitiation to Ganga Ma has been made by the mother of the groom. A mother who seeks a successful marriage for her son may pledge to Ganga Ma that when her son marries she will perform an offering for her. This, I have been told, is also intended to secure Ganga Ma's blessing for the marriage. A long ritual garland (*ar par ka mala*) is offered as propitiation when the wish has been fulfilled.[2] The ritual occurs in three stages and at three locations. The first stage is performed on the ghat close to the river, the second on the barren eastern side of the river and the final stage in midstream. Significantly, it is the boatmen who conduct this post-marital ritual – not the Brahmin priests. In the particular ceremony described here, my informant

---

2    A *manauti* may also be made for the success of a business or the birth of a son. In the latter, along with the offering of a ritual garland, the son is also symbolically offered to *Ganga Ma*.

(also the owner of the boat) had three other boatmen working as assistants. In this instance an older boatman known as Babaji performed the ceremony. As his nickname indicates, his appearance resembles that of a Baba or holy man (*sadhu*). Babaji is often employed on such occasions due to his devout appearance: long white beard and maroon loincloth.

The family performing the ceremony consisted of the mother who had made the *manauti*, her son and daughter-in-law, and six close family members, including a barber's wife. Besides the groom, all the participants were women. The first stage of the ritual, performed on the ghat, involved the consecration of the boat and the long ritual garland. Here Babaji assumed a role similar to that of a priest, serving as an intermediary between deity (in this case the boat) and worshipper. Babaji carefully instructed the mother how to make offerings to the prow (*sikah*) of the boat and the ritual garland. The ritual procedure and items used, such as turmeric paste, vermilion, marigolds and camphor, resembled the general manner in which any *puja* is performed for a deity. By the end of the ritual the boat looked like a fitting place of worship. Each member of the family was then instructed to perform *pranam* (gesture of respect or salutation) to the boat.

I asked the young owner of the boat why the boat receives this treatment and he replied that: 'One must treat the boat as a house of worship. To touch the boat with the forehead and hands is the same as one would do when going up the steps of a temple. This is because the boat is seen as a step to Ganga Ma'. Later,

**Figure 4.1    Ganga Pujaiya ritual: Babaji and the newlyweds (foreground) during the ritual**

another boatman expanded, saying that the boat is the goddess Tarini Ma and by performing *pranam* to the boat one touches the feet of God. I asked him if everyone who performs Pujaiya in Banaras does so and he replied: 'Everyone, regardless of caste must touch the feet of Ganga Ma and Tarini Ma'. He emphasized that boatmen also officiate these rituals for Brahmins, and that the worship of the boat ensures the safe sailing across the river.

The common word for boat is *naw*, whereas in the ritual context it is referred to as the goddess Tarini Ma. The name derives from the word *taran*, which is defined in the dictionary as follows: 'crossing over (as a river) and deliverance by crossing (the ocean of birth and rebirth), or a title of the Supreme Being' (McGregor 1993, 440). As mentioned, this notion of 'crossing a river' is a common metaphor in Hinduism; it represents the ubiquitous human journey through life and into the afterlife. The boat that carries the deceased across the ocean of creation to the point of rebirth is recurrent in devotional songs, myth and literature.

After performing *pranam* the mother was asked by Babaji to offer Rs.101 to the boat and garland respectively.[3] At this point the mother refused vehemently and a heated discussion developed. At length Babaji offered to lower the sum to Rs.101 in total. After further negotiation the mother finally agreed to pay Rs.61, which Babaji grudgingly accepted.

The party then boarded the boat and was carried to the other side of the river. Here a similar ritual sequence to the one conducted on the ghat was performed. This time, though, instead of worshipping the boat, three river goddesses – Ganga, Yamuna and Saraswati – were worshipped. When the ritual activities performed by the mother were completed, Babaji unexpectedly recited a Sanskrit mantra. The boatmen do not usually do this, as mantras are widely believed to be the privileged domain of Brahmin priests. Nonetheless some boatmen, like Babaji, do sometimes recite them.[4] Although no one could explain the precise meaning of the mantra to me (not even the ghat priests), it was said to be essential for the completion of the ritual and to bestow good luck. It seems that such recitations are employed to demonstrate and confirm the 'ritual authority' of the boatmen as skilful and competent religious specialists. And Babaji's ritual authority indeed seemed to be confirmed here, as the worshippers touched his feet with reverence, calling him *maharaj* (a title commonly used when referring to a Brahmin priest). However this extra performance came at a price. After completing his recitation, Babaji requested an additional payment, arguing that, as priests received *dakshina* from worshippers, so should the Khevats (boatmen).

Although the core price for the ritual had been negotiated at the outset, Babaji asked for additional sums of money to be offered after each phase. This is a familiar technique employed by both the boatmen and Brahmin priests in Banaras to exact as much money as possible from worshippers. However, it is also considered the

---

3    It is considered auspicious to offer a sum ending in the figure one.

4    Babaji told me that he had learned this mantra from wedding invitations. Other boatmen told me they learned it by watching Brahmin priests.

**Figure 4.2    Ganga Pujaiya ritual: mother of the groom performing the ritual on the other (eastern) side of the river**

priests'/ritual specialists' right (*haq*) to ask for this money as payment for their services.

The mother then asked Babaji to bless the newlyweds. Babaji placed a flower garland around their necks and applied a *tilak* (red dot) to their foreheads. The newlyweds then touched his feet. Babaji asked the bride to extend her garment forward so he could symbolically 'fill her lap' (*goda barhai*) and thus be blessed with a male child. He did this by filling the lap of the bride with sanctified food (*prasad*). Next, Babaji instructed the newlyweds to ask forgiveness from Ganga Ma for their sins and to protect them from any evil. The family then re-embarked and the party set off.

The final stage of the ceremony was performed midstream where the boatmen instructed the mother to throw money into the river as propitiatory offering (*nichawar*), which is said to ward off trouble for the participants in the ritual. While the mother of the groom was throwing coins to Ganga Ma the boatmen shouted 'Ganga Ma ki jai' ('Hail Ganga Ma') and all the participants replied in unison 'Jai'. The boat then ceremoniously circled three times and headed back to the ghat.[5] With the ceremony completed the satisfied newlyweds and the family

---

5    According to the boatmen the meaning of circling the boat three times is similar to the ritual circumambulation of a temple or deity (*parikrama*).

headed up the steps of the ghat, and the owner of the boat distributed the earnings to those boatmen who had participated in the Ganga Pujaiya.

## The Needle and the Sword: Conceptualizing the Role of Ritual Specialists

When I asked a Brahmin priest how the boatmen, given their low caste status, are permitted to conduct Ganga Pujaiya rituals he replied with poise: 'When you need a needle you cannot use a sword'.

One way in which this saying can be interpreted is in line with the formulations of David Mandelbaum (1966) and Lawrence Babb (1975) regarding the role and place of ritual specialists in Hindu society. According to them the role of the ritual specialist is consistent with a view of Hindu religion as two-fold. The first level is pan-Indian in its jurisdiction, associated with the higher, scriptural traditions and concerned with its sanctioning of social order. The second is local and oriented to the pragmatic needs of individuals (Babb 1975: 212–3). Accordingly, ritual specialists complement each other by operating in their respective domains.

Babb's observations are especially useful for understanding aspects related to the local shrines and deities in Banaras. For him the local deities fit into a purported structure underlying the Hindu religious system – based on foundational concepts like purity and pollution. The local protector deities worshipped en route to the River Ganga in neighbourhood shrines during the post-wedding ceremony are non-scriptural gods. These deities, Babb argues, are lower level deities (protectors) and are worshipped 'in the contexts of childbearing and marriage' because they are more accessible and more involved in human affairs, and have the capacity to ward off any harmful elements that can afflict newlyweds in this time of transition (Babb 1975, 243–5). As inferior gods in the hierarchical pantheon they demand a lesser degree of purity; hence there is no need for a priest.

Similarly, it could be argued that the boatmen are low caste ritual specialists who deal with minor deities (such as the boat in the form of the deity Tarini Ma) and officiate rituals that serve the practical needs of the local population with respect to marriage and for other domestic concerns such as birth and childrearing, illness, and economic livelihood. According to this interpretation, insofar as the boatmen perform priestly roles, their activities are confined to local settings, and do not amount to higher or proper priestly functions. Some of the details of the Ganga Pujaiya, as discussed later, may reinforce this interpretation – for instance its optional nature; the pivotal involvement of women; and the apparent acceptance by the local Brahmin priests of the boatmen's ritual aspirations.

In the case of the Ganga Pujaiya ritual the priest's enigmatic statement quoted above seems to reinforce the idea proposed by Mandelbaum and Babb: it suggests that Brahmin priests see themselves as 'sword-wielders', 'above' the performance of local, minor rituals requiring only the manipulation of a 'needle'. Or to put it another way, it implies that the role of ritual specialist was imparted or granted to the boatmen by the high caste priests. If this interpretation is correct, ritual serves to reproduce social hierarchy and labour relations and thus maintain the unswerving social order.

Babb's analysis echoes the structural and functional distinctions commonly made by orientalists and anthropologists alike. Caste is central, and the society revolves around religious principles of purity and pollution, as postulated by Dumont (1972) and his followers.[6] As Babb puts it, there is a divine hierarchy. In this view, overriding social structure determines the activities, behaviour and values of groups and individuals. All political and economic activities are subordinated to the ancient dominating religious structure, which maintains the hegemonic Brahminical order.

On the face of it, this line of argument is borne out by an analysis of the Ganga Pujaiya ritual process in the manner of Victor Turner (1969). We may see the boatmen assuming only a momentary priestly role in a 'liminal phase' of the wider wedding ritual. After this liminal phase, the normal hierarchical social order resumes. This interpretation, however, begs the questions of how the boatmen themselves interpret and negotiate their role; and how they are perceived by those using their services. For those involved, is Ganga Pujaiya a minor part of the marriage ceremony – or a central one? In the post-liminal phase is there an acceptance by the boatmen of a return to the ordained hierarchy?

My study shows that, for the mother at least, the Ganga Pujaiya is an important religious ritual. She believes that both the religious vow and subsequent ritual will influence her life, her son's marriage and future grandchildren.[7] As a result, the boatmen are viewed by her as important actors, indeed, as primary ritual specialists within the compass of the ceremony.

For the boatmen themselves the ritual is a way of gaining recognition for their unique role on the riverscape. Secondly, it is a means to gain control over a ritual space, often considered the domain of Brahmins. This is significant because the boatmen believe their role as ritual specialists has been granted to them, not by Brahminical sanctioning, but by virtue of their caste, occupation and relationship with Ganga Ma. Moreover, their claims and assertions are not designed to simply emulate Brahminical practices and support claims for higher status, as assumed under the logic of Sanskritization. Rather, these assertions are products of historical

---

6    The major criticism of Dumont's work concerns his overemphasis on structural abstractions that prioritize the stable and unchanging religious sphere over the ever changing economic and political ones. For a critique of Dumont's argument, see, for example, Dirks 2001; Gupta 2000, Searle-Chatterjee & Sharma (1994).

7    The fact that the participants in these rituals are mostly women could also suggest a gender division that corresponds to certain religious practices associated with tradition, family welfare and the domestic sphere. However I would argue, following Hancock, that by simply assigning lifecycle rituals to the traditional, domestic sphere, we are reproducing similar dichotomizing tropes (i.e. modernity/tradition' public/domestic) that limit further exploration into the concrete alternative meaning that such ritual performances hold for the participants. See Hancock 1999.

dynamics and ongoing politics within the boatman community as well as outside it over crucial resources. By firmly establishing their position as ritual specialists on the riverscape, the boatmen register their claim over physical space that is valuable beyond the ritual context.

The boatmen employ pan-Hindu symbols and myths as a resource because they intuitively understand that these constitute 'the single most important evaluative norm within Hinduism' (Fuller 1992, 27). Moreover, the boatmen have their own interpretations and emphasis within that tradition. They do not merely wish to take a place readymade for them, as it were, by the Hindu religious elite. Rather, they bolster their claim for control over sacred space, and pursue their quest for a more secure livelihood, on the basis of a version of Hinduism that is theirs, and in some measure shared with others – for example, the locals performing the ritual.

*The Ritual Performance*

Ritual and myth serve as the indigenous framework within which such claims over sacred space and secure livelihood are made. The success of the boatmen's claims to act as ritual specialists is, in part, dependent on the acceptance of such claims by other actors, such as those performing the rituals (i.e. newlyweds) and Brahmin priests. In the ritual described in the first part of the chapter I offer an account of how the local community recognizes the boatmen in their priestly roles within a ritual context, but there are limits to this recognition. On several occasions when asked to explain the difference between boatmen and priests in the Ganga Pujaiya ritual, people said that 'boatmen cannot chant the mantras'. This response derives from the common notion that chanting mantras is the exclusive mandate of the priests. According to the ancient Vedic tradition, low shudra castes are barred from reading and chanting mantras but, in the local ritual context the boatmen defy such authoritative injunctions.

As seen earlier, Babaji chanted mantras and blessed the participants in the post-wedding ceremony. His conduct of the ritual followed a prescribed order starting with the consecration of the boat (Tarini Ma), which assured the participants of his authority and knowledge. His use of mantras and blessing the bride indicate that the boatman's role is not merely one of assistant or ritual associate, but that of officiating priest. Indeed, Babaji faithfully (though perhaps with a hint of irony) imitates the Brahmin priests by using similar gestures and Sanskritic language (for example *dakshina*).

There are several ways that one may interpret Babaji's actions, all of them inevitably coloured by the anthropologist's position in relation to the 'subjects' in the field, and his or her intellectual and professional orientation (Thapan 1998, 6). For example, from a Subaltern Studies perspective, one could read Babaji's ritual performance not only as an imitation of priestly gestures, but also as public subversion and violation of priestly authority. However, this would reduce the discussion to the binary opposition between the dominant priest and subordinate boatman, disregarding the mixed intentions of the participants involved and the internal dynamics that exist within the subaltern category itself (Ortner 1995). As mentioned earlier (Chapter 3), there are power relations and internal differences within the boatman community itself – for example between the *ghatwars* and the *mallahis*. In this context, Babaji's ritual performance may be seen as an implicit assertion of his primacy over other casual workers (*mallahis*), who may be younger and stronger in rowing the boats, but are not as qualified as he is in ritual conduct.

The emphasis on power relations, should not be abstracted from the cultural and symbolic dimensions evident in the ritual performance. It may well be that by acting as an authoritative and competent ritual specialist Babaji is not trying to imitate a Brahmin priest, but rather attempting to dispel some of the common stereotypical ideas associated with the boatman community, such as that it is composed of low caste 'criminal types', only interested in the money of the worshippers.[8] At the same time, I am convinced that Babaji believes, as he told me in a conversation, that by mediating Ganga Ma for the worshippers, he is fulfilling and enacting his god-given right, privilege and duty (*haq*) to conduct rituals as a member of the Mallah caste. The following section will examine how the boatmen invoke caste identity, myth and other cultural symbols to enforce and assert their rights to conduct rituals and maintain control over sacred space.

## Myth, Caste and Identity

Caste is an important identity marker used by the boatmen to distinguish themselves from others and assert their role as ritual specialists. Boatmen often cite the story of Khevat from the epic Ramayana as a turning point for their caste within the social structure of Hindu society.[9]

While the Khevat myth is a marginal episode in the Ramayana, it nevertheless is a famous one, featuring a strong devotional (*bhakti*) theme. This is particularly so in North India and especially in Banaras where the most popular telling of the epic is known as Ramcharitmanas (the lake of the acts of Rama). Written by the sage poet Tulsi Das of Banaras in the 16th century, the *Manas*, as it is commonly called, is widely seen as a devotional text, and has been the subject of numerous retellings. As Phillip Lutgendorf (1989, 273) observes:

> Perhaps more than any other poem, the *Manas* functions as a script for cultural performance, reaching its largely illiterate audience thought such genres as ceremonial recitation (*path*); storytelling and oral exegesis (*katha*), and annual

---

8    Interestingly, some boatmen emphasized the difference between themselves and the *pandas* who have a notorious name in Banaras for their immoral behaviour and dishonest practices. See, for example, Havell, 2000 [1905] and Mehrotra, 1993.

9    Khevat, in this case a name, is also a term for a boatman/rower that derives from the verb *khena* – to row.

cycle of pageant plays (*Ramlila*), all of which continue to flourish and indeed proliferate in distinctively contemporary variants.

The following telling of the boatman episode (Khevat Prasang) is a fine example of the way in which a myth functions as a script for cultural performance. In this case the backdrop to the performance is a local setting, as boatmen consciously draw on the myth to reflect upon social life and construct their identity in a meaningful way.

Let me first recount the story as it was related to me by one boatman and is roughly similar to many of the other versions I heard during my fieldwork. Prince Rama (god incarnate), his brother Lakshmana and his wife Sita, recently banished into exile, arrive at the bank of the River Ganga. Upon arriving to the riverbank, Lord Rama summons Khevat (the boatman), and asks him to ferry them across to the other side. To Rama's surprise Khevat declines, unless Rama allows him to wash his feet. Khevat justifies his request by referring to the story of Ahalya, a beautiful woman, who was cursed by a sage and turned into a stone until she was restored to her human form by the sacred dust lacing the Lord's feet. The devoted Khevat realizes that if Rama touches his boat and it turns into a woman he will lose his livelihood. As Rama witnesses the commitment and devotion of the boatman,

**Figure 4.3**   **Colour Wall painting on Raj ghat, portraying the boatman (khevat) ferrying Lord Rama, Sita and Lakshmana across the Ganges.  On the top it is written, 'Sometimes even god depends on the services of devotees'**

he concedes. At the sight of Khevat washing Rama's feet all the gods of the Hindu pantheon shower flowers on the blessed boatman. Having washed God's feet with the sacred Ganga water, Khevat drinks it and distributes the rest of the water to his family. Khevat then ferries Lord Rama, Sita and Lakshmana across the river. Upon arrival on the other side Sita wants to pay the boatman his fee with all she has, her ring. The latter rejects her offer, saying to Rama: we are of the same profession, you carry people across the river of life (*samsara*) to the far shore of liberation (*moksha*) and I carry people from this bank of the river to the other side. A washerman never charges a fellow washerman. A barber does not take money from a fellow barber. Rama you are also a boatman (*tum bhi* Khevat), how can I charge you? When my day comes I ask only that you help me cross the river of life (*bahusagar*) to the far shore of liberation.

The myth itself is replete with devotional themes, with love and veneration of God, not knowledge, considered the ultimate path to liberation. This is further reinforced through the story of Ahalya, a woman who was graced by God. As Ramanujan (1991, 31) points out, 'her waking from the cold stone to fleshly human warmth, becomes an occasion for a moving *bhakti* (devotional) meditation on the soul waking to its form in god'. Likewise, the Khevat episode, portraying a low caste boatman's devotion to Lord Rama is suggestive of inclusive themes commonly found in devotional tradition. In the *Manas* such inclusion implies a purification of low castes incurred through contact with Rama (see also Hess 2001, 29). Khevat's washing of God's feet is symbolic, as it is considered a highly meritorious act. This was manifestly recognized by the gods who subsequently showered flowers on the devout boatman. Moreover, the act of the whole family drinking the water (*charan amrit*) suggests that all members of the community were also blessed and purified by God.

For the boatmen, the Khevat myth bears immense significance for their social identity and everyday life. The collective legitimatization of the boatmen as a community engaged in a god-sanctioned profession is evident both in the way boatmen retell the episode and their practice of their profession. When discussing the Khevat myth with several boatmen at Raj ghat, one concluded his telling of the myth saying, 'We are of the same community/caste [as Rama] and one Mallah will not take money from a member of his caste' (*hum ap ek biradry hai aur ek mallah dusra mallah se paisa nehi leta hai*).[10] Another boatman described the mythical reign of Rama (Ramraj) as one characterized by social justice and plenitude. For the boatmen the Khevat myth continues to have contemporary relevance as it signifies the transgression of their caste, so that the social degradation suffered under the caste system can no longer be justified after this event. As another boatman went on to explain, 'Previously we were considered a very low caste, people used to dig out the soil under which we sat and replace it with fresh soil, now we are respected

---

10    The episode has been popularized in the *bhajan* (devotional song) sung by Anoop Jalota (lyrics by pt. Ramchandra Bagora) called: 'Sometimes even the Lord depends on the services of devotees' (*kabhi kabhi Bhagwan ko bhi bhakto se kaam pare*).

**Figure 4.4     A wall painting of the episode from the Ramayana in which the boatman (Khevat) washes Lord Rama's feet, with Sita and Lakshman seated beside him, Bhadaini ghat**

by society'. Khevat's auspicious encounter with Rama marks a transformative event for the boatmen's collective social identity. For them the Khevat episode is evidence of their dignified roots and esteemed position within Hindu social order and religious tradition.

Such assertions by the boatmen are perhaps the most overt expression of their discontent and protest against caste ideology and local structures of domination. However, in order to further understand the subversive and manipulative potential that the Khevat myth holds, we must look at how it permeates the practice of everyday life and is articulated within the beliefs, ideas, attitudes and feelings of the boatman community in Banaras.

*The Cunning Khevat*

The narration, interpretation and appropriation of the Khevat myth informs the boatmen's everyday life, imbuing it with meaning and giving them a sense of their place in the world. Interestingly, while Khevat may be fortunate to have been blessed by Lord Rama, the way in which boatmen narrate the story highlights Khevat's agency in the encounter. I heard the story numerous times in my conversations with boatmen during my fieldwork, each one with slightly different inflections to suit contemporary sentiments. One of these tellings stood out when Khevat was referred to as *chalak* (calak), a word generally referring to a person who is 'active, quick, dexterous, clever, astute, cunning; vigilant' (McGregor 1993, 212). When I asked them to translate the word for me, one boatman said that Khevat's mention of the Ahalya incident in the story was, in reality, a ploy to gain access to Rama's feet. Another added that, while Khevat may have had practical concerns in mind, that is not losing his livelihood, he also wanted to fully exploit his encounter with God and please him. While I understood what they meant by Khevat 'tricking' God, it was not until I heard the story of how Khevat had previously failed in his attempt to reach God's feet, that I appreciated the full meaning of his devotional aspirations, as Santosh Nishad related to me:

> At that time Khevat was in his incarnation as a turtle. He wanted to reach the feet of Lord Vishnu who was taking rest in the Kshir Sagar (Ocean of Milk), lying on the Shesha Nag (the great Serpent god) and being massaged by Lakshmi. However, every time the turtle tried to get close to Vishnu's lotus feet the Shesha waved him off. Finally, Vishnu promised the turtle that he would meet him again during the incarnation of Ram. Now, Lakshman was the Nag and this is the reason why, when Khevat was summoned by Lakshman to ferry Ram, Sita and himself across the river Khevat refused. He knew that Lakshman would try to prevent him from touching God's feet and so he devised a plan.

Once again, in this telling the boatman is depicted as clever and calculating, but his intentions and acts are clearly motivated by his love and devotion to God. This ominous encounter with Lakshmana can be found in a booklet about the Khevat episode (see photo plates), narrated in the form of a devotional song (Kirtan) and widely available in the Bazaar and on the ghats of Banaras.[11] The following excerpt from the booklet follows an unpleasant standoff between Khevat and Lakshmana, who calls the boatman a 'crazy low caste fool' for refusing to ferry Lord Rama.

> Note - Dear devotees! The Lord becomes very sad upon hearing such words from His devotee and His brother and begins to ponder in His heart.
> Kirtan
>> 'Khevat and Lakshman have fought each other.
>> Now I am at a loss as to whom I should make prevail.
> Brother Lakhan [Lakshman] is my Sahodar (born from the same womb as I),
>> (yet) Khevat is also my devotee.
> All said and done, a devotee's devotion is the highest (noblest) thing in the world.
>> I shall say that which is right, after thinking it over first.
>> The love of one who serves (the Lord) is true
> and love contains phenomenal truth in side itself.'
>> Thinking this the Lord kept pondering in His heart.
>> 'Hear, Lakhan my words carefully.'
> Note - Dear devotees! The Lord, thinking thus, says to Lakhan as follows:

---

11    The way in which the episode is expounded in the booklet is reminiscent of those written by low caste political activists with an aim to increasing awareness and self respect among low castes across North India, see Narayan 2001.

Kirtan
>   This Khevat is not arrogant (Refrain)
>   I have nothing to do with caste; I am only interested in love.
> Irrespective of what one's caste, he who chants my name
> (I am with him)
>   I neither seek out fools nor wise men"
>   Says the Lord to Lakshman:
> 'I take people across the Bhava-sindhu (the vast, "oceanic" expanse of life on
> earth),
>   Hence I am a Mallah too.
>   I see everyone without discrimination (and) I do not care
> (about anyone's special qualities or privileges)
> Brother, do not speak words that would leave a lasting hurt.'
>   Says the Lord to Lakshman:
>   Love's greatness is eminent; love is the essence of this world.
>   I am unattainable without love (in one's heart),
>   and the whole world takes my name (calls out to me)[12]

In this bhakti-saturated account, Lakshmana's dismissal of Khevat serves to highlight the Brahminical view of caste as redundant for the true devotee prevails. When discussing the episode with boatmen, I was told that because Khevat refused payment (Sita's ring), the Lord remained forever in his debt. Another boatman concluded: "God resides in the devotee, and the devotee can even control God with his devotion" (*bhagwan, bhakt ke vash me rhete hai, aur bhakt bhagwan ko bhi vash mei kar leta hai*). The latter being a proverb I subsequently heard often in Banaras. Thus, the lowly boatman was able to manipulate and deploy clever tricks to win over the "powerful", and the godly.

Such cleverness or cunning (*chalak*) seems to enhance the character of Khevat.[13] That is, boatmen refer to his cleverness in a positive sense, in which Khevat's intentions and actions are wholly consistent with Hindu theology. Nevertheless, by exploiting the theme of devotion, boatmen creatively appropriate the myth to denote their dignified existence and elevate themselves in the caste hierarchy, inflecting it with their own aspirations, which eulogize the community and its morality. By recounting the story in this fashion boatmen make a clear statement about the legitimacy of their profession as valuable, commendable and indispensable. Further, the myth shows Khevat as a devoted, generous servant of the Lord himself – a quintessential quality in Hindu religious tradition.

The tactic of associating one's caste with a deity from time immemorial or from a mythical age to elevate its social status is of course a fairly common

---

12    The full 15-page version of the *Khevat Kirtan Anurag* was translated by myself and a translator from Hindi and Bhojpuri.

13    On the notion of cunning as a form of resistance, see Reed-Danahey 1993 and Scott 1990.

one in Hindu society (see Chapter 1). But Lord Rama referring to himself as a Mallah, highlights the parallel between Lord Rama's prerogative and their own calling, enabling them to define the boundaries of their community in terms of its sanctioned profession and its jurisdiction over the River Ganga. The important point to note here is that among Banaras boatmen such pan-Hindu symbols and beliefs have become not just a means of social legitimation but a way of explaining and defending their infiltration of the Brahmanical world of ritual – they too have a role sanctioned by the gods.

## Relationship with Ganga Ma

Another justification employed by the boatmen in support of their right to conduct rituals is their intimate association with Ganga Ma. Ganga Ma is an iconic symbol of Hindu civilization and national identity. As a river goddess, Ganga Ma embodies the universal qualities of virtue, high morality and purity, and she is venerated throughout the subcontinent (see Eck 1983; Kinsley 1986). She has also been used as a symbol of unity in independent India. In her discussion of the association between rivers, femininity and motherhood, Feldhaus (1995) suggests that rivers are commonly perceived by Hindus as places of fecundity, both in material and cultural terms. The River Ganga is also perceived as a mother who provides for all her children. Not surprisingly, therefore, the vows and rituals performed to Mother Ganga are often directed at shoring up family prosperity and welfare. Thus, we find that the offerings made in return for Mother Ganga's generosity and protection are usually ones seen as appropriate for a 'mother', such as saris and golden earrings (and even the symbolic sacrificing of children, as we shall see below). What is important to emphasize, though, is that the boatmen regard their relationship with Mother Ganga as unique and exclusive: that is, the River Ganga is perceived as *their* mother and provider not simply in ritual circumstances, but as part of their everyday encounters with the river. The river directly provides their food (fish and agricultural produce) and is their major source of livelihood (ferrying passengers). As such, the boatmen conceive their spiritual role (as her sons) in gendered and reciprocal terms. They believe they have been chosen to protect, guard and serve Mother Ganga. A brief examination of another life cycle ritual associated with the Ganges will further illustrate how the boatmen view their role in society and the ritual economy of Banaras.

Bachcha Khudana[14] is a ritual in which a young child (usually a boy) is offered to the river in an act of propitiation for Mother Ganga's help in the survival and wellbeing of the child as if he was her own (see also Feldhaus 1995, 122–6). The ritual involves throwing the child in midstream and his subsequent retrieval by a boatman. Thereafter the boatman returns the child to his family and receives credit in monetary and status terms. Apart from indicating a family's immense trust, faith

---

14   Literally, the term means 'causing the child to jump'.

and confidence in the boatmen, this ritual serves to reinforce the boatmen's own sense of place and identity. Boatmen regard the performance of this ritual as their *haq*; that is, they have a *moral obligation, duty* and *responsibility* to perform the ritual for the child, his family and Mother Ganga by virtue of their social/ritual identity. Such considerations also figure in what boatmen generally see as the demeaning aspects of their work – rituals associated with death – which involve the immersion of corpses and ashes into the River Ganga.

In Hinduism any association with death is polluting and carries social stigmas. Although the majority of bodies to be cremated in Banaras are taken to the main cremation ghats, occasionally dead bodies are brought to other ghats for immersion. Interestingly, despite the fact that boatmen often say that it is their *haq* (duty) to perform these tasks, in practice many boatmen, especially the more powerful *ghatwars*, avoid dealing with corpses personally, delegating the task to their *mallahis*. Others completely renounce their rights, preferring not to earn from such a stigmatized activity. In this way the more powerful *ghatwars* are able to assert a 'moral' and social supremacy over the weaker members of their community and present a 'cleaner' image, both to the rest of the community and to the outside world.[15]

Competition among the *ghatwars* has been fuelled, too, by changes in the city's riverscape economy, particularly by its rapidly growing tourist and pilgrimage industry. This has resulted in some boatmen becoming more prosperous than others, which in turn has enabled them to relinquish their rights to conduct death rituals. However, the economic changes taking place in the riverfront economy also mean that many boatmen feel less secure about the future of their livelihood. In this context, their assertion that plying boats on the river is their 'god-given' right by virtue of their inherent connection to Mother Ganga, is easily understood. Such claims are a way for the boatmen to gain broad social recognition and justify their maintaining a monopoly over river transportation and the more lucrative and respectable rituals associated with the Ganges, such as the Ganga Pujaiya.

The boatmen use the name Gangaputras (sons of the Ganga) to further declare themselves as a particularly privileged group of people closely associated with the river. As previously mentioned, however, the name Gangaputras is a contested one. Brahmin priests who live on the riverbank in Banaras also claim this name and refuse to acknowledge the boatmen's claim to this title. The boatmen often say that they are the original Gangaputras and have been since time immemorial. The name also figures in their caste journals as one of the numerous names of the

---

15    These perceptions and practices related to death appear consistent with studies done by Parry (1994) and van der Veer (1988) concerning gift giving in North Indian sacred centres between priests their patrons (*jajmans*) and the sins, impurities and moral perils associated with these gifts (*dan*). Such considerations further undermine the textbook understanding of Brahminical purity and supremacy within the caste system, particularly in the case of those officiating priests involved in the mortuary rites (Mahabrahmans) which are considered extremely degraded and relatively inferior to other Brahmins.

Mallah/Nishad caste. This can be interpreted, not only as overt contestation of priestly authority in Banaras, but as reclaiming their lost and suppressed origins and rights, which according to several boatmen, have been deliberately hidden by Brahmin priests and the authorities over the years.

One interview I conducted with a Brahmin (not a priest) and his wife after a Ganga Pujaiya ritual attests to the important role of the boatmen in the ceremonies.

> Q: Are the Mallahs like pandits (priests)?
> A: Yes, during particular times when they do Pujaiya for the boat, they are the *karndar* (steersmen and boatmen) and the *khevia* (a rower, boatman) of Gangaji.

> Q: How is it that the boatmen can bless a bride with a child and apply *tilak*?
> A: Because they are the *karndar* of Ganga and live on the bank they are considered the biggest devotees of Gangaji. That is the reason we ask the boatmen to give us *prasad* and bless us and to 'fill the lap' of a bride and ensure further happiness in the family.

> Q: So are they Gangaputras?
> A: No they are not, they try to prove it and force people to believe it, but to us Brahmins they will never say they are Gangaputras because we know they are not. But to those who don't know the truth, that is what they claim, and they prove it by referring to the Ramayana and the story of Khevat to show their importance and then they can ask for more *dakshina*.

From this account we can see the complexity of social interaction reflecting the ambiguous nature of social hierarchy. It is also evident that the boatmen do not operate in an autonomous subaltern domain separate from that of the priests. The fact that both Brahmins and boatmen share the same social space, and operate with similar gestures and mantras 'should suggest that the subaltern self [is] constantly in the process of production, mediated through symbols and processes both internal and external to the subaltern's moral and physical domain' (Sivaramakrishnan 1995, 405). In other words, the subversion of Brahminical authority is premised upon shared history and cultural codes, which are instrumental in the negotiation of power.

**Competing over Ritual Space**

To assure me that they legitimately operate as priests, the boatmen frequently cited the example of the Shitla Ma (goddess of Smallpox) temple, about 25 kilometres outside Banaras along the river. The goddess, Shitla Ma, is associated with common afflictions such as disease and human misfortune. Her worship is less elaborate and often involves witchcraft and other folklore practices. The practices in the temple of Shitla Ma confirm this assertion, but closer examination reveals other economic and political facets to the worship of the goddess. According to the lore of the boatmen/fishermen of the area, the image of the goddess that now adorns the temple was fished out of the water by their caste ancestors. Initially it was installed in a small shrine on the riverbank. However it seems that goddess was not happy with this arrangement, for she appeared to the boatmen in their dreams and demanded that they build a proper temple for her. The boatmen duly followed the godly injunction and the temple soon became a centre of worship for pilgrims from all over the district – bringing much money and offerings in kind to the boatman community. Not surprisingly the Brahmin priests of the area soon began to challenge the boatmen's right to officiate worship at the sacred site. But the boatmen refused to give way and not long ago there was a violent confrontation in which several boatmen and priests were killed. The matter is currently in court, but for now, the boatmen have been granted the sole right to perform rituals at the temple.

Apart from demonstrating how low caste/class peasants have challenged and resisted Brahminical domination, this incident offers other important insights. First, the ritual performance acts as a legitimizing device for the Mallahs; secondly, it shows that legitimacy derives not only from the classic (pan-Hindu) religious traditions, but also from the state; and finally, that caste/class conflicts are not caused by 'religious', 'cultural' or 'economic' factors acting in isolation, but by all three interacting dynamically.

*Indigenous Categories and Contested Pasts*

In his seminal article on temple politics in South India, Arjun Appadurai (1981b), and (1981b, 204) dispenses with sociological constructs and proposes an examination of an indigenous set of norms 'within which the charters of specific subgroups are constructed, defended and mutually evaluated' (1981b, 204). Just as Appadurai argues in relation to the South Indian temple, we have seen that there are different sources (textual and non-textual) that groups refer to when seeking to justify their authority and credibility for the charter in question. It is true that the authority of the classic religious cannon is imperative. However, documents reaffirming a group's authority, antiquity and legitimacy are not limited to the religious authority. In fact, more recent legal documentation from the colonial and postcolonial period is also of great importance to all parties involved in conflicts over ritual space and struggles for livelihood.

In our case it is difficult to trace exactly how and when the boatmen gained official recognition as ritual specialists in Banaras. Nevertheless it appears that, in seeking legal authority for their rights, the boatmen have followed a strikingly similar pattern to that of Brahmin and other higher-caste groups during the colonial period. In colonial writings there is clear evidence of competition among Brahmin groups over rights to conduct rituals and take shares in the offerings made by pilgrims on the ghats. The *Benares District Gazetteer* mentions the Gangaputras (Brahmin) as the most prominent group, noting that on several occasions they were challenged in the courts with respect to their monopoly over ritual rights on the ghats (Nevill 1909, 69–71). This is especially significant since formal recognition in places like the 'census, gazetteers, reports...came to represent the power of official discourse to name and fix the status of caste groups in local mindsets' (Das 2003, 10). Yet this colonial documentation does not mention the boatmen as one of the groups vying for control over the sacred space of the river or their role in the ritual economy of Banaras. As we have already seen, boatmen were classified officially as a criminal caste, which inevitably damaged their credibility and limited their access to official institutions. This may be one of the reasons why the boatmen's voices hardly figure in colonial records. Other reasons may include the fact that colonial perceptions of Indian society relied heavily on the views of Brahmin scholars, who were regarded by the British as the actual guardians of religious knowledge and practice in India, and the fact that Brahmin priests were the main custodians of the family genealogical records (*jajmans*) served as 'hard' evidence for caste claims in courts of law.

Although the boatmen state that it is their god-given right and privilege to conduct rituals on the riverscape, they add that these 'immemorial' rights have also been recognized and ratified by the government and, more recently, by the courts; and they claim that Ashish Manjhi, one of the most powerful and wealthy boatmen in Banaras who operates 25 boats on the main ghat, has the papers to prove it. This latter claim, at least, is true. In 1968 the chief civil court of Banaras ruled in Manjhi's favour in a case brought by him against the ghat priests. This decision set a precedent by formally recognizing the boatmen's rights as ritual specialists. Furthermore, while the court settlement awarded the priests from the ghat the right to pocket any items and money offered to them by worshippers on the ghat, it granted to Manjhi (and by implication his brother boatmen) all items designed for the worship of Ganga Ma (i.e., the river).[16] These rights are not yet set in stone. Nonetheless, as one lawyer told me, the very fact that a boatman has managed to produce a series of documents dating from the mid-twentieth century and stamped by the court's approval is valuable. It serves as a formal recognition of their customary rights to ply boats on the river and conduct rituals on the ghat and may provide the basis for refuting possible challenges from ghat priests in the future. Moreover, these documents have been useful in preventing boatmen – a conflicted and fractious group – from attempting to encroach on one another's territory. This is relevant to the frequent disputes over territory and passenger distribution discussed in the previous chapter.

Unlike the violent case concerning the Shitla Ma temple, here a boatman managed to establish his rights as a ritual specialist by reaching a negotiated settlement in court. The fact that the conflict was resolved and the position of

---

16   'The State v. Mata Prasad', Suit no.323 (1968), the Court of Civil Judge, Varanasi.

boatman subjugation mitigated, enabled a certain level of cooperation between the boatmen and ghat priests.

During my time in Banaras I did not see or hear of any disputes regarding Ganga Pujaiya on any of the major ghats in Banaras. In fact, there appears to be a degree of cooperation between the 'dominated' and the 'dominant'. On the major ghats the priests and boatmen share an elaborate secret language designed to communicate information regarding the economic status of pilgrims which allows them to maximize their asking price. Crossing the river costs on average between Rs.30 and Rs.50 per trip, whereas for ritual services the fees charged can exceed Rs.800, a total that does not include the offerings of gold earrings and other precious items that are routinely made to the river goddess – which begs the question of why the customers tolerate these hefty exactions.[17] There are several reasons. First, the Ganga Pujaiya is an auspicious occasion (a life-cycle event) where the newlyweds and their families are expected to provide generous payment to those serving them. Second, as we have seen, ritual boating is different from everyday boating as it empowers the boatmen to make certain claims over offerings made by the family and to use 'priestly' techniques for drawing money. Finally, on some ghats, there is a different system of passenger distribution for rituals (*pari*), which eliminates competition from other boatmen and allows boating prices to be very high. One could also argue, as do some locals, that the boatmen charge a high price for rituals simply because they can, and they can because their role as ritual specialists is socially and legally recognized.

The Banaras boatmen are watchful of anyone attempting to encroach upon their livelihood. The so-called 'dominated' needle is ever sharp. As already mentioned, according to the authorities, anyone can ply a boat and carry passengers on the river provided he has a licence to do so. Yet by restricting the trade to caste members possessing hereditary rights of access to the river, the boatmen have managed to repel repeated attempts from both outsiders and caste insiders to impinge on their livelihood. Thus, while caste is quickly brought to the fore when the boatmen need to reassert their role as ritual specialists against the priests, occupational identity becomes more prominent when disputes take place within the boatman community itself.


**Conclusion**

In this chapter I have discussed how rituals conducted by the boatmen of Banaras serve to empower the boatmen and interrupt priestly authority and, at the same time, reinforce their right to ply boats and operate as ritual specialists on the River Ganga. A number of issues of wider concern frame this chapter. The first relates to the overemphasis of the role of myth and ritual practice as a means to stabilize

---

17     During high season the average weekly income of a boatman working on one of the major ghats may range between Rs.400 and Rs.600.

and ensure the harmonious and integrated social order. Such interpretations, I have argued, inhibit nuanced and meaningful analysis of the discourse and practices of the Banaras boatmen, their clients and others engaged in the world of the ghats.

My second concern is with some aspects of 'resistance literature' that seek to highlight the agency of subordinate populations. Such literature harbours a potentially rich critique of the overly determined functional and symbolic models, furthering our understanding of politically sensitive issues, involving caste prejudice and relations of domination in the heart of Hindu India. However, in this case study I have sought to demonstrate that the boatmen should not be viewed as simply dispossessed subalterns operating in an independent domain and resisting Brahminical domination. My examination of the ritual practices involving boatmen, priests and other local actors shows that power relations exist both within and outside the boatman community. Thus, one finds that within the river economy boatmen are both dominated and dominant. They may contest Brahminical order and authority, yet at the same time imitate it and draw their strategic positioning from it. Boatmen continually construct their identity by selectively drawing from a variety of sources to empower themselves in relation to others. Moreover, claims over rights and control of sacred space do come from 'below'.

Indeed, boatmen are aware of their precarious position and are therefore at pains to emphasize their own dignified and valued status within the ritual economy of Banaras. As I have shown, they do so by highlighting their role in the Ramayana epic and proclaiming themselves as the 'true' Gangaputras. This is revealing of the complexity of their social life and the nature of their struggle. While the link between caste and occupation is fast dissolving across urban India, the Banaras boatmen seek to firmly maintain it; albeit by positioning themselves in a more distinguished position. For them, emphasizing their privileged connection to the river has both symbolic and practical consequences. Boatmen may reject certain elements in the ritual and caste hierarchy that label them lowly and impure, but at the same time strategically operate within the system itself to elevate their community status.

On a recent visit to Banaras I was amazed to see one of the most visible and central temples on the main ghat, which has been inoperative for years, renovated and occupied by a powerful boatman family from the ghat. This is certainly the most overt claim over sacred space and transgression of the Brahminical ritual domain that I have heard of in Banaras. Of course, as the boatman in charge related to me with dismay, his act has not been uncontested by local priests, with the latter lobbying the authorities in order to prevent him from re-establishing the temple. The boatman, however, has legal papers to prove his rightful ownership of the temple. His sons have since inaugurated the temple, conducting an elaborate and impressive worship: a clear display of their economic wealth and social status. No priests were invited to the event, although ironically, the boatmen presiding over the ritual wore the traditional attire of Brahmin priests and closely followed Brahminical ritual prescriptions. The temple has since been functional. Outside it is a large, almost life-size picture depicting Khevat ferrying Rama, Sita and

Lakshmana; with the name of the temple written above (Bhuneswar Mahadev) and the name of the ghat below (Prayag ghat). It is important to emphasize, however, that while such actions clearly subvert priestly authority, Banaras' ritual economy is still very much organized around the governing principles and values associated with orthodox religion. Boatmen are well aware of that and this, I would argue, is precisely the reason why the picture of Khevat is displayed in so many places along the ghats. Plying boats is thus seen and depicted not simply as manual labour, it is a vocation – a constant reminder to locals and pilgrims alike that boatmen occupy an important role in the 'sacred crossing' place of Banaras.

Chapter 5

# The Romance of Banaras: Boatmen, Pilgrims and Tourists

## The Tourist-cum-Anthropologist

As mentioned in the introduction to this book, my interest in tourism and the role of culture brokers, in part, derives from my own experiences as a frequent visitor to India under various guises: initially as a traveller, then as a tour guide and eventually as an anthropologist. Clearly, these 'shifting identities', to use Crick's term (1989), are not mutually exclusive. Moreover, my personal experiences as a traveller and tour guide provided me with a more emic perspective regarding tourist sensibilities and the way in which the tourist industry operates in India and Banaras in particular. Equally important, however, is to reflect on how such experiences influenced my work as an anthropologist and the often unconscious methodological implications this had for both the fieldwork and the writing of my research.

As an anthropologist I often felt the need to shed what I considered to be the 'superficial skin' of my tourist identity. While in the field, I found that the anthropological rite of passage, namely fieldwork (involving participant observation and learning the language), was indeed (or so I thought) an attempt to establish clear boundaries between myself and other tourists. Consequently, I spent most of my time in the field engaging with boatmen and other locals working on the ghats. For the boatmen, however, these two identities (tourist and anthropologist) were not necessarily incongruent – I was both. Although I did not conceal my third identity – that of tour guide – the matter was seldom discussed with boatmen. This was for a practical reason; I ceased working as a tour guide in 2000. In addition, I did not want to give the misleading impression that I could help boatmen in their business with my influence in the industry. Once again, this reflected my own insecurities at possibly being appropriated by boatmen for instrumental gain. Due to distancing myself from my tourist identity, my initial interaction with tourists was limited. It was not until the later stages of my research that I realized I had much more information regarding how boatmen perceive and interact with tourists, than about the tourists' own perspectives regarding boatmen. Interestingly, it proved much more difficult to break these imaginary barriers and engage with the tourists who frequent the ghats than I initially thought. Curiously enough, in my efforts to cross the boundaries I found myself operating in a similar manner to that of the boatmen. My interactions with tourists were generally brief and instrumental in nature. Another area of overlap between myself and some of the boatmen surfaced more clearly in the process of writing the ethnography, when

I discovered that we are both engaged in brokering, or translating, Banaras and its culture for others, whether for tourists or academics.

In this chapter I explore how boatmen mediate and broker Banaras and the riverscape for visitors to the city, including pilgrims, domestic tourists and foreign tourists. The first part of the chapter looks at the encounter between boatmen and pilgrims. It examines how, by drawing on their long experience with pilgrims, boatmen have developed a range of skills (leadership, communication, manipulation) to mediate the city for the visitors. This examination also illustrates how the boatmen have been able to translate and adapt such skills to the context of international tourism. The second part of this chapter focuses on the way tourists perceive Banaras in terms of their motivations, needs and wants. It begins by charting the historical background of travel and tourism to India and continues with a 'snapshot' of the various kinds of tourists who visit Banaras and their experiences and encounters with boatmen. Part three focuses on how boatmen themselves view tourists and looks at the strategies and tactics they have developed to satisfy the needs and desires of their foreign patrons and channel them to their advantage.

**Tourism and the Third World**

Contemporary studies of tourism in the 'Third World' have often sought to situate the uneven power relations embedded in tourism within the larger forces of world systems, globalization and nation building strategies (Markula 1997; Nash 1989; Palmer 1994, Wood 1997). Many of these studies have noted the far reaching economic, cultural and environmental consequences of tourism on local populations. Accordingly, there is an emphasis on the relations of domination informing guest-host encounters at the local level, in which, much like imperialism, wealthy Western tourists travel in search of the exotic. The tourists are then served and catered for by local communities who become increasingly dependent on their business (Bruner 1991; Silver 1993). In addition, such studies tend to privilege the guests as the purveyors of change, while the creative and innovative practices of the host group are rendered invisible.

A similar line of inquiry focuses on tourism and the process of commoditization, whereby tourists consume indigenous culture, which is often mediated for them through various institutions and people (Greenwood 1977; van den Bergh 1980). While such studies still maintain the view that tourism reproduces an asymmetrical power relationship between guests and hosts, attention is drawn to an intermediate group, generally called 'middlemen' or 'culture brokers', who operate outside the provisional categories of 'guest' and 'host' (Cohen 1982; 1985; Crick 1994, 162–3 ; Nash 1989). This category of mediators generally includes governments, guidebooks, travel agencies, tour guides, travel writers and people involved in the transportation industry.

More recently, scholars have argued for the need to consider the role of mediators as central to the development and promotion of the contemporary tourism business

(Chambers 2000, 11; Werner 2003, 2). Cynthia Werner notes that certain common tourist tropes are often replicated by mediators who seek to entice the tourist to their countries. Thus, local tour operators actively promote a romantic vision of the 'natives' in order to tap into tourists' desires. Local people are portrayed as leading a life steeped in tradition surrounded by natural landscapes and unaffected by the onslaught of modernity. Werner's analysis ultimately supports the argument that tourist marketing (whether promoted from abroad or at home) continues to condition and prescribe the terms of engagement between tourists and hosts. It involves the deployment of the dominant tourist discourse, which, emanating from Western countries, serves to reproduce a series of Orientalist tropes, largely produced and disseminated by the travel industry and media as well as travel talk (see Bhattacharyya 1997; Echtner & Prasad 2003). Although local elites are given agency and demonstrate a degree of control in the tourist discourse, subaltern locals involved in the tourist trade remain compliant. Thus, according to such accounts, locals have no choice but to adhere to the tourist discourse propagated by local elites who predominantly occupy the mediator positions in the tourist industry. Once again such an analysis suggests passivity on the part of the local people and dismisses or overlooks any ability they might have to counter and adapt to changes brought about by the dominant tourist discourse.

As I demonstrate in this chapter, the boatmen's role as culture brokers indicates that they are not simply passive recipients of the tourist discourse. I argue that it is on an interpersonal level that the dominant tourist discourse emerging from First World countries is often creatively appropriated, subverted and manipulated by marginal groups, such as the boatmen, to further their own economic and social interests. Thus, my contention is that the existence of uneven power relations does not necessarily entail the subordination and passivity of the 'other'. Indeed, as we shall see, the dominant tourist discourse is employed by boatmen; not only to differentiate between different categories of visitors, but also to enhance what might be called cultural service delivery for these visitors. This can be seen when we leave aside binary models that focus solely on the consequences of tourism on local populations and instead examine the actual ways in which individuals and groups relate to each other at the local level within the social spaces that Pratt (1988) identifies as 'contact zones'.[1]

---

1     The concept of 'contact zones' is described by Pratt (1988) as the 'social spaces where disparate cultures meet, clash and grapple with each other, often in highly asymmetrical relations of domination and subordination' (Pratt 1988, 4). For Pratt, whose main focus is travel writing during the colonial period, the notion of 'contact zones' provides a way of avoiding the binary categories that suggest a spatial and temporal separation between colonized and colonizer. Rather, she seeks to 'foreground the interactive, improvisational dimensions of colonial encounters so easily ignored by diffusionist accounts of conquest and domination' (1988, 7). For an insightful analysis of travel culture in India that employs Pratt's concepts of 'contact zones', see Matthiesson (1999).

## Touring the City of Banaras: The Boatmen as Mediators

The majestic setting of the holy city of Varanasi has for centuries captured the imagination of both pilgrims and foreign visitors. Among the plethora of books, travelogues and pictorial accounts portraying the city, one recent local publication clearly stands out. This comic book, written in English, is aptly titled: *A Pilgrimage to Kashi: History, Mythology and Culture of the Strangest and most Fascinating City in India* (Gol 1999). The comic scenes, illustrated in cartoon, provide a reliable and amusing take on the city's cultural, historical and social settings. Central to this beautifully crafted work is a boat ride on the River Ganga, employed as a narrative device through which the reader is introduced to the city.

The narrative follows the experiences of a middle-upper class Hindu family from Mumbai, that has come to the city to spread the ashes of a deceased relative. Upon their arrival at the train station the family is met by uncle Virendra who is a resident of Banaras. The uncle suggests a boat ride as the quickest and most convenient way to see the city. By making a pilgrimage along the river they will also be able to visit the major sacred bathing ghats. The family arrives at Assi ghat at sunrise to hire a boat. There they are promptly approached by a boatman. What follows is a comic description of the customary haggling between boatman and client. The family is then taken on the boat where Uncle Virendra explains the history and myths associated with the city, the ghats and the river. Thus, as the boat ride proceeds the reader is given a comprehensive view (through illustrations)

**Figure 5.1    A pilgrimage to Kashi (Banaras)**

*Source*: Gol (1999)

and explanation (through speech captions) of the sacred complex of Banaras. Familiar river scenes are shown as the boat ride progresses, such as a cow carcass floating in the river, the renowned cremation ghats and locals, as well as people performing ritual ablutions. Additional scenes show a boat packed with foreign tourists, suitably depicted wearing modern clothes and absorbed in photographing and filming the exotic scenery of the riverfront, as well as two young local men on the ghat attempting to initiate a conversation with two female backpackers.

**Figures 5.2 and 5.3   A pilgrimage to Kashi (Banaras) continued**
*Source*: GoI (1999)

**Figure 5.4	A pilgrimage to Kashi (Banaras)** *concluded*

Throughout the boat ride the boatman's explanations are equally informative, although they often differ from the uncle's classic view of the city. Thus, when uncle Virendra declares: 'The magnetism of sacred Banaras attracts great numbers of saintly men and women'; the boatman brazenly adds: 'Not only saints, the town is also full of crooks'. As the boat ride continues uncle Virendra becomes increasingly frustrated by the boatman, saying: 'This know-it-all boatman is getting on my nerves'. The constant interruptions with the boatman undermine the uncle's authoritative explanations. Finally, Uncle Virendra erupts and tells him to 'Shut up!'. Apart from the terse response of the uncle, the comic is instructive in several ways. First, it offers a condensed and amplified version of scenes from everyday life in Banaras (see McCloud 1994). Second, it shows that boatmen offer services beyond the strictly functional. That is, mediating the city for foreign and domestic visitors and thus operating as culture brokers. Third, it shows boatmen articulating their own representations of Banaras and local culture (in this case) at odds with those of local elites, who serve as the standard (designated) culture brokers.

**Interaction with Pilgrims**

There are a number of ways in which boatmen engage with pilgrims in the role of culture brokers. They perform a range of services, from the purely functional, (i.e., transport, taking people from one place to another) to activities less connected to boating, such as organizing hotel accommodation, arranging music lessons and taking pilgrims/tourists shopping. As mentioned previously, the city of Banaras has been a major centre of pilgrimage for more than two millennia. Since the advent of railroads built during the colonial period and improved communication networks across the subcontinent, pilgrimage in India has expanded markedly. Contemporary pilgrimage is organized in the style of package tours. Pilgrims (many of them villagers from all over India) may visit more than twenty holy sites across the country in as many days. Such haste means that pilgrims generally stay in Banaras for no more than one day. After spending a night or two in Banaras the typical pilgrimage package tours will continue on to the next destination, often Gaya or Allahabad/Prayag. The primary pilgrim destination in Banaras is the holy Vishvanath temple, easily accessed from Lalita ghat. Other stops commonly found on the Banaras pilgrims' programme are the major sacred bathing ghats, such as Manikarnika, Dashashvamedh, and Assi ghat. These ghats also serve as stopover points where pilgrims can continue to other temples within the city. Assi ghat is often a major stopping point for pilgrims, who walk on foot (barefoot) to take *darshan* (auspicious site) at several temples located nearby, such as Tulsi Manas Mandir, Durga Temple or the Sankat Mochan Temple. Less often, pilgrims venture on boats up river to Ramnagar, where the Maharaja's palace is located. Boats are therefore extremely useful as they provide the fastest and most convenient form of transport from site to site. In the past decade more boatmen have begun operating motorboats (as opposed to rowboats only) to accommodate the needs of these numerous pilgrims, due to the brief duration of their visits.

Some pilgrims coming to the city are connected to, and reside with a hereditary priest (*tirth puruhit*), while others reside in the numerous pilgrim hostels (*dharamsalas*) across the city. Both priests and hostels make the necessary arrangements for the pilgrims to visit the essential sacred sites. Boatmen may receive passengers through their connections with pilgrim hostels and hereditary Brahmin priests. On some ghats pilgrim groups are assigned to respective boatmen according to a rotation system (*pari*). Pilgrims, often travelling in small groups, who are not affiliated with any institution or person acting on their behalf, are much more vulnerable to local chicanery (see Parry 1994). Upon arriving at the main ghat area (Dashashvamedh ghat) they are closely monitored by boatmen and local ghat priests. These ghat functionaries have developed an elaborate secret language designed to communicate in coded terms the socio-economic status of pilgrims and the potential for economic gain from them. As we shall see, such practices of observing and objectifying visitors are significant for understanding tourist-host relations. In the case of mass pilgrim package tours, their local affiliations make the pilgrims less susceptible to such trickery. Time limitations mean they follow a tight itinerary adhering to a commonly prescribed route consisting of worship at the major temples and bathing ghats.

The boatmen have the closest interaction with these groups of pilgrims as their services extend beyond providing transport and include services similar to those of a tour guide. Following Cohen (1985), it is useful to examine the role of tour guides as leaders and mediators. Cohen identifies instrumental and social components of leadership. The instrumental component includes a tour guide's duty to ensure the 'smooth accomplishment of the tour'. The social component refers to the guide's 'responsibility for the cohesion and morale of the touring party' (Cohen 1985, 11–12). We see the instrumental mode when boatmen fulfil their roles of leading pilgrims safely to and from places of worship and ensuring no one drowns or slips while bathing in the river. The social mode is visible when boatmen prompt the pilgrim party to shout familiar slogans, such as 'Ganga Ma ki – Jay' (Victory to Mother Ganga) or 'Hara Hara Mahadev' (Hail Lord Shiva), thus creating and contributing to a feeling of excitement, elation and expectation among the pilgrims.

Cohen further suggests a division between interactional and communicative elements as aspects of mediation. The first denotes the guide's role as 'middleman between his party and the local population, sites and institutions' (Cohen 1985, 13). The communicative element applies to the tour guide's task as culture broker, drawing attention to, interpreting and explaining places of interest for the visitor. Such activities may 'have manipulative significance' given that the information provided 'is rarely purely neutral' (Cohen 1985:14–15). Both types of mediation apply to the boatmen as informal tour guides.

Operating as unauthorized tour guides, boatmen cross the boundaries between what has often been called the formal and informal sectors in the pilgrimage/ tourist industry. On the one hand their profession squarely falls within the ambit of the formal sector, as they are registered and licensed to carry passengers. On the other hand, the nature of their work features some of the characteristics commonly attributed to the informal sector. Their boating businesses are small and family owned. Boatmen are relatively poor, as are many of those working in the sector. This generates a highly competitive environment, where people employ a range of innovative skills, usually acquired outside formal institutions, to eke out a living.

One example of such a skill is the practical knowledge of the major Indian languages spoken by pilgrims gained through informal learning and years of experience. The same is true of the manner in which they selectively impart information about various sites along the riverfront. On one occasion when I joined a group of pilgrims from the western state of Maharashtra, one of the boatmen stopped the motorboat and ceremoniously pointed towards Ram ghat. In a mixture of Marathi-Hindi he informed the pilgrims of the ghat's religious significance in an excited tone. 'This is the very ghat where Lord Rama and Sita (his wife) departed on a boat to perform a pilgrimage (*yatra*), just as you are doing'. He then briefly narrated the story, duly emphasizing that, following the legendary boat ride where the boatman offered his humble services to Lord Rama, who in return blessed the boatman (Khevat) and gave him a donation (*dan*) for his service and devotion. The boatman then took out a brass pot, filled it with auspicious river water (Ganga jal), and began sprinkling the pilgrims while imploring them to make a similar offering themselves: '*Khevat dan dena; Khevat dan dena*' (give a donation to the boatman), blessing those who put coins into the golden pot. The boatman was in this way able to collect Rs.170 – a considerable sum.

Here the boatman suggests a parallel between Lord Rama's mythical pilgrimage and that of the pilgrims, to his advantage. Pilgrims are not unaware of such tactics, however, and some remarked upon his craftiness. Despite this, most felt compelled to donate some coins.[2] Such practices are akin to what Appadurai (1990, 101) calls 'coercive subordination'. For example, a practice where the subordinate (in the extreme case, beggars) bless and praise 'their (potential) benefactors' trapping them in 'the cultural implication of their roles as superiors, that is, in the obligation to be generous'. It is important to note, however, that for the boatmen a position of subordination is assumed strategically. In their capacity as culture brokers boatmen also assume a position of authority when guiding pilgrims, selectively informing them about the city.

The popular scene of the encounter between Khevat and Rama is found in various posters, available throughout the city's bazaars, which boatmen paste to their boats. Thus, they connect 'the place with the story', similar to what Hawley (1981, 25) describes in his account of the *pandas* of Vrindhavan. While such explicit depictions of the role of Khevat provide the preamble for pilgrims to embark on their pilgrimage, it is in watching boatmen perform this role that one gains a sense of how they manipulate the mythological narrative to their own advantage.

Nevertheless, the boatmen's performance should not be viewed simply as salesmanship or a selling ploy; it holds further importance and efficacy for all those involved when the 'performance arena' is taken into consideration. By acting out the role as Khevat, boatmen consciously draw on common images, metaphors, symbols, values and experiences consistent with Hindu tradition. In fact, many of the pilgrims themselves perceive their own pilgrimage as a re-enactment of a sacred journey. When I inquired amongst pilgrims as to why they perform the pilgrimage, common answers included, 'for the name/sake of Ram'(*Ram ke nam par*) and 'to cross the ocean of life' (*bahosagar se par hone ke liye*) or 'for salvation' (*ud-dhar ke liye*).[3] Many added that they intended to carry holy Ganga water (*Ganga jal*) home for the benefit of their families.[4]

---

2    Such behaviour seems to reinforce Gold (1988) and Parry's (1994) observations regarding pilgrims' expectations from their encounters and engagements with those 'predatory' ritual specialists who occupy pilgrimage centres. Parry, who supports Gold's view about the perceived merit inherent to such unpleasant exchanges, adds that in Banaras the greedy priests' actions constitute an essential part of the pilgrimage experience. As his metaphorical account suggests: 'The pilgrim is (quite explicitly) a temporary renouncer; his pilgrimage an act of *tapasya* (an ascetic austerity). Priestly rapacity is (implicitly) part of his bed of nails and the more painful the renunciation, the greater its spiritual "fruit"' (1994, 121).

3    Other common answers were to fulfill a vow (*manauti*), or for the sake of the ancestors.

4    In my conversations with pilgrims visiting Banaras about their motivations for performing the *yatra* (pilgrimage), *moksha* and taking *darshan* were recurring themes, see

Respectively, boatmen reaffirm the view that the pilgrims are partaking in a divine journey and must therefore be treated with respect. They pride themselves in being responsible for the pilgrims' safety and security during their journey. For example, boatmen claim to always cast a keen eye across the ghats to make sure that when pilgrims perform ritual ablutions their belongings are kept safe. On one of my excursions with a pilgrimage group, the boatmen warned his passengers before they left the boat about the overcrowded alleys leading to the Vishvanath Mandir (Shiva's Golden Temple), telling them to mind their belongings and walk in a straight line. He ended with a proverb: 'Remember, where there are crowds, you will find god and where god resides demons (*raksha*) also dwell'.

The boatmen's role as informal guides should not be underestimated. They play a vital role in directing pilgrims to various temples, minding their belongings and providing them access to religious paraphernalia and souvenirs. Such advice and direction serves to establish a degree of trust, much needed for the smooth operation of a tour. Establishing such trust is an indirect way of gaining control and exercising manipulation, which boatmen are careful to exploit, for example, when taking pilgrims to certain shops (from which they receive commission) en route to temples.[5] Gopal, a boatman from the main ghat explained the techniques of manipulating pilgrims as ageless, a matter of using one's wits.

> It's very simple really, we even did the same thing to Lord Ram, so with humans it is not so difficult. The boatman was very clever when he ferried Ram, Sita and Lakshman across the river because he refused to take the ring from Sitaji as payment for his services. At the beginning Lord Ram was confused but then understood and embraced the boatman who won his heart. Ramchandraji was charmed by the boatman's talk. If you are looking for an honest boatman you won't find one, even Lord Ram could not. You may also be tricked, beware!

The above discussion shows some of the skills and strategies employed by boatmen (e.g., leadership, communication, manipulation), and illustrates the agency that underpins their interactions with pilgrims. Likewise, boatmen interact with a variety of visitors to the city, including domestic and foreign tourists;

---

also Gold (1988).

5    As in other pilgrimage cities in India, Banaras has a variety of facilities and services catering for the needs and wants of pilgrims. Along the routes to the major pilgrimage attractions and next to temples are numerous shops and stalls selling ritual paraphernalia. There are also additional items along these routes to entice the pilgrim, ranging from cheap souvenirs, glossy pictures of the gods, toys, pots of holy Ganga water, beads and brassware, to expensive cloth and the famous Banaras silk *saris*. The boatmen who guide the groups through the alleys of Banaras receive a commission from the shop owners' takings. This may amount to a small sum, such as that received from the *phulwalla* (flower vendor) who sells items for worship, such as flowers, rice and coconuts or it may be a substantial amount in the case of *sari* shops.

and each set of relationships demonstrates the diverse ways in which boatmen exercise agency. In the following section I examine some of the differences that exist between pilgrims and tourists visiting the city, in terms of their needs, wants and expectations, to demonstrate the shifting strategies employed by boatmen to advance their own needs and aims. I then go on to give a brief account of colonial perceptions of Banaras to provide a historical background to contemporary tourist perceptions and practices. Distinctions between the needs and practices of Banaras pilgrims and tourists (domestic and foreign), as well as between colonial and contemporary tourists, will be drawn on in order to highlight the ways in which boatmen creatively adapt their strategies to different contexts.

## Perceptions of Banaras

Tourists can be roughly divided into three categories: package holiday tourists, domestic tourists and foreign backpackers.[6] Boatmen have more to do with the latter two categories since package tours have private formal guides and their boat rides booked in advance. Applying the category of domestic tourism to the Indian context is somewhat problematic because it is often hard to clearly distinguish between pilgrimage and tourism. Nevertheless, there are some distinct characteristics that are worth noting. Domestic tourists largely come from the socially mobile urban middle class of Indian society and generally visit Banaras for longer periods than pilgrims (several days). They often travel in small groups (such as families), coming to the city during national holidays. Both pilgrims and tourists buy souvenirs that capture and symbolize their time in Banaras. Although the purpose of their travel may differ (as much as it overlaps), both pilgrims and tourists use boats. It is important to stress, however, the different nature of their interactions with boatmen. Pilgrims generally travel en masse and pay much less than tourists. Boatmen therefore fill their boats as much as possible when transporting pilgrims in order to make a trip worthwhile. The price for pilgrims is generally fixed in advance, whereas with tourists it is much more flexible. The manner in which domestic tourists visit Banaras and interact with the boatmen is, in these respects, more comparable to that of foreign tourists. The same could be said of their motivations, needs and desires that in turn affect the way in which boatmen interact and deal with them.

Like the middle class family described in the comic book, many domestic tourists' experience of Banaras often combines both religious and tourist practices. On several occasions, domestic tourists told me that despite their modern sensibilities, which due to pollution fears prevent them from bathing in or drinking

---

6    Clearly domestic tourists also participate in 'package tours', although this is uncommon. The division of tourists outlined above, is therefore more for analytical purposes than an accurate description of the diverse domestic and foreign types of tourists coming to Banaras.

the sacred river water, visiting the city is still a spiritual and religious experience for them. In other words, one experience does not necessarily displace the other; on the contrary, for many domestic tourists the tourist experience is enhanced and complemented by the religious one. Likewise, it is not uncommon to spot a foreign tourist participating in ritual activities and morning ablutions in the river. As Gopal Manjhi noted:

> The Japanese and Koreans who come to Banaras, also visit Gangaji to worship and perform rituals. I have seen this many times, they are less interested in taking photos. These tourists even buy flower garlands and lamps, recite mantras and worship the sun. This is because they have faith, they believe... The *angrez*, he is more interested in listening to stories about the ghats, the Maharajas, the burning ghats or the level pollution in the river. So you see there are different types of tourists, some stay for a month, or for six months while others come only for a day or two.[7]

Indeed, tourists' motivations and experiences, whether domestic or foreign, should not be conceived in binary terms, such as sacred and profane. As Smith has argued (1992, 2), the sacred and spiritual motivations for travel should not be 'restricted to the pilgrim'. One of the primary motivations underlying modern tourism, contends MacCannell (1976), is the search for an authentic experience. This, he argues, is partly the result of the 'instability and inauthenticity' of modernity, which is characterized by alienation, loss of meaning and nostalgic yearning for the past. MacCannell (1976, 42–48) suggests that the practice and motivations underlying tourism bear much in common with religious experience and ritual conduct. Other scholars have noted the interface between modern tourism and pilgrimage, arguing that the search for the sacred and spiritual is a central feature of the tourist journey (Graburn 1989; Smith 1992; Turner & Turner 1978). Spiritual and religious experiences are often part of the 'multiple and changing motivations of the travellers, whose interests and activities may switch from tourist to pilgrim and vice versa' (Smith 1992, 4). Not surprisingly, tourist destinations have often been marketed as places of spirituality, purity and personal transformation (Bruner 1991). The need to experience an authentic setting underlies what Urry characterizes as the 'tourist gaze'. The tourist gaze, he argues, is premised upon difference, 'constructed in relation to its opposite' (Urry 1990, 2). It is not surprising, then, that Banaras, with its riverfront vista and exotic ritual practices and oriental scenes captures the imagination of foreign visitors. However, the tourist gaze, as Urry reminds us, is itself contingent upon historical and social circumstances.

---

7    Boatmen commonly use the word *angrez* when referring to Western looking tourists.

**Figure 5.5     Western tourists taking a boatride along the river, Banaras**

*Colonial Perceptions of Banaras*

The mode of travel, motivations, expectations and experiences of colonial travellers to Banaras were, in part, different from those of the contemporary traveller.[8] Perhaps the most important difference is how the contact zone was described and experienced by colonial travellers. In colonial travelogues and guidebooks the city is exotic and its inhabitants were commonly described as essentially different from Europeans. (see, for example, Caine 1898; Havell 1905; Minturn 1858, 138). One of the best known travel guides, written by W.S Caine called *Picturesque India: A Handbook for European Travellers*, provides a detailed description of the city and riverscape. It also offers travel advice to the European traveller:

> Ghats, platforms and piers are alive with pilgrims from every part of India, in a variety of costume, and every stage of dress and undress... Crows, kites, pigeons and parrots circle round the heads of this kaleidoscopic crowd... Every morning, during his stay at Benares the European traveller should take a boat and row slowly down in front of the ghats. The guides belonging to Clark's Hotel, which is the best in the city, will make the necessary arrangements. It is a great advantage to secure introductions in Benares to some educated Hindu

---

8    On colonial travelogues and the expansion and marketing of tourism during the colonial and postcolonial periods, see Ramusack (1994; 1995).

gentleman, or missionary who has been for some time resident in the town. The professional guides all over India are very inferior, and cannot do more than show the way through the bazaars, point out notable buildings, and keep a sharp eye on tips and commissions. Every turn of the street, every step of the ghat, every group on the platforms present some incident exciting the greatest curiosity, which can only be satisfied by someone versed in the customs of Hindu religion (1898, 202–303).

The population was there to be gazed upon from a distance; Banaras embodied the primitive past while the activities and practices of the locals provided a colourful and animated backdrop to this magnificent stage: a living museum worthy of being visited, observed and commented upon by the colonial traveller; the tourist gaze served to reinforce the authority and superiority of the knowledgeable and rational European traveller.[9] As the above quotation suggests, locals served as the backdrop and local guides were no better than petty tricksters. Hence, as suggested by Caine, the mediator or tour guide for the European traveller should only be a member of the elite.

While many of the imperial depictions of the Orient avoid mentioning close interaction with locals, contemporary tourists to Third World countries actively search for such encounters (Echtner & Prasad 2003). The contact zone becomes the focus of attention; and the locals the objects of desire and consumption. Postcolonial travel literature on India and the Indian experience is replete with tourist-host encounters.[10] This change emerged most strikingly in the 1960s for the 'hippie' generation.

Much has been written about the 1960s and 1970s counterculture period during which Westerners sought to experience India through spirituality, drugs, music, food, clothing and encounters with the locals. Julie Stephens, for instance, argues that India signified freedom and an opportunity to 'counter all restrictions of "Western" culture…[it] came to be seen as an "uncontaminated" place, far from the polluting influences of money; a place beyond the market where the ethic of "free" could flourish supreme' (Stephens 1998, 53). The perception of India as the 'antithesis' of the West was shared by both the hippie generation and the colonial one. Under the colonial gaze India was perceived as backward, its inhabitants less evolved and therefore in need of being redeemed (the 'civilizing mission') and disciplined by the colonial regime and its 'superior' culture. The 1960s counterculture, however, celebrated the lack of material modernity as a sign of spirituality, concerned, as counterculture was, with renouncing the acquisitiveness and accumulation of material possessions and achieving a harmony with nature. Such perceptions of India as a place of discovery (and self-discovery) and

---

9    Peter Friedlander (2004) has eloquently demonstrated the need to acknowledge the variety of gazes and experiences of colonial travellers in India during early the colonial period.

10    See, for example, Newby (1966); Jayapal (2000).

spirituality continue to inform travel discourses and patterns of consumption.[11] An examination of the experiences of contemporary travellers in the contact zone, reveals the often unpleasant gap between representations and reality.


**Experiencing Banaras: The Sacred and the Profane**

Lisa, a woman from Germany, told me about her motivations and experience of the city:

> I came to learn Sanskrit. I love this place. The river is wonderful, no cars, silent, fresh air, open space, and when the sun comes out there is always a kind of lazy Sunday afternoon atmosphere…One boatman I met, he works to live, and does not live to work, like we do in West…The only thing that bothers me here are the motorboats that create noise and air pollution.

For a person on holiday, such as Lisa, who does not need to work to provide for her family, it is easy to experience the riverfront as a spiritual vacation spot. For Lisa, the boatmen are objectified. They embody and delineate the contrast between East and West. Uneven economic relationships between tourists and locals obviously contribute to the way in which the former exercise their gaze upon the different and underprivileged 'reality' of India. This 'reality' is seen, experienced, consumed and constructed on preconceived notions about India and the 'other'.

Lisa complained about the presence of motorboats on the river, saying that they pollute the riverscape. For her, these motorboats are signs of the corrupting forces of modernity and 'progress'. Such corrupting foreign influences are never depicted or portrayed in travel advertising and representations of the holy city. In the comic book, pilgrims figure as part of the riverfront scenery, but motorboats are conspicuously absent. For tourists, motorboats spoil the atmosphere of the riverfront. They puncture the romantic notion of Banaras as a place suspended in time, authentic, unchanging and pure. Tourists, whose information comes mainly from brochures and travel agencies, are unaware that these motorboats are vital to the boatmen's livelihood, especially for those who live and operate their boats from distant ghats where tourists rarely go, providing services for pilgrims. Ironically, it

---

11    For example, in one of the brochures of the latest campaign launched by the Department of Tourism (Government of India) known as *Incredible India*, one finds a long list of things to do in India, such as 'Wear a sari. Learn to walk all over again… Eat food off a banana leaf…Try paan…Fly a kite…Attend an Indian wedding. Live in an Ashram… Buy bangles…Pay homage to the Ganges…Pick up the art of bargaining…' (Department of Tourism, Ministry of Tourism and Culture, Government of India, New Delhi, October 2002).

is the pious package-tour pilgrims who use motorboats in order to complete their pilgrimage itinerary according to plan.

Several tourists I spoke to expressed dismay and disappointment with their experience of the riverscape and their interactions with boatmen. When I explained my research topic to one tourist, he responded by asking: 'Is your research about the cheating by boatmen?' On another occasion a Canadian backpacker said that his expectations had largely derived from tales told by friends at home and fellow travellers in India. They had praised the unique experience of boating and the special atmosphere on the River Ganga, including the releasing of candles (*diyas*) into the river at dusk. Arriving at the city, he went directly from the train station to the riverfront to catch the sunrise and morning religious ceremonies. He recounted his experience:

> Boatmen kept approaching me and asking 'Hello! You want boat? you want boat?' I wanted to take a boat by myself as I thought it would be special, but I really don't like the constant hassling and discussions about money. For me, Banaras is supposed to be a holy place—the cremations, the Ganga, the boats— but when it's all about cheating and money, money, money, I just shut off.

By now the nagging question 'Hello! Boat?' should sound familiar to the reader. In this chapter, however, I am more concerned with the tourist perspective in the encounter. Here we have a dissonance resulting from the unmet expectations of the tourist, whose image of Banaras was based on exotic representations and tourist tales. It may well be that those who told the Canadian about Banaras were equally disillusioned by the constant pestering of the boatmen. The sense that remains is mixed. On the one hand, tourists seek an authentic and spiritual experience of India, one portrayed by a series of romantic images (photographs, literature, tourist brochures). On the other hand, there is the profane image of India as a place where one must bargain.[12]

The image of the boatmen as aggressive bargainers corresponds to a wider imagery that figures in depictions of the Orient as mischievous and conniving.

---

12　Consider, for example, Eric Newby's (1966) fascinating account of travelling down the River Ganges, *Slowly Down the Ganges*, which is full of stories about his encounters with the locals along his journey. Upon arrival to Banaras, Newby describes the early morning scene with an enthusiasm similar to that of other travel writers. Newby, however, notes his disappointment and frustration at the relentless bargaining by the boatman his party employed.

'Here we hired a boat to take us down as far as Malviya Bridge and then back again upstream to the southern outskirts of the city. (At Banaras the Ganges flows from south to north). The boatman was a taciturn fellow, but we continued to make use of his services while we were in Banaras. One would have thought that by doing so a great deal of haggling would have been avoided but at each fresh encounter he looked at us as if he had never seen us before and the whole tedious business of striking a price had to be gone through afresh' (Newby 1966, 215).

Bargaining is seen as unpleasant and dishonest conduct by many Westerners, who associate such behaviour with poverty, greed and expediency (Geertz 1979; Herrmann 2003, 242). Such ideas may tell us as much about ourselves as about the exotic 'other'. As Herrmann (2003, 246) observes: 'Americans equate fixed prices with equality, fairness, and rationality, and bargaining with inequality, unfairness and irrationality'. Such behaviour becomes even more dissonant when India comes to be associated with notions of spirituality and purity. Compare, for example, the following passage in which Noa, an Israeli girl, relates her experience of Varanasi:

> You have to argue and bargain for everything! It spoils the atmosphere of holiness. At the same time, I can understand them, they are poor people and I am not angry with them. We need to have compassion, but really what did I ask for except to pay the real price.

Noa's experience is not unique. These ideas about 'India' continue to inform tourist sensibilities, expectations and responses. In this case, Noa finds it hard to come to terms with people trying to exact more money than she would like to pay because she is a tourist. She is disappointed that her 'hosts' exhibit such materialistic tendencies.[13] Moreover, she is upset at being treated like an ignorant tourist unaware of local prices. Disillusionment results from fantasies about Banaras as a spiritual place, poverty as a sign of virtue (rather than greed), and its inhabitants as quaint, generous and forthcoming. In spite of the unpleasant and disliked practice of bargaining, many tourists actually speak of this as being part of the real, difficult and authentic experience of India – in a manner akin to a 'rite of passage'. As Noa explained: 'When I arrived in India, other travellers said that one should only go to Banaras after having travelled in India for some time, since Varanasi is the real India and there are no concessions!'. In a way, Noa's frustrations were eased by the fact that her experience confirmed the representation of Varanasi as a difficult and challenging place.

As Bourdieu (1984) suggests, consumption is a form of communication as well as a means of social differentiation. Consuming the local in its many forms serves to enhance the consumer's cultural capital, a matter of great significance when one is travelling and relating to fellow travellers.[14] Sørensen (2003, 856)

---

13　Trojanow's (2001) recent critique of travelogues of India written by such prominent European intellectuals as Günter Grass is instructive:

'Evidently, an author who is sick of consumer society has composed a fantasy of indulgence. But this fantasy is light years away from the aspirations of the slum dweller, who is saving up for a TV, on which he can admire the local and foreign consumer and the consumer goods for which he is striving'.

14　I use the notion of cultural capital here in the broader sense to denote the way in which some tourists seek to enhance their status amongst their fellow travellers by their adoption of certain patterns of consumption. For example, dress codes or the fact that many

calls this 'road status', which is secured by 'paying "local prices", getting the best deal, travelling off the beaten track, [suffering] long term travel, diseases, dangerous experiences, and more'. Consuming the local also serves to demarcate and differentiate the 'traveller' from the 'tourist' who is mocked for seeing India through the window of a bus.[15]

We find, then, that like the anthropologist (as mentioned in the introduction of the book), travellers too are engaged in performing their own 'rites of passage' in an effort to differentiate themselves from other tourists. Travellers actively seek a range of physical (fatigue, illness, danger, sex) and emotional (elation, satisfaction) experiences of the local as part of their wider consumption of local culture. Travellers' insistence on paying 'local prices' is related to how they perceive themselves in relation to the 'other'. Indeed many travellers do not see themselves consumers but learners, joining in, not wanting to be conspicuously different from the local people. However, for some there is a considerable tension in this attempt. The 'cultural capital' they accumulate contributes to an illusion of being in control. The feeling of unease at being tricked and manipulated reflects the way in which myth and reality collide in the contact zone.


## Tourist-Boatman Transactions

The strategies employed by boatmen in their encounters with tourists are informed by their passenger distribution system, as well as their ability to operate as culture brokers, mediating and negotiating the city for the tourists. As mentioned in Chapter 3, in order to regulate passenger distribution along the riverfront, the boatmen operate a unique work system based on a territorial arrangement of the riverfront, which is divided according to the different ghats. Each ghat space is considered the exclusive territory of a specific group of resident boatmen (*ghatwars*). In turn, a boatman is always associated with a specific ghat, which serves as his base and place of work. As such, there are no 'loose' boatmen operating in Banaras.

### *The Boli System: Classifying and Objectifying Visitors*

As previously outlined, the initial moment of encounter between boatman and visitor (potential passenger) occurs on the ghat or, more broadly, in its immediate vicinity. On most ghats, boatmen are strategically placed to gauge the tourist's moves and intentions as s/he enters the ghat space. As a tourist arrives, s/he is immediately spotted, pegged and subsequently assigned to a particular boatman. That boatman then approaches the tourist to ask if s/he would like to take a boat

---

tourists avoid the more luxurious means of travel in favour of 'rougher' ones, thus evincing their knowledge of and capacity to consume the local.

15    'Local' items are typically produced specifically for travellers. Rarely do locals eat or wear items such as the bags and clothes for sale in markets'.

ride. In other words, from the moment of entry onto the ghat the boatmen closely observe a visitor's activities and intentions. This surveillance of the unsuspecting tourist is part of a broader method of passenger distribution.

The act of identifying and bidding for passengers is known as *boli*. The method of distributing passengers is based on spatial classifications within the ghat territory itself. The first stage concerns bidding for a potential passenger (*savari*). As a potential passenger enters the ghat, the *ghatwars* 'call out' the place from which s/he emerges, for example, 'passenger coming from temple', or 'passenger coming from the pandit's house', or 'passenger from the riverfront'. This calling is strictly between the boatmen themselves, in terms unfamiliar to other Indians and without the knowledge of the potential passenger. At Assi ghat, for example, boatmen are situated on a cliff with a bird's eye view. They must be located there to participate in the auction-like activity.[16] The boatman who first identifies and calls for the potential passenger then has the right to approach him/her or send his worker (*mallahi*) to do so.

These spatial terms used to designate clients represent the physical environment as perceived by the boatmen, and serve to divide the ghat space into many sub-sections. They set the ground rules for participation and inclusion. Part of a common pool of signs and shared conceptual maps based on an agreed vocabulary and knowledge, they are essential for those working on the ghat as boatmen. A boatman who is not from Assi ghat is not likely to understand the full meaning of this language, primarily because he is not familiar with the particular ghat space. Others would be perplexed simply because the boatmen speak quickly in local dialect and in a semi-coded manner. In other words, it is the boatmen who control and manipulate the encounter with the tourists on the ghat.

The tourist becomes an object of observation and judgment, thereafter becoming the 'property' of a particular boatman and price negotiation is restricted. On numerous occasions I observed tourists who were displeased with the price offered by a boatman. Rejecting him, they ceremoniously walked off in search of a lower price unaware that the boatman who next approached them was from the same family. The price subsequently offered is then usually lowered a little to appease the tourists, permitting them to come away thinking that they have controlled the transaction.

Foreign tourists may come expecting to engage in a ritualized bargaining. What the tourist is unaware of is that this ritual interaction is institutionalized as part of a larger system of social interaction pertaining to the boatman community. Moreover, a similar system applies to all other potential passengers (locals and domestic tourists), though the interaction will differ according to passenger 'type'. Determining passenger 'type' is integral to the way boatmen secure their

---

16    Interestingly, on the main ghat (Dashashvamedh) other features are added to describe the potential passenger, for example 'the one with the red hat, black pants arriving from the temple'. This is due to the large flow of people, which necessitates additional forms of identification.

livelihood. Prior to the actual spoken encounter the boatman seeks to 'define the situation' (Goffman 1974, 13). He calculates a set of factors: an assessment of the potential passenger according to age, gender, clothing, nationality and conduct. This is similar to the way in which boatmen and priests communicate in coded terms to gauge and assess a pilgrim's socio-economic status.

Boatmen are keen observers when it comes to guessing a tourist's nationality from afar. Boatmen will start the price negotiation according to nationality. For an Israeli, the starting price will be much higher. They know, as they told me many times, that Israelis are hard bargainers and argumentative (and that, as one boatman said, 'Israeli women are just as tough as the men'). Koreans were seen as stingy and rude, Americans nice and polite, as were the British and Australians. A number of studies across the world (Crick 1994; Evans-Pritchard 1989; Sweet 1989; van den Bergh 1980) have shown similar patterns whereby locals stereotype foreign tourists in terms of their behaviour, dress and nationality: an activity that also informs/shapes the actual encounter with foreigners. In our case, the construction of national stereotypes based on limited interaction serves to illustrate how the boatmen themselves objectify and perceive the 'other'. The manner in which backpackers dress and interact with each other as well as with locals is often mocked by them. In my conversations with them, some boatmen found the clothing and matted hair sported by backpackers or 'hippie' tourists, as well as the unkempt, ragged and immodest look of such travellers, both perplexing and ridiculous.

Another area of judgment by boatmen concerns gender. Within the local framework of gender relations women occupy the domestic sphere. A family's status may be tarnished if the women work outside the home. Some Indian men therefore view foreign women from the outset as somewhat 'loose', their behaviour not respectable.[17] This is further compounded by varying ideas of what constitutes proper and improper dress. Many foreign women protest at being stared at and harassed by local men. One German woman told me of the frustration she felt at having to keep her guard up, despite her efforts to follow local conduct and dress codes. The majority of foreign tourists, however, seem oblivious of local conventions. Some women wear skimpy worn-out clothing, have their hair loose and smoke in public, all of which are considered inappropriate behaviour in traditional and sacred places. Tourist insensitivities or indifference to local sensibilities may derive from the playful and pleasure seeking conduct that characterizes much

---

17    There are many reasons why local men perceive foreign women (especially Western) as highly promiscuous and often morally corrupt. This stereotype possibly derives from the many movie advertisements spread across the city on billboards in which blonde, voluptuous Western women are shown seeking sexual pleasure. It is also no secret that pornographic movies starring Western women circulate freely in India.

tourism. For some women tourists, the carefree, liminal phase of travel also opens up other possibilities, including sexual relationships with boatmen.[18]

For their part, the 'hosts' not only bluntly gaze at foreign tourists, but also make jokes about their looks and conduct among themselves and even directly in front of them. Some boatmen classify foreign women in national terms according to their sexual prowess. This may be a case of male boasting mixed with feelings of frustration. However, such experiences also enable the boatmen to reflect on their own culture and gender relations. When I asked one boatman whether he would like to marry a foreign woman, he adamantly answered: 'No, I will only marry an Indian woman. Indian women don't go around with other men; an Indian wife will remain loyal to her husband and will provide him company until the end. Now, I am just playing with foreign women'.

I suspect, however, that despite such claims, boatmen often feel restricted by their culture and traditional attitudes to sex and marriage patterns.[19] At the same time, they seem ambivalent about what they perceive as the promiscuity characteristic of foreigners. Indeed, the stories told by some young boatmen of their sexual interludes with Western women are reminiscent of Bowman's (1989) provocatively titled article 'Fucking Tourists', where he interprets Palestinian male tales of sexual encounters with foreign women as more than simply designed to enhance one's status amongst peers. Rather, as Bowman argues, such stories should be seen 'as a means of imagining and acting out power' at the personal level by locals, who are otherwise in a position of socio-economic inferiority (Bowman 1989, 79). In our case, the uneven power relations are obvious: the boatmen remain in Banaras while the foreign women come and go as they please. The women are mobile, wealthy and (seem to be) in control of their lives. Boatmen feel excluded and restricted in their movements. Not only are they unable to visit foreign countries, but in their own environment they are barred from escorting tourists outside the riverscape and old city. In fact, boatmen seen working as unlicensed guides outside the proximity of the riverfront are subject to police harassment and run the risk of prosecution. Consequently, this is perceived by the boatmen as systematic persecution by the authorities, one that does injustice to both the hosts and the guests:

> When I walk around with tourists the police often stop me and ask: 'If you are a guide then where is your licence?' You see, when tourists come from far away countries, having spent so much money to come and see Varanasi, they want to know about Indian culture and Varanasi. Now, I am a Hindu and a local, so I can

---

18　Tucker (1997, 113–114) makes a similar argument, suggesting that for the female tourist in Turkey 'the liminal experiences of tourism allow for certain moral constraints present in normal life to be put aside'. At the same time, such relationships contribute to the strengthening of local male sexual identity.

19　Cf. Cohen (1971) for a similar case amongst Arab boys of Israel.

tell them about the temples, the different gods and the culture – it is my duty to explain these things.

Likewise, en route to a family birthday party at the grandparent's household of one of my main informants, I was surprised when he suggested we travel in separate cycle rickshaws to avoid harassment on the way – even though I assured him that I would vouch for his credibility.

Boatmen are well aware of the fact that some tourists are becoming increasingly impatient with the many locals trying to cheat them or sell them something for an inflated price. They are also aware of the negative perceptions that tourists have of them, as Anil explains:

> I know that some tourists think boatmen are like mosquitoes always bothering them, but you must understand that after September 11 hardly any tourists came to Varanasi. Nowadays the hotels are once again full, but the hotel managers tell the tourists that they should only pay Rs.45–50 for a boat ride, while they ask for ten times as much for a room in their hotels. What? Is the hotel room made of gold and our boats of stone?! So when tourists want a boat ride they always think we are cheats, but we are also entitled to earn a living, we are not beggars!

Anil's observations demonstrate a good understanding of how the tourist industry operates and how global considerations have a direct impact on his livelihood. He is equally aware of the effects such factors have on his daily encounters with tourists. Some boatmen try to neutralize the unpleasant feelings surrounding the initial encounter with suspicious tourists. On many occasions I witnessed boatmen telling tourists 'pay as much as you wish at the end of the boat ride'. Then again, some boatmen negotiate a lower price, but once on the boat employ all their persuasive and manipulative techniques to compel the passenger to pay a larger sum. On the boat, boatmen will engage with the passenger to get an impression of his/her wants and needs and length of stay. On this basis they then offer to negotiate Hindi, Yoga or music lessons, as well as a range of other services. They will often make an extra effort to establish rapport with tourists who intend staying for a longer period of time (i.e., more than three days). This is because once a boatman establishes rapport with a tourist, the next time s/he enters the ghat space, s/he is no longer part of the *boli* pegging system. The tourist then falls into the 'known passenger' category (much like Miss West in Mishra's novel) and is automatically designated to that boatman.[20]

During my initial months in the field I was also labelled as a 'known passenger' of my main informant at Assi ghat. I was therefore seldom approached by other boatmen to take a boat. As this clearly hindered my own research I explained the matter to my informant and eventually decided to initiate a rotation system

---

20    Geertz (1979), Herrmann (2003, 241) suggests that a 'softer style' of bargaining maybe 'used to establish long term trading relationships or "clientization"'.

of my own (a *pari* of sorts) so that I could familiarize myself with the rest of the community. Conversely, while venturing to more distant ghats, I often took a more 'passive' stance where my (incognito) tourist identity proved useful for 'first hand' experiences of how boatmen engage with me both on the ghat and in the boat.

The encounter in the boat is a significant one for the boatmen, as it affords room for manoeuvre outside the pressures of the initial encounter. Gopal's account shows how boatmen manipulate tourists:

> As boatmen we have to be sensitive to the moods of the customer. In the morning, for example, all the tourists want to take a boat ride to see the sunrise, so during this time I will try and extract as much money as I can from the tourist. Yes, we are like cheats, and the good cheater knows exactly which key will work in which lock. Mallahs are even sharper tricksters than pandits [priests] because we do sweet cheating. I mean we are like snake charmers playing the flute and controlling the snake (*nagin* – female snake). First we grant the snake elation (*mast*) and then we catch her and take out the poison. Similarly, when we interact with the pilgrims or tourists, we first provide our services and then extract the money. We try and do all we can to please the passengers, so they relax on our boats and experience joy, just like a snake enjoys the dance, and thus we are able to gain their trust. You see, we don't simply ply the boats, we are also guides.

Indeed, a boatman provides the passenger with a range of services, including the provision of cultural products, which contribute to and hopefully enhance the experience of boating. These services demonstrate to the tourist the abilities of the boatman as a guide. He informs the tourist, interprets and clarifies things regarding matters that even formal tour guides are often unfamiliar with.[21] The following conversation I had with a French couple illustrates how a boatman-tourist relationship typically develops:

> Q: How did you decide to take a boat?
> A: A boatman came and asked whether we wanted to take a boat ride and we agreed. It was very interesting. At first he took us along the riverfront explaining about the burning ghats and the reasons why some corpses are cremated and others are not, like babies and holy men. He also took us to the Nepali temple and showed us around the streets. Later the boatman suggested we see the evening ceremony on the main ghat; so we arranged to meet him in the evening. He waited for us next to the hotel. He is an older boatman, a very kind person. The following day the same boatman arranged to meet us and take us to the

---

21   A vivid example of the various levels of guidance, a kind of hierarchy of mediation, is given in the documentary film *Boatman* (Rossi 1993). In the film the boatman acts as a local guide, reflecting on both the 'strange' tourists as well as Hindu culture.

> Ramnagar fort across the river. He showed us around and took us to the museum.
> Afterwards he took us to have a very tasty *lassi* drink near the fort.

A British tourist recounted a similar experience:

> …from the boat the boatman showed us the cremation ghats and explained about
> karma in Hinduism, the cost of wood for cremations, and the quantity of wood
> needed. It was a good experience. I feel I understand more about Indian culture
> now.
>
> Q: Can I ask how much he charged?
> A: He charged Rs.70 per hour, but I paid more because he worked like a guide.

These conversations show that the services provided by the boatmen far exceed the physical labour of rowing. Boatmen are aware of the tourists' search for 'authenticity', such as going to places uncontaminated by other tourists. They often offer tourists a visit to their homes to meet their families, thus providing the tourist with a 'backstage' glimpse into Indian culture – the 'real India'. In addition, by telling tourists their own personal stories, the boatmen (whether consciously or not) destabilize the generic representation of indigenous people as passive objects commonly found in guidebooks (see Bhattacharyya 1997, 288). In fact, many boatmen showed me photos and letters they had received from tourists with whom they had established good relationships. Such personalized relationships seem to add to the quality of the tourist experience and cultural capital ('road status') and to the boatmen's sense of themselves.[22]

The accumulation of cultural capital by tourists is reminiscent of the colonial period where resources and capital produced in the peripheries were taken back to the centres of power. However, it should not be forgotten that just as this process of production involved exploitation, remittance and profit, it also generated wealth in the colonial outposts in terms of employment opportunities, education and social mobility. Boatmen are similarly aware of the opportunities provided by tourism. The cultural capital accumulated by tourists and produced as part of the tourist discourse is also available to, generated by, and exploited by locals, such as the boatmen.

Many boatmen are becoming increasingly aware of how the tourist discourse operates, especially through travel talk and electronic communication. Some

---

22    I should qualify this point, for the cultural capital acquired by boatmen from association with tourists is often overstated. As mentioned, some tourist/travellers are considered strange, both in terms of their dress and behaviour, for example, their talking to beggars and associating with lepers. Such behaviour is considered lowly and undignified. In other words, tourists may transgress socio-cultural boundaries and this can mean that local people who interact with them do not necessarily gain credit, but on the contrary, are also looked down upon.

boatmen have acquired business cards, mobile phones and e-mail accounts with the assistance of tourists.[23] When backpackers arrive in the city equipped with such a business card, they head directly to the riverfront to avoid the hassles associated with arriving in Banaras (e.g., being led to an unwanted guest house by a rickshaw driver). A tourist who has heard of a boatman's credentials from fellow travellers is less suspicious of him and the initial encounter is more pleasant. Such an encounter also means the boatman gains a 'known passenger'. The initial interaction is more amicable and rapport more easily attained. Establishing trust and cultivating a personal relationship with tourists often yields unpredicted/unanticipated benefits. One such case is a close, long-standing friendship between a young boatman from the main ghat area and Ineka, a Dutch woman in her 40s. Ineka had come to Banaras for the first time five years previously. Here in her words is the story of her initial encounter with a boatman called Sundar:

> My first encounter with Sundar was at the road crossing near the main ghats. I was looking in the Lonely Planet guide to find out how to get to the Golden Temple when a young man approached me asking if I needed help. Well, you know, by that time I was already two months in India and was familiar with such hassling, so I said 'No, just go, go away (*'chello, chello'*)'. He answered, 'Madam, I don't want money, just to help you'. I knew their tricks and said, 'Go away, I am a big girl'. So then he looked at me, and caught me with a sentence that I think must work well with many tourists. He said, 'Madam, I like your face, I want to help you, why do you tourists always think we want to cheat you?' So I thought, 'Wow, maybe some people are really kind and not just after my money'. I looked at his face and I saw a young man and said 'Alright, I want to go to see the Golden Temple.' He took me there and to other places and finally I said; 'Well now I want to pay you for your services.' I was surprised when he refused any payment, so then I invited him for a drink. I asked what his job was and he replied, 'I am a boatman and tourist guide'. So I said, 'Okay, then maybe tomorrow you can show me Varanasi and then I can pay you.' We arranged to meet the following day and he took me on a really nice tour with his boat to see the ghats and temples.

Ineka and Sundar have maintained a close relationship since then. Ineka has helped Sundar in many ways, teaching him to read and write English, and assisting him with financial difficulties. Over the years, Ineka has sent Sundar enough money to purchase a small house. She and her family come to Banaras once every two years and Sundar has come to be considered as one of her 'sons'. They have travelled around India together and she took Sundar on his first flight. Such close relationships between boatmen and tourists are not altogether rare

---

23    One card has a picture of the main temple on Prayag ghat and written on the side is the name of the boatman and his place of residence: 'Anil Manjhi, Prayag ghat, Dashashwamedh, Varanasi, Requested; everybody for "BOATING" Please contact here'.

or novel. In his memoirs the well-known scholar Alain Danielou describes his time in Banaras (early 20th century) and mentions his close relationship with a boatman (Danielou 1987, 130–132). This relationship, I have come to know, was maintained over several decades through correspondence and financial assistance given to the boatman. It is important to note, however, that interpreting long term relationships between boatmen and foreign tourists as economically beneficial does not negate or discount the value of friendship.[24] The two dimensions often overlap rather than contradict each other. It would therefore be misleading to suggest that Sundar's continuing relationship with Ineka was based purely on financial gain. Such considerations may indeed provide the initial impetus for a boatman to approach a tourist; however, it is also clear that there is a potential in the relationship that cannot be anticipated in advance and should not be reduced to its economic dimension alone. The 'contact zone' also has a personal and affectual dimension.


## Conclusion

A close examination of how boatmen operate and mediate the city for tourists and pilgrims clearly reveals the multidimensional nature of their work. The boatmen's services are never solely confined to the purely instrumental function of transporting passengers on the river. Their other functions involve ensuring the security and safety of pilgrims, as well as operating as culture brokers. Much of the way in which India, tourists and the tourist experience is represented, especially perhaps in the discourse emanating from the tourist industry, is undoubtedly beyond the control of local actors. However, as I have argued throughout, such unequal power relations do not entail the passivity and subordination of locals. It is in the contact zone where we can gauge the innovative strategies employed by boatmen to deal with tourists, their needs, wants and fears. Here, the boatmen cleverly exercise a significant degree of control and agency over 'guest-host' interactions and transactions. The boatmen may be the object of the tourist gaze, but the tourist is also under the object of the boatmen's gaze, subjected to typological examination (and at times ridicule), allowing the boatmen to critically reflect on foreign culture, as well as their own. This does not result in any overall change in the balance of the power, but it does mean that the transactional relationship is not overwhelmingly one-way in favour of the non-locals/outsiders.

The way in which some boatmen engage with tourists demonstrates a good understanding on their part of the tourist discourse, that is, the search for an authentic and local experience. Their multiple roles as informal tour guides, commission-

---

24    Cf. Adams (1996) for a similar point regarding the binding and reciprocal nature of such long term relationships between foreigners and Sharpas, which she argues cannot be explained by reducing such relations into simple binaries, such as backstage/onstage; utilitarian/free-exchange, genuine/fake (friendship).

paid agents and friends mean they are able to influence, manipulate and enhance the visitors' experience of the city. Although some boatmen clearly benefit from their interactions with tourists in terms of economic gain, it is nevertheless important to bear in mind that in some cases genuine and long-lasting relationships are forged that remain of great personal and social significance to the parties.

While this chapter has explored the interactions between boatmen and tourists at the interpersonal level, we must reiterate that such transactions occur within the wider public space of the riverscape. On one level, the work of the boatmen involves ferrying pilgrims and tourists across the riverscape, and providing a range of functional and cultural services. On another level, their livelihood is directly influenced and shaped by institutions and individuals, both inside and outside their immediate community (including the modern state, the tourist and pilgrimage industries and their own community). Thus, in order to maintain and protect their livelihood, boatmen are engaged in a difficult balancing act that involves meeting the needs and wants of their valuable clients, and at the same time, avoiding confrontation by complying (at least publicly) with government regulations and other non-state actors' interests.

By looking at the effects of these 'two levels', we can better understand this micro-level analysis of tourist-host interactions, and how it affects the day-to-day work practices of the boatmen. Such a consideration demonstrates the complex dynamics involved in the construction of the community's identity as boatmen, and of the boatmen's attempt to make meaning and sense of their lives within the constraints of their insecure situation in Banaras.

# Conclusion

In early October 2005, 18 boatmen were captured and arrested by the Dashashvamedh ghat police for operating as 'fake tour guides' for pilgrims and foreign tourists. The news of the arrests quickly spread across the riverfront. A large group of boatmen congregated on the main ghat, calling for the police to stop harassing their community. By evening a local congress leader had also arrived to join the protest in front of the Dashashvamedh police post. The boatmen demanded the release of the arrested persons and the immediate dismissal of all charges. The following morning a meeting was convened at the ghat and the boatmen decided to stage an indefinite strike, halting all boating on the river in the city, and subsequently shutting down the main fish and vegetable market in Banaras. According to newspaper reports, the arrests had been made in response to the demands by the Government Approved Tourist Guide Association (GATGA) for legal action against unlicensed guides operating in the city.

The boatmen continued their strike and protests over the following days, threatening to refuse participation in the upcoming popular festival of Durga Puja unless their demands were met. This was a serious threat, as thousands of pilgrims from across India would arrive in Banaras for the occasion to perform a ritual immersion of the goddess Durga in the River Ganga. The boatmen and their boats were essential for what is considered the climax of the Durga Puja celebrations, where elaborate images of the goddess are loaded onto boats for immersion. Clearly, the boatmen themselves stood to loose much money from such collective action.

The authorities became increasingly concerned by this threat, with the police superintendent issuing a warning to the boatmen, published in local newspapers, of his intention to bring boatmen from the neighbouring villages to take their place during the festival. Accordingly, any local boatman attempting to prevent the village boatmen from working or 'wreak havoc' would be charged and arrested under the 'gangster act'. Nevertheless, the standoff continued and on the fourth day of the strike, one day before the impending immersion ritual (13th October), the police yielded to the boatmen's demands, releasing the arrested boatmen and dropping all charges. It seemed that the village boatmen were united with their 'brothers' in their strike and the authorities were left with no choice but to acquiesce.

The above incident encapsulates many of the themes discussed in this book. The arrests of the boatmen echo the historical pattern, whereby the boatman community has been progressively marginalized and stigmatized both socially and economically. This pattern continues to inform contemporary official perceptions of boatmen who have become an easy target for state discrimination and persecution. Indeed, the arrests also remind us of the colonial period in which the boatman caste and community were considered criminally disposed and their members described as 'thieves, imposters and swindlers', a charge not too different from this recent one, claiming boatmen were 'posing' as fake tour guides.

This ominous encounter with local authorities appears to reaffirm the boatmen's perceptions of the state as an instrument manipulated by elite (e.g., GATGA) interests, while subordinate groups are systematically persecuted and degraded. More specifically, boatmen view and experience such denigration as further evidence of the way in which the authorities, and particularly the local police, seek to entrench their economic and social marginalization. However, boatmen deploy a range of methods to resist state intervention and encroachments on their rights and livelihood.

What began as a spontaneous protest against the arrests of 18 boatmen soon turned into a mass demonstration, systematically organized under the various caste associations. In launching the campaign to free the arrested men, the community demonstrated strategic sophistication and planning appropriate for such open political action. Local newspapers were notified of the community's intended actions and demands through press releases and a full strike was implemented across the river, essentially bringing parts of the city to a halt.

Sustaining the closure of the largest fish market and nearby vegetable market of Banaras, located just above the main ghat, is not an easy achievement. Such an operation is possible, however, because members of the community operate and manage the fish market and many of the vegetable sellers and suppliers rely on boats for the transportation of their goods.

By implementing a strike and shutting down the fish and vegetable markets, boatmen made a clear statement, not confined to the 'hidden transcripts', and demonstrated their central role in the city's economy. In doing so, they shifted from covert, everyday forms of resistance, such as fishing at night or operating as informal tour guides, to overt resistance and a direct challenge to state authority. This was a strategic shift rather than a substantive one. That is, the people intimately involved and familiar with the river economy, including local Brahmins and the police, remain perfectly aware that fishing, for example, continues to be practised by boatmen clandestinely, but as long as boatmen maintain a certain veneer of discreetness, such actions are, if not condoned, at least tolerated. Once this tacit understanding has been disturbed, however, boatmen are free to, or perhaps compelled to employ other means of resisting state domination, sending a powerful message signalling their dissatisfaction.

*Arenas of Resistance*

Boatmen are conscious of several potential arenas where they can exert their influence by withdrawing their services; these acts demonstrate a fairly sophisticated level of coordination. Such open, non-violent, direct actions occur in several arenas or socio-politically charged spaces, including the river, ghats and the city's main market. By shutting down the central markets, boatmen were able to utilize wider resources and people (including the women and children of the community), subsequently affecting the local sector of the population and disrupting the economy of Banaras, and their cause was thus propelled onto a much larger stage than of the ghats and river – their usual turf.

Withholding participation in the riverscape arena had both symbolic and material consequences. Boatmen were able to effectively highlight their indispensable role in the ritual economy of Banaras as their actions severely disturbed the substantial population of tourists and pilgrims. Such actions were powerfully articulated at the ghat level, where boatmen staged public meetings and mass protests. As I have shown, the ghats are negotiated spaces, occupied by various ghat functionaries, including boatmen, priests, and the local police, all of whom participate in the prospering tourist and pilgrimage industry, and where a social dynamic remains largely intact. As such, the agency displayed by boatmen should not be reduced to that of resistance; it is equally the agency of production – the production of space, ritual boundaries, delineation of territory and the insertion of oneself into a social dynamic. By simultaneously renouncing their role as ritual associates, but maintaining their presence on the ghat and, in fact, dominating it with their mass protests, the boatmen became a forceful entity, claiming a stake in the river economy and disrupting the existing social and symbolic order.

I have argued that the above incident necessarily involved a shift from covert to more overt forms of resistance. This raises two questions: why do the boatmen resort to everyday forms of resistance if they can achieve more with large scale strikes and demonstrations? And what are the circumstances that promote the switch from everyday modes of resistance to open, explicit, coordinated political action? The answers must take into account both the micro-level analysis, concerning the internal dynamics of the boatman community, their experiences, agency and modes of resistance, as well as the broader social and historical context – one in which state action, caste identity and market economy constitute the structures of domination.

## Micro-level Analysis

It is misleading to view these as evolutionary stages, whereby everyday forms of resistance develop into overt and more confrontational forms of protest, or as Scott (1985) argues, everyday forms of resistance have an incremental effect, eventually undermining domination. Rather, this shift from using 'weapons of the weak' type resistance to more overt ones signals the crossing of a threshold; an event has occurred which the boatmen perceive as a fundamental threat to their community and identity as boatmen. Moreover, covert and overt forms of resistance are not mutually exclusive, for they often co-exist, with the weapons of the weak being employed alongside more coordinated efforts by institutional political action instigated by the caste associations.

The commonplace strategies deployed by boatmen, such as fishing, operating motorboats, cultivating and offering their services as unlicensed tour guides, are sufficient because boatmen have a vested interest in maintaining a low-key dynamic. It is also true that some boatmen are prospering, and such everyday tactics are meant to avoid inconvenience and harassment, without causing damage or upsetting the balance of power. These are indeed, as Scott rightly observes useful individual self-help mechanisms and remain so as long as the informal rules governing the 'cat and mouse' games between police and boatmen continue to be operative. But when such an implicit understanding is disturbed, for example, in the form of a blanket ban on motorboats, fishing, or arrests, the games come to an abrupt stop as the entire way of life of the boatmen is at stake. This is no longer simply an inconvenience to individuals, but an existential threat to the very essence of the community and their livelihood practices, where state actions may fundamentally redefine them. It is this threshold that generates mass protest and open political action.

Everyday forms of resistance are therefore not about instigating change, and the shift should not be simply seen as one of scale. Rather, it is about a change of intention. The ritual economy of Banaras is underpinned by a dynamic status quo, whereby each group is constantly vying for a better position, stamping its ground, asserting its authority and affirming its identity. Accordingly, for boatmen this identity and agency is evident through a range of activities, such as storytelling, performing rituals, and interpreting and occupying the riverscape on their own terms, to fit with their particular needs and wants. Such re-appropriation of symbolic and material order artfully subverts the cultural forms, ideas and structures generated by the state and religious authorities. Having said that, at the level of everyday life boatmen are equally careful not to undermine the status quo; they realize that all groups are necessary for ensuring the smooth operation of the ritual economy of Banaras. Instead of overt conflict between groups, what we find is a productive friction amongst the social actors that exists within the sphere of interaction of the riverfront.

In other words, there is an implicit, dynamic normative order, whereby each group is constantly creating and sustaining its identity. The October 2005 arrests were an aggressive breach of this status quo, a pre-emptive action designed to curtail another group's identity – the boatmen. Such action necessitated a shift in the mode of action, for everyday resistance, with its low yield friction, back and forth movement has been interrupted abruptly. The overt exercise of power by the police signalled a change of intention. No longer was this a matter of negotiating spheres of interaction based on implicit rules of engagement. This was a clear breach of the tacit order, where the role of boatmen within the social ecology of the river economy was seriously threatened. For boatmen, resisting such actions was therefore not about enacting change, but rather withstanding it, with the aim of maintaining the dynamics of the status quo.

Local authorities are equally implicated in this productive friction underpinning the status quo. Indeed, this incident is another example of the non-coherent nature of the state, with its divergent levels, discourses and practices. As I have shown, boatmen have been subjected to various state policies that have severely impinged on their livelihood, such as the banning of sandmining, and restrictions on fishing and cultivation. Such policies, however, were a product of national initiatives, shaped by development discourse and wider national and international concerns, which had implications at the local level. Likewise, the arrests of the boatmen were a result of pressures from above; in this case the Government Approved Tourist Guide Association. While local authorities must flex their muscles occasionally to show that they implement policies, at the level of everyday life, they too have a stake in maintaining a balanced ritual economy.

Within this dynamic all parties, including priests, boatmen and local authorities, try to make small gains. However, they all recognize and agree, much like in an ecological system, that it is the mutually dependant nature of this system that enables its operation. It may well be that for this reason everyday forms of resistance remain operative. This is not to say that the authorities are placating boatmen by giving them concessions; the opposite is the case, boatmen are actively engaged in reasserting their identity, carving a niche for themselves within the local ritual, economic and political structures of Banaras, constantly verifying their presence, by employing various tactics and strategies to enhance their position within the these structures. Importantly, however, within the productive friction the local authorities are also waging their low yield, low-intensity skirmish, in order to keep the boundaries alive and dynamic. That is, state actors have a vested interest in maintaining the informal social mechanisms which lubricate and sustain the ritual economy of Banaras, while making sure that no one group oversteps its mark. What is at stake is not a status quo where each group is seeking to displace or wear down its opponents (an attrition warfare of sorts), but rather tapping into this productive friction sustaining the interface between groups as a space offering people opportunities to aspire for more.

The arrest of the 18 boatmen forced the community to unite and declare their shared agenda forcefully in Banaras' most public places, its riverfront and its markets. Significantly, the arrests took place on the main ghat, where a police post is located overlooking the ghat. The presence of policemen on the main ghat has long been a sore point for boatmen, constantly under the gaze of the authorities, who pester them and interfere in their negotiations with passengers. I often witnessed policemen telling tourists how much they should pay the boatmen for their services. In addition, police harass boatmen for operating as informal tour guides not only for Western tourists, but also when escorting pilgrims to the various temples in the city – an activity boatmen and their patrons consider part of their services.

On occasion policemen stop boatmen leading pilgrim groups along the narrow lanes of Banaras and publicly warn the already apprehensive pilgrims to be aware of the "cheating" boatmen. Such insult is compounded by the fact that when pilgrims report their bags and wallets lost, police immediately suspect the boatmen of theft. The boatmen describe such incidents with a mixture of humiliation, frustration and anger largely directed towards the police. This is not surprising, for boatmen regard themselves the guardians of pilgrims and of local knowledge in Banaras, by virtue of their long standing association with the city and the River Ganga. Hence, the arrests of the boatmen were seen as an assault on their identity, and a strong reminder of their shared experience of degradation and discrimination.

This shared experience of subordination was particularly evident on this occasion, as the police did not differentiate between class, status or location of boatmen involved. In fact, amongst those arrested were both *ghatwars* and *mallahis*, several of whom belonged to powerful *ghatwar* families from the main ghat. Hence, the open protest was itself a product of a specific type of subordination that generated greater uniformity amongst boatmen, underpinned by long standing anger, and feelings of moral indignation. It was fuelled not only by concern for the individuals who were in custody (in an Indian jail) but by the day-to-day experience of subordination, in the form of encroachment on their livelihood and subjection to humiliation and punishment by the authorities and local elites.

So far I have suggested that we need to examine modes of domination and how they are interpreted by the subaltern group to understand the shift from covert to overt forms of resistance. The fact that the arrests were indiscriminate generated a consensus amongst the boatmen. The arrests were perceived as an existential threat to the community as a whole rather than an inconvenience to individuals. Once identified as such by the community it then became necessary for resistance to take on a different form – a more effective, open, collective one. Moreover, the structures for launching such resistance were already in place in the form of community/caste associations and the work system. The latter was particularly useful as it operated in a space that could not be controlled by the administrative authority of the state. Informed by moral economic precepts, the work system enabled boatmen to exercise their power materially and symbolically, highlighting their indispensable role in the ritual economy of Banaras.

Ironically, in this case boatmen exercised agency by withdrawing their services as ritual specialists at a key moment in the ritual calendar of Banaras; serendipity perhaps, but the occasion presented itself in a way that was ingeniously exploited. It is important to reiterate that insisting on the right to operate as ritual specialists, however, is not only a matter of material interests, but also endows boatmen with a meaningful existence within the broader Hindu social order, as well as a legitimate role within the ritual economy of the riverscape. Thus, boatmen who may in the past have accepted (reluctantly maybe) Brahminical authority and domination are less inclined to do so nowadays. As I have argued, such actions should not be simply viewed as rebellious/subversive acts against Brahminical domination, for everyday relations between boatmen and priests at the local level are more complex. It has also to do with the struggle over meaning and identity of the boatmen; their sense of who they are, including their place within a mythical and religious order constructed through stories, deities and rituals. They are *Gangaputras*, and they are part of a meaningful framework in which priests also have a firmly acknowledged place. They have a vocation celebrated and sealed in the story of Lord Rama and

Khevat. Therefore, boatmen have the right and duty to challenge those who deny or ignore the 'truth' and significance of the shared myth and history.

## Macro-level Analysis

Equally important is to acknowledge how the localized, everyday experience is intrinsically connected to broader social and historical contexts associated with modernity. The socio-political changes taking place in modern India, such as caste uplift movements, positive discrimination policies, and the low castes' political success in UP have an impact on the local level and significant influence on the hopes and aspirations of subaltern communities. It may well be that Fuller's claim that 'equality is progressively displacing traditional hierarchy as a compelling value' (2004, 161) would be contested by boatmen, pointing out with justification that they are still discriminated against, and that 'some people are more equal than others'. However, this very objection, using the modern concepts of equality and rights, would vindicate his point. In other words, it is the modern values of social justice, equality, and a democratic polity that are at the root of such responses. These democratic ideals are continuously promoted and disseminated through various channels, including the boatmen's own caste journals, local rallies and community events, which often refer to the injustices done to them by the elites, including Brahmins and government officials. In addition, in modern India low caste/class communities are becoming increasingly confident, a factor that also supports Fuller's claim. As we have seen boatmen are contesting their exclusion and celebrating their (suppressed) role in both traditional (e.g., in the stories of Eklavya and Khevat) and modern India (e.g., as loyal and worthy freedom fighters). As such they aspire to be acknowledged as worthy participants in Indian modernity.

The expansion of market forces is also changing the way in which caste is valued and viewed, generating new meanings and possibilities for resistance for subordinate people. This too contributes to the shift between individual and open collective action. The potential opportunities of the market fundamentally change the boatmen's perspective, offering significant incentives for achieving social and economic security, which has been denied to them both individually and communally.

While boatmen may in the past have rejected their marginalized role in the ritual hierarchy, the folktales and legends and myths of their extolled vocation are no longer simply about enhancing the dignity of the downtrodden, they are also a means to secure their livelihoods in a modernising environment, where traditional networks, structures and institutions are becoming increasingly vulnerable. Andre Beteille (1997) rightly observes that the conventional association between caste and occupation is fast dissolving in urban India, and caste no longer has the same meaning, moral basis and economic implications it had in the past. This is also the case with regards to boatmen, but in their particular context of Banaras – a pilgrimage centre and stronghold of Hindu traditions – there is an ironic twist to the story.

Boatmen have now become a commodity, their profession is valued economically, and there are numerous social actors, including commercial entrepreneurs and other outside communities, who are willing to take on the boating business for the financial benefits it offers. While the lowly ritual status and stigmatized association attached to their community remains operative amongst some local actors, the practice of running a boat is seen more as an economic activity, largely separate from such stigmas. In order to protect their monopoly on the boating industry boatmen must, ironically perhaps, refer back to traditional idioms and structures, both as a means to enhance their social status, and equally importantly, to secure their livelihood from the potential threat of market economy and competition. As *Sons of the Ganga* and the loyal devotees of Prince Rama, boatmen have re-appropriated pan Indian symbols in ways that enable the community to claim engagement in a sacred vocation since 'time immemorial'. As such, it is their privilege and duty as boatmen to operate as ritual associates and tour guides on the Ganga. While their identity is culturally mediated and constructed, and its essential qualities strategically conceived, this does not make it less significant or valid. Thus, when the authorities arrest members of the community on the pretext of operating as impostors, disguised as 'fake tour guides', boatmen take to the streets, deploying whatever means they have at their disposal to oppose what they perceive as a threat to their identity and an attempt to deprive them of their customary, symbolic and material rights.

I began this study reflecting on Pankaj Mishra's novel *The Romantics*, set in Banaras, where an encounter with a boatman, Ramchand, is portrayed from two distinct angles. Miss West's orientalizing gaze is pitted against a more sober view of the narrator, alerting us to the cultural and economic constrictions in Indian society, barring any meaningful encounter between the boatman (conceived as part of a collective) and himself on equal grounds. While it is under Miss West's gaze that the boatman has at least the potential to exercise agency, his acts betray a mute, subservient and docile personality, matched by his physically able, immaculate body – naturally accustomed to sun-drenched labour on the Ganga. My intervention in this encounter was to shift the focus, foregrounding the lives and practices of Ramchand and his fellow boatmen as a subaltern community uniquely situated at the juncture of tradition and modernity in contemporary India. Boatmen provide a particularly interesting case study as they appear to be the 'classic' traditional caste, with a distinct occupation and ritual position in the social hierarchy. At the same time, by virtue of their unique occupation and geographical location, they are exposed to the ongoing processes of political and economic modernization, and, more recently, economic and cultural globalization. As boatmen, they have a historical and continuing relationship with traditional institutions associated with the sacred city (e.g., rituals, pilgrimage, the death industry), and can trace the origins of their vocation to the time of Lord Rama. These institutions are continuously changing as a result of wider social, political, economical and cultural shifts taking place in modern India. The boatmen and their community are also changing, fewer and fewer boatmen fish for subsistence, and more are converting their rowboats into motorboats. As a group closely associated with the tourist industry boatmen are increasingly exposed to foreign capital, culture and ideas. Such elements, I would argue, contribute to what scholars call fragmented identities, insofar as they do not form a coherent story; they are discursive, disparate elements that come into play on the riverscape, and as such affect the way boatmen perceive their community, identity, livelihood and the world around them, and their future in it.

Throughout this book I have referred to the boatmen as subalterns, which I believe, captures their historical experience as an oppressed and disadvantaged group. At the same time, however, I have also shown that boatmen consciously present themselves as a subaltern community, disenfranchised by state discourse and action and invalidated by caste structure. These claims, I have argued, are necessarily partial truths, for while they certainly constitute part of the everyday lives and experiences of boatmen, such experiences are always mediated by wider forces, social discourses and interactions. At the most general level, they are part of a broader discourse of subalternity that exists and circulates, not only among world intellectuals, but also within the context of caste politics, forcefully resurrected since the early 1980s in the caste uplift movements (cf. Khan 1994). This is evident in the recent victory of the Bahujan Samaj Party (BSP) in the UP elections. The triumph of the BSP, a party dominated by the so-called low castes, has been described in a leading Indian newspaper as a spectacular display

**Figure 6.1    The author with the boatmen of Assi ghat**

of 'subaltern' power.[1] Importantly, however, it is only because the party has been able to widen its support base, by securing the votes of the upper castes (especially Brahmins) that it was able to succeed in the elections. Such developments necessarily undermine any clear distinctions between dominant and subordinate groups in modern India. At a more local level, boatmen are also aware of the potential benefits associated with subaltern identity, as bearers of 'tradition', which they are careful to selectively appropriate, for example, by contributing to and enhancing the modern experience of foreign visitors to Banaras.

In late 2006 three more budget flight companies began flying to Banaras; making it one of the most accessible cities in India, with direct international flights from Nepal and Thailand. Such changes are certain to have implications for the ritual economy of Banaras, and while boatmen remain disadvantaged in the 'traditional' and 'modern' sense, their innovative strategies and ability to adapt is itself an indication that, rather than simply being victims of change and marginalization, they are increasingly asserting themselves as active citizens within Indian history, culture, and society.

---

1    *The Hindu*, Editorial 12 May 2007.

# Glossary

| | |
|---|---|
| *arati* | A ritual weaving of an oil lamp before a deity |
| *bhakti* | Devotion, devotional love to a deity |
| *boli* | Pegging system of passengers used by boatmen |
| *dakshina* | Payment given for ritual service (generally for Brahmin priests) |
| Eklavya Nishad | Prince of the Nishad tribe who in the Mahabharata became a great archer |
| Ganga | Known by its anglicised name as the Ganges River, also revered as the Goddess Ganga, Ganga Ma (lit. Mother Ganga) |
| Ganga Pujaiya | Ritual worship performed for the goddess, Ganga |
| ghat | Landing steps leading to the river, bathing place |
| *ghatwar* | Resident (ghat) boatman, generally a boat owner |
| Guha Raj Nishad | The king of the Nishad tribe found in the Ramayana, also known as Nishadraj |
| *haq* | Duty, obligation, right |
| *jati* | Caste |
| Khevat | The name of the boatman who encountered the divine prince in the Ramayana; also a name of the boatmen caste (*jati*) spelled 'Kewat' in colonial writings |
| Mahabharata | One of the great Indian epics |

| | |
|---|---|
| Mallah | One of the general caste names associated with the boatmen |
| *mallahi* | Non-resident boatman, worker, also called driver (of a boat) |
| Manjhi | Boatman, title/surname attached to boat owner |
| *manauti* | Vow of propitiation to a deity |
| *moksha* | Salvation, liberation from the endless cycle of death and rebirth (*samsara*) |
| *naw* | Boat |
| *naw walla* | Boatman, one who plies a boat |
| Nishad | The name of a tribe of a hunter/fisher people found in the Ramayana and Mahabharata, also one of the general caste names associated with the boatmen |
| *panda* | Pilgrim priest |
| *pari* | Rotation system used for ferrying passengers |
| *prasad* | Consecrated offerings, often sanctified food |
| *puja* | Worship |
| Ramayana | The Indian epic recounting the life of the divine prince Rama |
| *savari* | Passenger |
| *samaj* | Society, group, council |
| *samiti/ sabha* | Association |
| *tirtha* | Crossing place, ford, pilgrimage centre |
| *yatri* | Pilgrim |
| *yatra* | Pilgrimage |

# Bibliography


Adams, V. (1996), *Tigers of the Snow and Other Virtual Sherpas: An Ethnography of Himalayan Encounters* (Princeton: Princeton University Press).

Adas, M. (1980), '"Moral Economy" Or "Contest State"? Elite Demands and the Origins of Peasant Protest in Southeast Asia', *Journal of Social History* 13:4, 521–546.

Agarwal, A. & Narain, S. (eds) (1985), *The State of India's Environment, 1984–5: The Second Citizens' Report* (New Delhi: Centre for Science & Environment).

Ahmad, I. (1971), 'Caste Mobility Movements in North India', *Indian Economic and Social History Review* 8:2, 164–191.

Ahmed, S. (1991) Questioning Participation: Culture and Power in Water Pollution Control the Implementation of the Ganga Action Plan at Varanasi. *Faculty of Social and Political Science* (Cambridge: University of Cambridge).

Alam, M. & Subrahmanyam, S. (eds) (1998), *The Mughal State 1526–1750* (New Delhi: Oxford University Press).

Alexander, R. M. G. (1856), *The Rise and Progress of British Opium Smuggling: The Illegality of the East India's Company's Monopoly of the Drug* (London: Judd & Glass).

Alley, K. (1994), 'Ganga and Gandagi: Interpretations of Pollution and Waste in Banaras', *Ethnology* 33:2, 127–145.

Alley, K. (2002), *On the Banks of the Ganga: When Wastewater Meets a Sacred River* (Ann Arbor: University of Michigan Press).

Alter, S. J. (1992), *The Wrestler's Body: Identity and Ideology in North India* (Berkeley: University of California Press).

Amin, S. (1984), 'Gandhi as Mahatma: Gorakhpur District, Eastern up, 1921–2', in Guha, R. (ed.) *Subaltern Studies III: Writing on South Asian History and Society* (Delhi: Oxford University Press), pp.1–61.

Amin, S. (1989), 'Editor's Introduction', in Amin, S. (ed.) *A Glossary of North Indian Peasant Life by William Crooke* (Delhi: Oxford University Press), pp.xviii–xlii.

Anderson, B. (1998), *The Spectre of Comparisons: Nationalism, Southeast Asia and the World* (New York: Verso).

Appadurai, A. (1981), *Worship and Conflict under Colonial Rule: A South Asian Case* (London: Cambridge University Press).

Appadurai, A. (1981b), 'The Past as a Scarce Resource', *Journal of Royal Anthropological Institute* 16: 201–219.

Appadurai, A. (1988), 'Putting Hierarchy in Its Place', *Cultural Anthropology* 3:1, 36–49.

Appadurai, A. (1990), 'Topographies of the Self: Praise and Emotion in Hindu India', in Lutz, C. & Abu-Lughod, L. (eds) *Language and the Politics of Emotion* (Cambridge: Cambridge University Press), pp.92–112.

Appadurai, A. (1996), *Modernity at Large: Cultural Dimensions of Globalization* (London: University of Minnesota Press).

Arnold, D. (1979), 'Looting, Grain Riots and Government Policy in South India', *Past and Present* 84:111–145.

Arnold, D. (1984), 'Famine in Peasant Consciousness and Peasant Action: Madras 1876–8', in Guha, R. (ed.) *Subaltern Studies III: Writings on South Asian History and Society* (Delhi: Oxford University Press), pp.62–115.

Arnold, D. (1989), 'The Ecology and Cosmology of Disease in the Banaras Region', in Freitag, S. (ed.) *Culture and Power in Banaras: Community, Performance, and Environment, 1800–1980* (Berkeley: University of California Press), pp.246–267.

Arnold, T. (2001), 'Rethinking Moral Economy', *The American Political Science Review* 95:1, 85–95.

Bacon, T. (1837), *First Impressions and Studies from Nature in Hindostan: Embracing an Outline of the Voyage to Calcutta, and Five Years Residence in Bengal and the Doáb, from 1831 to 1836* (London: W.H. Allen).

Bardhan, P. (1984), *The Political Economy of Development in India* (Oxford: Blackwell).

Barrier, N. (ed.) (1981), *Census in British India: New Perspectives* (New Delhi: Manohar).

Barth, F. (ed.) (1969), *Ethnic Groups and Boundaries: The Social Organization of Culture Difference* (Bergen: Universitets-forlaget).

Baviskar, A. (2002), *Seminar* No. 516 (web edition http://www.india-seminar. com/semframe.html), accessed 28 April 2008.

Bayly, C. A. (1983), *Rulers, Townsmen and Bazaars: North Indian Society in the Age of British Expansion, 1770–1870.* (Cambridge: Cambridge University Press).

Bayly, C. A. (1985), 'The Pre-History of Communalism: Religious Conflict in India, 1700–1860', *Modern Asian Studies* 19:2, 177–203.

Bayly, S. (1999), *Caste, Society and Politics in India from the Eighteenth to the Modern Age* (Cambridge: Cambridge University Press).

Bernal, V. (1994), 'Peasants, Capitalism and (ir)Rationality', *American Ethnologist* 21:4, 792–810.

Bernal, V. (1997), 'Colonial Moral Economy and the Discipline of Development: The Gezira Scheme and "Modern" Sudan', *Cultural Anthropology* 12:4, 447–479.

Bernstein, H. (1960 (1987)), *Steamboats on the Ganges* (Calcutta: Orient Longman).

Bhattacharyya, D. P. (1997), 'Mediating India: An Analysis of a Guidebook', *Annals of Tourism Research* 24:2, 371–389.

Bourdieu, P. (1982), *Outline of Theory of Practice* (Cambridge: Cambridge University Press).

Bourdieu, P. (1984), *Distinction: A Social Critique of the Judgment of Taste* (Cambridge: Harvard University Press).

Bowman, G. (1989), 'Fucking Tourists: Sexual Relations and Tourism in Jerusalem's Old City', *Critique of Anthropology* 9:2, 77–93.

Bruner, E. (1991), 'Transformation of Self in Tourism', *Annals of Tourism Research* 18: 238–250.

Caine, W. S. (1982 (1898)), *Picturesque India: A Handbook for European Travellers* (Delhi: Neeraj Publishing House).

Carroll, L. (1978), 'Colonial Perceptions of Indian Society and the Emergence of Caste(S) Associations', *Journal of Asian Studies* 37:2, 233–250.

Cashman, I. R. (1975), *The Myth of Lokmanya: Tilak and Mass Politics in Maharashtra* (Berkeley: Berkeley University Press).

Certeau, M. de (1988), *The Practice of Everyday Life* (Berkeley: University of California Press).

Chakrabarty, D. (1983), 'Conditions for Knowledge of Working-Class Conditions: Employers, Government and the Jute Workers of Calcutta, 1890–1940', in Guha, R. (ed.) *Subaltern Studies III: Writing on South Asian History and Society* (Delhi: Oxford University Press), pp.259–310.

Chakrabarty, D. (2001), 'Open Space/Public Space: Garbage, Modernity and India', *South Asia: Journal of South Asian Studies* 14:1, 15–31.

Chambers, E. (2000), *Title Native Tours: The Anthropology of Travel and Tourism* (Prospect Heights: Waveland Press).

Chatterjee, P. (1993), *The Nation and Its Fragments: Colonial and Postcolonial Histories* (Princeton: Princeton University Press).

Chatterjee, P. (1997), *A Possible India: Essays in Political Criticism* (Delhi: Oxford University Press).

Chaturvedi, N. (ed.) (2000), *Mapping Subaltern Studies and the Postcolonial* (London: Verso).

Coccari, D. (1989), 'Protection and Identity: Banaras's Bir Babas as Neighbourhood Guardian Deities', in Freitag, S. (ed.) *Culture and Power in Banaras: Community, Performance, and Environment, 1800–1980* (Berkeley: University of California Press), pp.130–146.

Cohen, E. (1971), 'Arab Boys and Tourist Girls in a Mixed Jewish Arab Community', *International Journal of Comparative Sociology* 12:4, 217–233.

Cohen, E. (1982b), 'Thai Girls and Farang Men: The Edge of Ambiguity', *Annals of Tourism Research* 9: 403–428.

Cohen, E. (1985), 'The Tourist Guide', *Annals of Tourism Research* 12:5–29.

Cohen, L. (1998), *No Aging in India: Modernity, Senility and the Family* (New Delhi: Oxford University Press).

Cohn, B. (1996), *Colonialism and Its Forms of Knowledge: The British in India* (London: Princeton University Press).

Cohn, B. (1998 [1987]), *An Anthropologist among the Historians and Other Essays* (New Delhi: Oxford University Press).

Comaroff, J. (1985), *Body of Power, Spirit of Resistance: The Culture and History of a South African People* (Chicago: University of Chicago Press).

Comaroff, J. & Comaroff, J. (1988), 'Through the Looking-Glass: Colonial Encounters of the First Kind', *Journal of Historical Sociology* 1:1, 6–32.

Contrusi, J., A (1989), 'Militant Hindus and Buddhist Dalits: Hegemony and Resistance in an Indian Slum', *American Ethnologist* 16:3, 441–457.

Cooper, F. (2002), 'Conflict and Connection: Rethinking Colonial African History', in Ludden, D. (ed.) *Reading Subaltern Studies: Critical History, Contested Meaning, and the Globalization of South Asia* (London: Anthem South Asian Studies), pp.256–303.

Crick, M. (1989), 'Shifting Identities in the Research Process: An Essay in Personal Anthropology', in Perry, J. (ed.) *Doing Fieldwork: Eight Personal Accounts of Social Research* (Geelong: Deakin University Press), pp.24–40.

Crick, M. (1994), *Resplendent Sites, Discordant Voices: Sri Lankans and International Tourism* (Camberwell: Harwood Academic Publishers).

Crick, M. (1995), 'The Anthropologist as Tourist: An Identity in Question', in Lanfant, M., Allcock, B. & Bruner, E. (eds) *International Tourism: Identity and Change* (New Delhi: Sage), pp.205–223.

Crooke, W. (1906), *Things Indian: Being Discursive Notes on Various Subjects Connected with India* (New York: Charles Scribner's Sons).

Crooke, W. (1974 (1876–96)), *The Tribes and Castes of the North-Western Provinces, 4 vol.* (Delhi: Cosmo Publications).

Dalmia, V. (1999 [1997]), *The Nationalisation of Hindu Traditions: Bharatendu Harichandra and Nineteenth-Century Banaras* (London: Oxford).

Dalrymple, W. (2003), *White Mughals: Love and Betrayal in the Eighteenth-Century India* (New York: Viking).

Danielou, A. (1987), *The Way to the Labyrinth: Memories of East and West* (New York: New Directions).

Darian, G. S. (1970), 'The Economic History of the Ganges to the End of Gupta Times', *Journal of the Economic and Social History of the Orient* 13:1, 62–87.

Das, V. (1995), 'Communities as Political Actors: The Question of Cultural Rights', *Critical Events: An Anthropological Perspective on Contemporary India* (New Delhi: Oxford University Press), pp.84–117.

Das, V. (2003), 'Social Sciences and the Publics', in Das, V. (ed.) *The Oxford Companion to Sociology and Social Anthropology* (New Delhi: Oxford University Press), pp.1–29.

Datta, N. (1999), *Forming an Identity: A Social History of the Jats* (New Delhi: Oxford University Press).

Derné, S. (1995), *Culture in Action: Family Life, Emotion and Male Dominance in Banaras, India* (New York: SUNY Press).

Dirks, N. (1991), 'Ritual and Resistance: Subversion as Social Fact', in Haynes, D. & Prakash, G. (eds) *Contesting Power: Resistance and Everyday Social*

*Relations in South Asia* (Berkeley: University of California Press), pp.213–238.

Dirks, N. (1996), 'Reading Culture: Anthropology and the Textualization of India', in Daniel, V. & Peck, J. M. (eds) *Culture/Contexture: Explorations in Anthropology and Literary Studies* (Berkeley: University of California Press), pp.275–295.

Dirks, N. (2001), *Castes of Mind: Colonialism and the Making of Modern India* (Princeton: Princeton University Press).

Doron, A. (2008), 'The Forgotten People: India's Most Backward Castes and the Nishads of Uttar Pradesh', In Lakha, S. & Taneja, P. (eds) *Democracy, Development and Civil Society in India* (Melbourne: Refereed Conference Proceedings, University of Melbourne, Australia, September 20, 2007).

Dumont, L. (1972), *Homo Hierarchicus: An Essay on the Caste System and Its Implications* (London: Paladin).

Echtner, C. & Prasad, P. (2003), 'The Context of Third World Tourism Marketing', *Annals of Tourism Research* 30:3, 660–682.

Eck, D. (1983), *Banaras: City of Light* (London: Routledge & Kegan Paul).

Edelman, M. (2005), 'Bringing the Moral Economy Back In... To the Study of 21st-Century Translational Peasant Movements', *American Anthropologist* 107:3, 331–345.

Edwards, S. M. (1924), *Crime in India* (London: Oxford University Press).

Elliot, H. M. (1985 (1870)), *Encyclopedia of Caste, Costumes, Rites and Superstitions of the Races of Northern India* (Delhi: Sumit Publications).

Escobar, A. (2001), 'Culture Sits in Places: Reflections on Globalism and Subaltern Strategies of Localization', *Political Geography* 20:2, 139–174.

Evans-Pritchard, D. (1989), 'How "They" See "Us": Native American Images of Tourists', *Annals of Tourism Research* 16: 85–105.

Feldhaus, A. (1995), *Water and Womanhood: Religious Meanings of Rivers in Maharashtra* (New York: Oxford University Press).

Foucault, M. (1982), 'The Subject and Power', in Dreyfus, H., L & Rabinow, P. (eds) *Beyond Structuralism and Hermeneutics* (Chicago: The University of Chicago Press), pp.208–226.

Foucault, M. (1998), *The History of Sexuality Vol 1: The Will to Knowledge* (London: Penguin Books).

Freitag, S. (1985), 'Collective Crime and Authority in North India', in Yang, A. (ed.) *Crime and Criminality in British India* (Tuscon: University of Arizona Press), pp.140–163.

Freitag, S. (ed.) (1989), *Culture and Power in Banaras: Community, Performance, and Environment, 1800–1980* (Berkeley: University of California Press).

Freitag, S. (1991), 'Crime in the Social Order of Colonial India', *Modern Asian Studies* 25:2, 227–261.

Friedlander, P. (2004) Travel Talk: Phrases for Travellers in India, in Cribb, R. (ed.) *Asia Examined: Proceedings of the 15th Biennial Conference of the ASAA, 2004, Canberra, Australia.*

Fuller, C. J. (1984), *Servants of the Goddess: The Priests of a South Indian Temple* (Cambridge: Cambridge University Press).

Fuller, C. J. (1988), 'Hinduism and Scriptural Authority in Modern Indian Law', *Comparative Studies in Society and History*, 225–248.

Fuller, C. J. (1992), *The Camphor Flame: Popular Hinduism and Society in India* (Princeton: Princeton University Press).

Fuller, C. J. (2003), 'Caste', in Das, V. (ed.) *The Oxford Companion to Sociology and Social Anthropology* (New Delhi: Oxford University Press), pp.477–501.

Fuller, C. J. (2004), *The Renewal of the Priesthood: Modernity and Traditionalism in a South Indian Temple* (New Delhi: Oxford University Press).

Fuller, C. J. & Harriss, J. (2000), 'For an Anthropology of the Modern Indian State.' in Fuller, C. J. & Benei, V. (eds) *The Everyday State and Society in Modern India* (New Delhi: Social Science Press), pp.1–30.

Gadgil, M. & Guha, R. (1999), *This Fissured Land: An Ecological History of India* (New Delhi: Oxford University Press).

Gal, S. (1995), 'Language and the "Arts of Resistance"', *Cultural Anthropology* 10:3, 407–424.

Galanter, M. (1992), *Law and Society in Modern India* (Delhi: Oxford University Press).

Gandhi, R. (1987), *Selected Speeches and Writings* (New Delhi: Publication Divisions).

Gardner, R. dir (1985), *Forest of Bliss* (Boston: Harvard University).

Geertz, C. (1979), 'Suq: The Bazaar Economy in Sefrou.' in Geertz, C., Geertz, H. & Rosen, L. (eds), *Meaning and Order in Moroccan Society: Three Essays in Cultural Analysis* (Cambridge: Cambridge University Press), pp.123–244.

Giddens, A. (1984), *The Constitution of Society: Outline of the Theory of Structuration* (Berkeley: University of California Press).

Gilmartin, D. & Lawrence, B. (eds) (2002), *Beyond Turk and Hindu: Rethinking Religious Identities in Islamicate South Asia* (New Delhi: India Research Press: India Research Press).

Goffman, E. (1974), *The Presentation of Self in Everyday Life* (London: Penguin Books).

Gol. (1999), *A Pilgrimage to Kashi-Banaras, Varanasi, Kashi: History, Mythology and Culture of the Strangest and Most Fascinating City in the World* (Varanasi: Indica Books).

Gold, A. (1988), *Fruitful Journeys: The Ways of Rajasthani Pilgrims* (Berkeley: University of California Press).

Gooptu, N. (1997), 'The Urban Poor and Militant Hinduism in Early Twentieth-Century Uttar Pradesh', *Modern Asian Studies* 34:4, 879–918.

Gooptu, N. (2001), *The Politics of the Urban Poor in Early Twentieth-Century India* (Cambridge: Cambridge University Press).

Graburn, N. (1989), 'Tourism: The Sacred Journey', in Smith, V. (ed.) *Hosts and Guests: The Anthropology of Tourism* (Philadelphia: University of Pennsylvania Press), pp.21–36.

Greenwood, D. (1977), 'Culture by the Pound: An Anthropological Perspective on Tourism as Cultural Commoditization', in Smith, V. (ed.) *Hosts and Guests: The Anthropology of Tourism* (Philadelphia: University of Pennsylvania Press), pp.171–185.

Guha, R. (1982), 'On Some Aspects of Historiography of Colonial India', in Guha, R. (ed.) *Subaltern Studies I: Writing on South Asian History and Society* (Delhi: Oxford University Press), pp.1–8.

Guha, R. (1983), 'The Prose of Counter-Insurgency', in Guha, R. (ed.) *Subaltern Studies II: Writing on South Asian History and Society* (Delhi: Oxford University Press), pp.1–43.

Gupta, A. (1995), 'Blurred Boundaries: The Discourse of Corruption, the Culture of Politics, and the Imagined State', *American Ethnologist* 22:2, 375–402.

Gupta, A. & Ferguson, J. (1992), 'Beyond "Culture": Space, Identity, and the Politics of Difference', *Cultural Anthropology* 7:1, 6–23.

Gupta, A. & Ferguson, J. (1997), 'Discipline and Practice: "The Field" As Site, Method, and Location in Anthropology', in Gupta, A. & Ferguson, J. (eds) *Anthropological Locations: Boundaries and Grounds of a Field Science* (Berkeley: University of California Press), pp.1–45.

Gupta, D. (1985), 'On Altering Ego and Peasant History: Paradoxes of the Ethnic Option', *Journal of Peasant Studies* 13:1, 5–24.

Gupta, D. (2000), *Interrogating Caste: Understanding Hierarchy and Difference in Indian Society* (New Delhi: Penguin).

Gupta, D. (2001), 'Everyday Resistance or Routine Repression? Exaggeration as Stratagem in Agrarian Conflict', *Journal of Peasant Studies* 29:1, 89–108.

Hall, S. (2001), 'Foucault: Power, Knowledge and Discourse', in Wetherell, M., Taylor, S. & Yates, J. S. (eds) *Discourse Theory and Practice: A Reader* (London: Sage), pp.72–81.

Hancock, M. (1999), *Womanhood in the Making: Domestic Ritual and Public Culture in Urban South India* (Boulder: Westview Press).

Hannerz, U. (1985), 'The Informal Sector: Some Remarks', in Skar, O. H. (ed.), *Anthropological Contributions to Planned Change and Development* (Goteborg: Acta Universitatis Gothoburgensis), pp.143–153.

Hansen, T. (1997), 'Inside the Romanticist Episteme', *Thesis Eleven* 48, 21–42.

Hansen, T. (2000), 'Governance and Myths of State in Mumbai', in Fuller, C. J. & Bennei, V. (eds) *The Everyday State and Society in Modern India* (New Delhi: Social Science Press), pp.31–67.

Hardiman, D. (1982), 'The Indian Faction: A Political Theory Examined', in Guha, R. (ed.) *Subaltern Studies I: Writing on South Asian History and Society* (Delhi: Oxford University Press), pp.198–231.

Hardiman, D. (1984), 'Adivasi Assertion in South Gujarat: The Devi Movement of 1922–3', in Guha, R. (ed.) *Subaltern Studies III: Writings on South Asian History and Society* (Delhi: Oxford University Press), pp.196–230.

Hardiman, D. (1996), 'Usury, Dearth, and Famine in Western India', *Past and Present* 152, 113–156.

Hart, G. (1991), 'Engendering Everyday Resistance: Gender, Patronage, and Production Politics in Rural Malaysia', *Journal of Peasant Studies* 19:1, 93–121.

Havell, E. (2000 (1905)), *Benares the Sacred City: Sketches of Hindu Life and Religion* (Delhi: Book Faith).

Hawley, J. (1981), *Sur Das: Poet, Singer, Saint* (Princeton: Princeton University Press).

Hay, S. (ed.) (1991), *Sources of India Tradition: Modern India and Pakistan* (Vol. 2) (New Delhi: Penguin Books).

Haynes, D. (1989), 'Review: The Artisans of Banaras: Popular Culture and Identity, 1880–1986. By N. Kumar', *Pacific Affairs* 62:3, 416–418.

Haynes, D. & Roy, T. (1999), 'Conceiving Mobility: Weavers' Migrations in Pre-Colonial and Colonial India', *Indian Economic Social History Review* 36:1, 35–67.

Herrmann, G. (2003), 'Negotiating Culture: Conflict and Consensus in U.S. Garage Sale Bargaining', *Ethnology* 42:3, 237–253.

Hess, L. (2001), 'Lovers' Doubts: Questioning the Tulsi Ramayana', in Richman, P. (ed.) *Questioning Ramayanas: A South Asian Tradition* (Berkeley; London: University of California Press), pp.25–47.

Highmore, B. (2002), 'Introduction: Questioning Everyday Life', in Highmore, B. (ed.) *The Everyday Life Reader* (New York: Routledge), pp.1–34.

Hornell, J. (1924), 'The Boats of the Ganges', *Memoirs of the Asiatic Society of Bengal* 8:3, 171–198.

Hutton, J. (1857), *A Popular Account of the Thugs and Dacoits: The Hereditary Garotters and Gang Robbers in India* (London: W.M.H. Allen and Co).

Jafferlot, C. (1998), 'The Bahujan Samaj Party in North India: No Longer Just a Dalit Party', *Comparative Studies of South Asia and the Middle East* 18:1, 35–52.

Jain, K. (2004), 'Mascularity and Its Ramifications: Mimetic Male Bodies in Indian Mass Culture', in Srivastava, S. (ed.) *Sexual Sites, Seminal Attitudes: Sexualities, Masculinities, and Culture in South Asia* (New Delhi: Sage Publications), pp.300–341.

Jain, M. (1996), 'Backward Castes and Social Change in U.P. and Bihar', in Srinivas, M. N. (ed.) *Caste: Its Twentieth Century Avatar* (New Delhi: Penguin), pp.135–151.

Jayapal, P. (2000), *Pilgrimage: One Woman's Return to a Changing India* (New Delhi: Penguin Books).

Jeffrey, C. & Lerche, J. (2000), 'Dimensions of Dominance: Class and State in Uttar Pradesh', in Fuller, C. J. & Benei, V. (eds) *The Everyday State and Society in Modern India* (New Delhi: Social Science Press), pp.91–114.

Jenkins, L. (2003), 'Another "People of India" Project: Colonial and National Anthropology', *The Journal of Asian Studies* 62:4, 1143–1170.

Justice, C. (1997), *Dying the Good Death: The Pilgrimage to Die in India's Holy City* (New York: SUNY).

Kahn, J. (1994), 'Subalternity and the Construction of Malay Identity', in Gomes, A. (ed.) *Modernity and Identity: Asian Illustrations* (Bundoora: La Trobe University Press), pp.23–41.

Kaplan, M. & Kelly, J. (1994), 'Rethinking Resistance: Dialogics of "Disaffection" in Colonial Fiji', *American Ethnologist* 21:1, 123–151.

Katz, M. J. (1993), *The Children of Assi: The Transference of Religious Traditions and Communal Inclusion in Banaras.* (Göteborg: Department of Religious Studies.).

Kaviraj, S. (1991), 'On State, Society and Discourse in India', in Manor, J. (ed.) *Rethinking Third World Politics* (London: Longman), pp. 72–99.

Kaviraj, S. (1997), 'The Modern State in India', in Doombos, M. & Kaviraj, S. (eds) *Dynamics of State Formation: India and Europe Compared* (Thousand Oaks: Sage), pp.225–250.

Kaviraj, S. (1999), 'On the Construction of Colonial Power: Structure, Discourse, Hegemony', in Kaviraj, S. (ed.) *Politics in India* (Delhi: Oxford University Press), pp.141–158.

Kinsley, D. (1986), *Hindu Goddesses: Visions of the Divine Feminine in the Hindu Religious Tradition* (Berkeley: University of California Press).

Kondo, D. (1990), *Crafting Selves: Power, Gender, and Discourses of Identity in a Japanese Workplace* (Chicago: University of Chicago Press).

Kumar, N. (1995 (1988)), *The Artisans of Banaras: Popular Culture and Identity, 1880–1986* (New Delhi: Orient Longman).

Kumra, V. K. (1995), 'Water Quality in the River Ganges', in Chapman, G. P. & Thompson, M. (eds) *Water and the Quest for Sustainable Development in the Ganges Valley* (London: Mansell), pp. 130–140.

Linkenbach, A. (2000), 'Anthropology of Modernity: Projects and Contexts', *Thesis Eleven* 61:41–63.

Ludden, D. (ed.) (2002), *Reading Subaltern Studies: Critical History, Contested Meaning, and the Globalization of South Asia* (London: Anthem South Asian Studies).

Lukens-Bull, R. (1999), 'Between Text and Practice: Considerations in the Anthropological Study of Islam', *Marburg Journal of Religion* 4:2, 1–21. (www.uni-marburg.de/religionswissenschaft/journal/mjr/lukensbull.html. Last accessed 15 June 2007).

Lutgendorf, P. (1989), 'The View from the Ghats: Traditional Exegesis of a Hindu Epic', *The Journal of Asian Studies* 48:2, 272–288.

MacCannell, D. (1976), *The Tourist: A New Theory of the Leisure Class* (Berkeley: University of California Press).

Mahajan, J. (ed.) (1994), *Ganga Observed: Foreign Accounts of the River* (New Delhi: Virgo Publications).

Malkki, L. (1992), 'National Geographic: The Rooting of Peoples and the Territorialisation of National Identity among Scholars and Refugees', *Cultural Anthropology* 7:1, 24–44.

Malkki, L. (1997), 'New Culture: Transitory Phenomena and Fieldwork Tradition', in Gupta, A. & Ferguson, J. (eds) *Anthropological Locations: Boundaries and Grounds of a Field Science* (Berkeley: University of California Press), pp.86–101.

Mandelbaum, D. (1966), 'Transcendental and Pragmatic Aspects of Religion', *American Anthropologist* 69:1174–91.

Manu, Doniger, W. & Smith, B. K. (1991), *The Laws of Manu: With an Introduction and Notes/Translated by W. Doniger with B. Smith* (New York: Penguin).

Markula, P. (1997), 'As a Tourist in Tahiti: An Analysis of Personal Experience', *Journal of Contemporary Ethnography* 26:2, 202–225.

Massey, D. (2004), 'Geographies of Responsibility', *Geografiska Annaler: Series B, Human Geography* 86:1, 5–18.

Matthiesson, J. (1999), *Doing the India Trip: Myths and Paradoxes of a Travel Culture*. Department of History. Melbourne, University of Melbourne.

Mawdsley, E. (2004), 'India's Middle Classes and the Environment', *Development and Change* 35:1, 79–103.

McCloud, S. (1994), *Understanding Comics: The Invisible Art* (New York: Harper Perennial).

McGregor, R. (ed.) (1993), *The Oxford Hindi-English Dictionary* (Oxford: Oxford University Press).

Mehrotra, R. (1993), 'Sociology of Secret Languages', in Singh, R. P. B. (ed.) *Banâras (Varanasi): Cosmic Order, Sacred City, Hindu Traditions* (Varanasi: Tara Book Agency), pp.197–214.

Mehta, D. (1997), *Work, Ritual, Biography: A Muslim Community in North India* (New Delhi: Oxford University Press).

Menon, R. (1997), 'Ganga Clean-Up: Monumental Failure', *Indian Today* January 14, 103–107.

Metcalf, T. (1995), *Ideologies of the Raj* (Cambridge: Cambridge University Press).

Mines, D. (2002), 'Hindu Nationalism, Untouchable Reform, and the Ritual Production of a South Indian Village', *American Ethnologist* 29:1, 58–85.

Minturn (Jr), R. (1858), *From New York to Delhi by Way of Rio De Janeiro, Australia and China* (New York: D. Appelton & Co.).

Mishra, P. (1999), *The Romantics* (London: Picador).

Mitchell, T. (1990), 'Everyday Metaphors of Power', *Theory and Society* 19:5, 545–577.

Mittelman, J. & Chin, C. (2005), 'Conceptualizing Resistance to Globalization', in Amoore, L. (ed.) *The Global Resistance Reader* (London: Routledge), pp.17–27.

Moore, D. (1992), 'Contesting Terrain in Zimbabwe's Eastern Highlands: Political Ecology, Ethnography, and Peasant Resource Struggles', *Economic Geography* 69:4, 380–401.

Moore, D. (1997), 'Remapping Resistance: 'Ground for Struggle' and the Politics of Place', in Pile, S. & Keith, M. (eds) *Geographies of Resistance* (London: Routledge), pp.87–106.

Moore, D. (1998), 'Subaltern Struggles and the Politics of Place: Remapping Resistance in Zimbabwe's Eastern Highlands', *Cultural Anthropology* 13:3, 344–381.

Moore, D., Kosek, J. & Pandian, A. (eds) (2003), *Race, Nature, and the Politics of Difference* (Durham Duke University Press).

Moore, E. (1998), *Gender, Law, and Resistance in India* (Tuscon: The University of Arizona).

Motichand, K. (1931), *Benares and Its Ghats* (Allahabad: Kashi Tirth Sudhar Trust, Benares).

Naidu, B. (1996 [1915]), *The History of Railway Thieves with Illustration & Hints on Detection* (Madras: Higginbothams Limited).

Narayan, B. (2001), 'Heroes, Histories and Booklets', *Economic and Political Weekly* 36:41, 3923–3934.

Nash, D. (1989), 'Tourism as a Form of Imperialism', in Smith, V. (ed.) *Hosts and Guests: The Anthropology of Tourism* (Philadelphia: University of Pennsylvania Press), pp.37–52.

Nevill, H. R. (ed.) (1909), *Benares: A Gazetteer. Vol. Xxvi of the District Gazetteers of the United Provinces of Agra and Oudh.* (Allahabad: Government Press.).

Newby, E. (1966), *Slowly Down the Ganges* (London: Hodder & Stoughton).

Nigam, S. (1990), 'Disciplining and Policing the 'Criminals by Birth', Part 1: The Making of a Colonial Stereotype – the Criminal Tribes and Castes of North India', *The Indian Economic and Social History Review* 27:2–3, 131–164, 257 287.

O'Hanlon, R. (2002), 'Recovering the Subject: Subaltern Studies and Histories of Resistance in Colonial South Asia', in Ludden, D. (ed.) *Reading Subaltern Studies: Critical History, Contested Meaning, and the Globalization of South Asia* (London: Anthem South Asian Studies), pp.135–186.

Olivelle, P. (2008, March), 'Crime and Punishment in Ancient India: Ideology of Rebirth and the Making of the Body'. Seminar presented on March 5 at the *South Asia Seminar Series*, RSPAS, Australian National University.

Ortner, S. (1995), 'Resistance and the Problem of Ethnographic Refusal', *Comparative Studies in Society and History* 37: 173–193.

Ortner, S. (2001), 'Specifying Agency: The Comaoffs and Their Critics', *Interventions* 3:1, 76–84.

Osella, F. & Osella, C. (2000a), *Social Mobility in Kerala: Modernity and Identity in Conflict* (London: Pluto Press).

Osella, C. & Osella, F. (2000b), 'The Return of King Maharani: The Politics of Morality in Kerala', in Fuller, C. J. & Benei, V. (eds) *The Everyday State and Society in Modern India* (New Delhi: Social Science Press), pp.137–162.

Palmer, C. (1994), 'Tourism and Colonialism: The Experience of the Bahamas', *Annals of Tourism Research* 21:4, 792–811.

Pandey, G. (1983), 'Rallying Round the Cow: Sectarian Strife in the Bhojpuri Region, C.1888–1917', in Guha, R. (ed.) *Subaltern Studies II: Writing on South Asian History and Society* (Delhi: Oxford University Press), pp.60–129.

Pandey, G. (1984), "Encounters and Calamities': The History of a North India Qasba in the Nineteenth Century', in Guha, R. (ed.) *Subaltern Studies III: Writing on South Asian History and Society* (Delhi: Oxford University Press), pp.231–270.

Pandey, G. (2000), 'Voices from the Edge: The Struggle to Write Subaltern Histories', in Chaturvedi, N. (ed.) *Mapping Subaltern Studies and the Postcolonial* (London: Verso), pp.281–299.

Parish, S. (1997), *Hierarchy and Its Discontents: Culture and the Politics of Consciousness in Caste Society* (Delhi: Oxford University Press).

Parry, J. (1974), 'Egalitarian Values in a Hierarchical Society', *South Asia Review* 7:2, 95–121.

Parry, J. P. (1993), 'Ghosts, Greed and Sin: The Occupational Identity of the Banaras Funeral Priests', in Singh, R. P. B. (ed.) *Banaras: Cosmic Order, Sacred City, Hindu Traditions* (Varanasi: Tara Book Agency), pp. 179–196.

Parry, J. (1994), *Death in Banaras* (Cambridge: Cambridge University Press).

Parry, J. (2000), 'The 'Crisis of Corruption' and the 'Idea of India': A Worm's Eye View', in Pardo, I. (ed.) *The Morals of Legitimacy* (Oxford: Berghahn Book), pp.27–55.

Pile, S. (1997), 'Opposition, Political Identities and Spaces of Resistance', in Pile, S. & Keith, M. (eds) *Geographies of Resistance* (London: Routledge), pp.1–32.

Pinch, W. (1996), *Peasants and Monks in British India* (Berkeley: University of California Press).

Pinch, W. (1999), 'Same Difference in India and Europe', *History and Theory* 38:3, 389–407.

Pintchman, T. (2005), *Guests at God's Wedding: Celebrating Kartik among the Women of Benares* (New York: SUNY Press).

Prakash, G. (1995), 'Writing Post-Orientalist Histories of the Third World: Indian Historiography Is Good to Think', in Dirks, N. (ed.) *Colonialism and Culture* (Ann Arbor University of Michigan Press), pp.353–388.

Pratt, L. M. (1988), *Imperial Eyes: Travel Writing and Transculturation* (London: Routledge).

Radhakrishna, M. (2001), *Dishonoured by History: 'Criminal Tribes' and British Colonial Policy.* (Hyderabad: Orient Longman).

Raheja, G. & Gold, A. (1994), *Listen to the Heron's Words: Reimagining Gender and Kinship in North India* (Berkeley: University of California Press).

Ramanujan, A. K. (1991), 'Three Hundred Ramayanas: Five Examples and Three Thoughts on Translation', in Richman, P. (ed.) *Many Ramayanas: The Diversity of a Narrative Tradition in South Asia* (Berkeley: University of California Press), pp. 22–49.

Ramusack, B. (1994), 'Tourism and Icons: The Packaging of the Princely States of Rajasthan', in Asher, C. E. B. & Metcalf, T. R. (eds) *Perceptions of South Asia's Visual Past* (New Delhi: Oxford & IBH Pub. Co.), pp.235–255.

Ramusack, B. (1995), 'The Indian Princes as Fantasy: Palace Hotels, Palace Museums, and Palace on Wheels', in Breckenridge, C. A. (ed.) *Consuming Modernity: Public Culture in a South Asian World* (London: University of Minnesota Press), pp.66–89.

Reed-Danahay, D. (1993), 'Talking About Resistance: Ethnography and Theory in Rural France', *Anthropological Quarterly* 66:4, 221–229.

Richards, J. (1993), *The Mughal Empire* (Cambridge: Cambridge University Press).

Risley, H. (1969 [1915]), *The People of India* (Delhi: Mushiram Manoharlal Oriental Publishers).

Rosi, G. Dir (1993), *Boatman* (Italy).

Rudolph, S. & Rudolph, L. (1987), *In Pursuit of Lakshmi* (Chicago: Chicago University Press).

Scott, J. (1976), *The Moral Economy of the Peasant: Rebellion and Subsistence in Southeast Asia* (New Haven: Yale University Press).

Scott, J. (1985), *Weapons of the Weak: Everyday Forms of Peasant Resistance* (New Haven: Yale University Press).

Scott, J. (1989), 'Everyday Forms of Resistance', in Colburn, D. F. (ed.) *Everyday Forms of Peasant Resistance* (New York: M.E Sharp), pp.1–33.

Scott, J. (1990), *Domination and the Arts of Resistance: Hidden Transcripts* (New Haven: Yale University Press).

Scott, J. (2000), 'The Moral Economy as an Argument and as a Fight', in Randall, A. & Charlesworth, A. (eds) *Moral Economy and Popular Protest: Crowds, Conflict and Authority* (London: Macmillan Press), pp. 187–208.

Searle-Chatterjee, M. (1979), 'The Polluted Identity of Work: A Study of Benares Sweepers', in Wallman, S. (ed.) *Social Anthropology of Work* (London: Academic Press), pp.269–286.

Searle-Chatterjee, M. & Sharma, U. (1994), 'Introduction', in Searle-Chatterjee, M. & Sharma, U. (eds) *Cotextualising Caste: Post-Dumontian Approaches* (Oxford: Blackwell), pp. 1–24.

Shah, A. (1996), 'The Judicial and Sociological View of Other Backward Classes', in Srinivas, M. N. (ed.) *Caste: Its Twentieth Century Avatar* (New Delhi: Penguin), pp.174–194.

Shankar, S. (1994), 'The Thumb of Ekalavya: Postcolonial Studies and The "Third World" Scholar in a Neocolonial World', *World Literature Today* 63:3, 479–487.

Sherring, M. A. (1974 (1872)), *Hindu Tribes and Castes as Represented in Benares* (Delhi: Cosmo Publications).

Silver, I. (1993), 'Marketing Authenticity in Third World Countries', *Annals of Tourism Research* 20:302–318.

Sivaramakrishnan, K. (1995), 'Schools and Scholars: Situating the Subaltern: History and Anthropology in the Subaltern Studies Project', *Journal of Historical Sociology* 8:4, 395–429.

Sivaramakrishnan, K. (2005), 'In Focus: Moral Economies, State Spaces, and Categorical Violence: Anthropological Engagements with the Work of James Scott', *American Anthropologist* 107:3, 321–402.

Smith, B. (1991), 'Introduction', in *The Laws of Manu* (New York: Penguin).

Smith, V. (1992), 'Introduction: The Quest in Guest', *Annals of Tourism Research* 19:1, 1–17.

Soja, E. (1989), *Postmodern Geographies: The Reassertion of Space in Critical Social Theory* (London: Verso).

Somers, R. M. (1994), 'The Narrative Constitution of Identity: A Relational and Network Approach', *Theory and Society* 23:5, 605–649.

Sørensen, A. (2003), 'Backpacker Ethnography', *Annals of Tourism Research* 30:4, 847–867.

Stephens, J. (1998), *Anti-Disciplinary Protest: Sixties Radicalism and Postmodernism* (Cambridge: Cambridge University Press).

Sweet, J. (1989), 'Burlesquing "The Other" In Pueblo Performance', *Annals of Tourism Research* 16:62–75.

Tandon, R. & Mohanty, R. (2000), Civil Society and Governance: A Research Study in India. New Delhi, Society for Participatory Research (PRIA), (http://www.eldis.org/static/DOC10892.htm, last accessed 16 March 2005).

Thompson, E. P. (1967), 'Time, Work-Discipline and Industrial Capitalism', *Past and Present* 38:56–97.

Thompson, E. P. (1971), 'The Moral Economy of the English Crowd in the Eighteenth Century', *Past and Present* 50:1, 76–136.

Thompson, E. P. (1991), *Customs in Common* (New York: New Press).

Tiwary, S. (2001), 'Caste and the Colonial State: Mallahs in the Census', *Contributions to Indian Sociology* 35:3, 319–354.

Tolen, R. (1991), 'Colonizing and Transforming the Criminal Tribesman: The Salvation Army in British India', *American Ethnologist* 18:1, 106–125.

Toutain, P. (1985), *Benares* (Paris: UBS Publishers).

Trawick, P. (2001), 'The Moral Economy of Water: Equity and Antiquity in the Andean Commons', *American Anthropologist* 103:2, 361–379.

Trojanow, I. (2001), 'Imperial Politics in the Progressive Gaze', *The Hindu* 3.

Tsing, A. (1993), *The Realm of the Diamond Queen* (Princeton: Princeton University Press).

Tucker, H. (1997), 'The Ideal Village: Interactions through Tourism in Central Anatolia', in Abram, S., Waldern, J. & Macleod, D. (eds) *Tourists and Tourism: Identifying with People and Places* (Oxford: Berg), pp.107–128.

Turner, V. (1969), *The Ritual Process* (New York: Cornell University Press).

Turner, V. & Turner, E. (1978), *Image and Pilgrimage in Christian Culture: Anthropological Perspectives* (Oxford: Basil Blackwell).

Urry, J. (1990), *The Tourist Gaze: Leisure and Travel in Contemporary Societies* (London: Sage Publications).

van den Bergh, P. (1980), 'Tourism as Ethnic Relations: A Case Study of Cuzco, Peru', *Ethnic and Racial Studies* 3:4, 375–390.

van der Veer, P. (1988), *Gods on Earth: The Management of Religious Experience and Identity in a North Indian Pilgrimage Centre* (London: Athlone Press).

Vanaik, A. (1990), *The Painful Transition: Bourgeois Democracy in India* (London: Verso).

Varmma, R. C. (1962), *Manaka Hindi Kosa (5 Vol)* (Allahabad: Hindi Sahitya Sammelana).

Vidyarthi, L. et al. (1979), *The Sacred Complex of Kashi* (Delhi: Concept Publishing Company).

Werner, C. (2003), 'The New Silk Road: Mediators and Tourism Development in Central Asia', *Ethnology* 42:2, 141–161.

Williams, R. (1986), *Marxism and Literature* (Oxford: Oxford University Press).

Wood, R. (1997), 'Tourism and the State: Ethnic Options and Constructions of Otherness', in Picard, M. & Wood, R. (eds) *Tourism, Ethnicity, and the State in Asian and Pacific Societies* (Honolulu: University of Hawai'i Press), pp.1–34.

Yang, A. (1985), 'Issues and Themes in the Study of Historical Crime and Criminality: Passages to the Social History of British India', in Yang, A. (ed.) *Crime and Criminality in British India* (Tucson: University of Arizona Press), pp.1–25.


**Newspapers, Magazines and Booklets**


*Amar Ujala*, daily newspaper, Lucknow (Hindi).

*Dainik Jagran*, daily newspaper, Kanpur (Hindi).

*Down to Earth*, fortnightly magazine, New Delhi (English).

*India Today*, weekly magazine, New Delhi (English).

*The Hindustan*, daily newspaper, New Delhi (Hindi).

*Times of India*, daily, New Delhi (English).

*The Hindu*, daily, New Delhi (English).

*Khevat Anurag*, (n.d.) booklet, Narayan & Co, Patna (Hindi and Bhojpuri).

*Nishad Jyothi*, monthly magazine, Lucknow (Hindi).

*Sri Ram*, (n.d.) booklet, Gita Press, Gorakhpur (Hindi).

*Sri Ramacaritamanaasa: With Hindi Text and English Translation*, (1999) Gita Press, Gorakhpur.


**Websites in English**


*Times of India*, on the Web, (http://timesofindia.indiatimes.com/articleshow/852146.cms, accessed 16 March 2005.

*The Hindustan* on the Web, (http://www.hindustantimes.com/2004/Oct/05/5983_
     1043328,00430001.htm, accessed 15 March 2005.

**Cases**

Suit no. 146, the Court of Additional Civil Judge, Benares (1949).
The State v. Mata Prasad, Suit no. 323, the Court of Civil Judge, Varanasi (1968).

# Index

cultural capital, 155–6, 162

*dakshina* (fee), 67–8, 118, 120, 124, 133
Dalmia, Vasudha, 26
Danielou, Alain, 164
Dashashvamedh ghat, 55–6, 88–90, 99,
    *100*, 101, 145, 167,
  as main ghat, 66, 106, 114, 135–7, 161,
    171–2
devotion (*bhakti*)
  to gods, 18, 73, 80, 116, 125–130, 146,
    172,
  to guru, 67–8
Dirks, Nicholas, 24
divers (*gotakhors*) (*see* boatmen)
domination, 2, 4, 10–15, 46, 67–9, 79, 90,
    116–7, 128, 140, 168–172 (*see
    also* agency, hegemony, resistance,
    state)
Dumont, Louis, 123

Eck, Diana, 115
Edelman, Marc, 83
Eklavya Nishad, 67–71, 173

festivals, 6–8, 41, 111, 167
Foucault, Michel, 14, 40, 46
Fuller, C. J., 173

Galanter, Marc, 103
Gandhi, Indira, 56
Gandhi, Rajiv, 58–9, 66, 79
Ganga, as river Ganges, 7, 22–30, 35,
    38–47, 53–66, 73, 77, 82, 106, 110,
    153
Ganga water (*Ganga jal*), 146–7
  as cultural symbol, 59, 72–80, 131
  and environmental pollution, 60–65,
    72–5, 150 (*see also* boatmen,
    Ganga Action Plan, Gangaputras;
    gods and goddesses)
Ganga Action Plan (GAP), 18, 57–66, 79,
    95
Gangaputras ('sons of the Ganges'), 55,
    72–3, 99, 132–137, 172
Geertz, Clifford, 110
ghats, 6–11, 16, 43, 59, 84–90, 101,
    112, (*see also* Assi, Cremation,

Dashashvamedh, Nishad Raj, Raj
    ghats)
gods, goddesses, classification of,
    122–3
Durga, 167;
Ganga Ma, 116, 118, 120–5, 131, 135
Rama, 1, 32, 37, 70, 107, 116, 126–9,
    137, 146–8;
Shitla Ma, 100, 133–5 (*see also* boats,
    rituals)
*ghatwars* (resident boatmen), 84–98,
    103–114, 125, 132, 157 *(see also*
    boatmen)
Giddens, Anthony, 9
Gooptu, Nandini, 41, 42, 45
Gramsci, Antonio, 14
Gupta, Akhil, 3
Guha, Ranajit, 12

*haq* (duty, obligation, property right),
    110–1, 114, 132
Hansen, Thomas, 67
Hardiman, David, 82
Hawley, John, 147
hegemony, 14
Herrmann, Gretchen, 155
Hinduism, 29, 118–120, 124, 132

identity, 2–3, 12–8, 69, 80, 99, 117, 125–8,
    132–7, 170–176 (*see also* boatmen,
    caste, myth)

Kashi, 62, 175, 142 (*see* Banaras)
Kaviraj, Sudipta, 79
Kinship, 12–4, 52, 67, 80, 106, 112 (*see
    also* Ganga, *ghatwars*)
Kumar, Nita, 17, 115

Linkenbach, Antje, 77
Lutgendorf, Philip, 125

MacCannell, Dean, 150
Mahabharata, 67–8
Malkki, Lisa, 4, 5
Mallah, 1, 16–7, 53, 56, 65, 84, 111, 127,
    133
  and colonialism, 27–39 (*see also*
    boatmen, caste, Nishad)